Scaling Networks
Lab Manual

Cisco Networking Academy

ılıılı.
CISCO.

Cisco Press
800 East 96th Street
Indianapolis, Indiana 46240

Scaling Networks Lab Manual
Cisco Networking Academy

Copyright © 2014 Cisco Systems, Inc.

Published by:
Cisco Press
800 East 96th Street
Indianapolis, IN 46240 USA

Printed in the United States of America

First Printing December 2013

ISBN-13: 9781587133251

ISBN-10: 1587133253

Warning and Disclaimer

This book is designed to provide information about Scaling Networks. Every effort has been made to make this book as complete and as accurate as possible, but no warranty or fitness is implied.

The information is provided on an "as is" basis. The authors, Cisco Press, and Cisco Systems, Inc. shall have neither liability nor responsibility to any person or entity with respect to any loss or damages arising from the information contained in this book or from the use of the discs or programs that may accompany it.

The opinions expressed in this book belong to the author and are not necessarily those of Cisco Systems, Inc.

Trademark Acknowledgments

All terms mentioned in this book that are known to be trademarks or service marks have been appropriately capitalized. Cisco Press or Cisco Systems, Inc., cannot attest to the accuracy of this information. Use of a term in this book should not be regarded as affecting the validity of any trademark or service mark.

This book is part of the Cisco Networking Academy® series from Cisco Press. The products in this series support and complement the Cisco Networking Academy curriculum. If you are using this book outside the Networking Academy, then you are not preparing with a Cisco trained and authorized Networking Academy provider.

For more information on the Cisco Networking Academy or to locate a Networking Academy, please visit www.cisco.com/edu.

CISCO.

Feedback Information

At Cisco Press, our goal is to create in-depth technical books of the highest quality and value. Each book is crafted with care and precision, undergoing rigorous development that involves the unique expertise of members from the professional technical community.

Readers' feedback is a natural continuation of this process. If you have any comments regarding how we could improve the quality of this book, or otherwise alter it to better suit your needs, you can contact us through email at feedback@ciscopress.com. Please make sure to include the book title and ISBN in your message.

We greatly appreciate your assistance.

Publisher	**Paul Boger**
Associate Publisher	**Dave Dusthimer**
Business Operations Manager, Cisco Press	**Jan Cornelssen**
Executive Editor	**Mary Beth Ray**
Managing Editor	**Sandra Schroeder**
Project Editor	**Seth Kerney**
Editorial Assistant	**Vanessa Evans**
Cover Designer	**Mark Shirar**
Compositor	**TnT Design, Inc.**

CISCO

Americas Headquarters
Cisco Systems, Inc.
San Jose, CA

Asia Pacific Headquarters
Cisco Systems (USA) Pte. Ltd.
Singapore

Europe Headquarters
Cisco Systems International BV
Amsterdam, The Netherlands

Cisco has more than 200 offices worldwide. Addresses, phone numbers, and fax numbers are listed on the Cisco Website at www.cisco.com/go/offices.

Contents

About This Lab Manual

Scaling Networks Lab Manual contains all the labs and class activities from the Cisco Networking Academy course of the same name. It is meant to be used within this program of study.

More Practice

If you would like more practice activities, combine your Lab Manual with the new *CCNA Routing and Switching Practice and Study Guide* ISBN: 9781587133442

Other Related Titles

CCNA Routing and Switching Portable Command Guide ISBN: 9781587204302 (or eBook ISBN: 9780133381368)

Scaling Networks Companion Guide ISBN: 9781587133282 (or eBook ISBN: 9780133476408)

Scaling Networks Course Booklet ISBN: 9781587133244

Command Syntax Conventions

The conventions used to present command syntax in this book are the same conventions used in the IOS Command Reference. The Command Reference describes these conventions as follows:

- **Boldface** indicates commands and keywords that are entered literally as shown. In actual configuration examples and output (not general command syntax), boldface indicates commands that are manually input by the user (such as a **show** command).

- *Italic* indicates arguments for which you supply actual values.

- Vertical bars (|) separate alternative, mutually exclusive elements.

- Square brackets ([ ]) indicate an optional element.

- Braces ({ }) indicate a required choice.

- Braces within brackets ([{ }]) indicate a required choice within an optional element.

Chapter 1 — Introduction to Scaling Networks

1.0.1.2 Class Activity – Network by Design

Objective

Explain the need to design a hierarchical network that is scalable.

Scenario

Your employer is opening a new, branch office.

You have been reassigned to the site as the network administrator where your job will be to design and maintain the new branch network.

The network administrators at the other branches used the Cisco three-layer hierarchical model when designing their networks. You decide to use the same approach.

To get an idea of what using the hierarchical model can do to enhance the design process, you research the topic.

Resources

- World Wide Web access
- Word processing software

Directions

Step 1: Use the Internet to find information and take notes about the Cisco three-layer hierarchical model. The site should include information about the:

a. Access layer

b. Distribution layer

c. Core layer

Step 2: In your research, make sure to include:

a. A simple definition of each hierarchical layer

b. Three concise facts about each layer

c. Network device capabilities needed at each layer

d. A detailed graphic that shows a full, three-layer hierarchical model design

Step 3: Create a simple table to organize and share your research with another student, group, the class, or instructor.

1.2.1.8 Lab – Selecting Switching Hardware

Objectives

Part 1: Explore Cisco Switch Products

Part 2: Select an Access Layer Switch

Part 3: Select a Distribution/Core Layer Switch

Background / Scenario

As a Network Engineer, you are part of a team that selects appropriate devices for your network. You need to consider the network requirements for the company as they migrate to a converged network. This converged network supports voice over IP (VoIP), video streaming, and expansion of the company to support a larger customer base.

For a small- to medium-sized company, Cisco hierarchical network design suggests only using a two-tier LAN design. This design consists of an access layer and a collapsed core/distribution layer. Network switches come in different form factors, and with various features and functions. When selecting a switch, the team must choose between fixed configuration or modular configuration, and stackable or non-stackable switches.

Based on a given set of requirements, you will identify the Cisco switch models and features to support the requirements. The scope of this lab will limit the switch models to campus LAN only.

Required Resources

PC with Internet access

Part 1: Explore Cisco Switch Products

In Part 1, you will navigate the Cisco website and explore available switch products.

Step 1:   Navigate the Cisco website.

At www.cisco.com, a list of available products and information about these products is available.

a.   From the home page, click **Products & Services** > **Switches**.

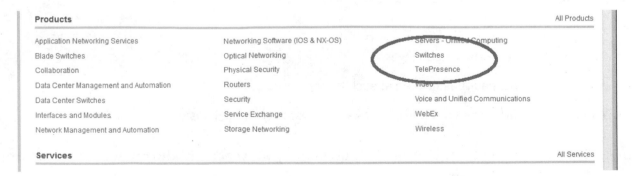

Step 2:   Explore switch products.

In the Feature Products section, a list of different categories of switches is displayed. In this lab, you will explore the campus LAN switches. You can click different links to gather information about the different switch models. On this page, the information is organized in different ways. You can view all available switches by clicking **View All Switches**. If you click **Compare Series**, the switches are organized by types: modular vs. fixed configuration.

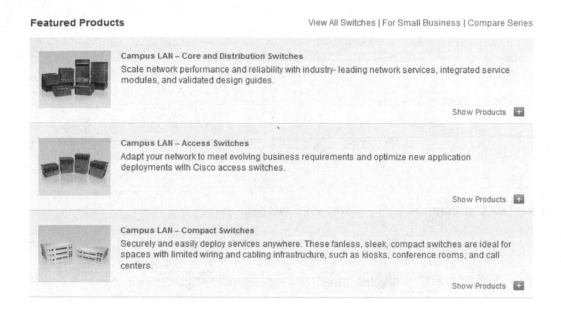

a. Click the heading **Campus LAN – Core and Distribution Switches**.

List a few models and some of features in the table below.

Model	Uplink Speed	Number of Ports/Speed	Other Features

b. Click the heading **Campus LAN – Access Switches**.

List a few models and some of features in the table below.

Model	Uplink Speed	Number of Ports/Speed	Other Features

c. Click the heading **Campus LAN – Compact Switches**.

List a few models and some of features in the table below.

Model	Uplink Speed	Number of Ports/Speed	Other Features

Part 2: Select an Access Layer Switch

The main function of an access layer switch is to provide network access to end user devices. This switch connects to the core/distribution layer switches. Access switches are usually located in the intermediate distribution frame (IDF). An IDF is mainly used for managing and interconnecting the telecommunications cables between end user devices and a main distribution frame (MDF). There are typically multiple IDFs with uplinks to a single centralized MDF.

An access switch should have the following capabilities: low cost per switch port, high port density, scalable uplinks to higher layers, and user access functions and resiliency. In Part 2, you will select an access switch based on the requirements set by the company. You have reviewed and become familiar with Cisco switch product line.

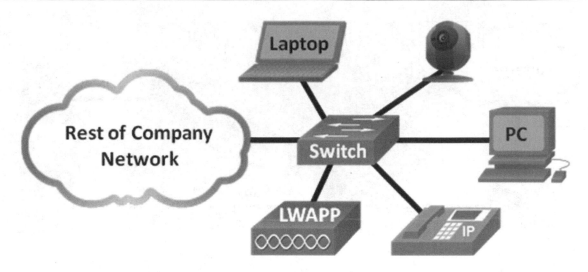

a. Company A requires a replacement access switch in the wiring closet. The company requires the switch to support VoIP and multicast, accommodate future growth of users and increased bandwidth usage. The switch must support a minimum of 35 current users and have a high-speed uplink. List a few of models that meet those requirements.

_____

_____

b. Company B would like to extend services to a conference room on an as-needed basis. The switch will be placed on the conference room table, and switch security is a priority.

_____

_____

Part 3: Select a Distribution/Core Layer Switch

The distribution/core switch is the backbone of the network for the company. A reliable network core is of paramount importance for the function of the company. A network backbone switch provides both adequate capacity for current and future traffic requirements and resilience in the event of failure. They also require high throughput, high availability, and advanced quality of service (QoS). These switches usually reside in the main wiring closet (MDF) along with high speed servers, routers, and the termination point of your ISP.

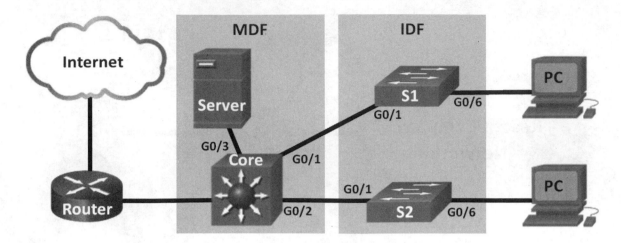

a. Company C will replace a backbone switch in the next budget cycle. The switch must provide redundancy features to minimize possible downtime in the event that an internal component fails. What features can accommodate these requirements for the replacement switch?

_____

_____

b. Which Cisco Catalyst switches would you recommend?

_____

c. As Company C grows, high speed, such as 10 GB Ethernet, up to 8 uplink ports, and a modular configuration for the switch will become necessary. Which switch models would meet the requirement?

_____

Reflection

What other factors should be considered during the selection process aside from network requirements and costs?

_____

_____

1.3.1.1 Class Activity – Layered Network Design Simulation

Objective

Explain the need to design a hierarchical network that is scalable.

Scenario

As the network administrator for a very small network, you want to prepare a simulated-network presentation for your branch manager to explain how the network currently operates.

The small network includes the following equipment:

- One Cisco 2911 series router
- One Cisco 3560 switch
- One Cisco 2960 switch
- Four user workstations (PCs or laptops)
- One printer

Resources

- Packet Tracer software

Directions

Step 1: Create a simple network topology using Packet Tracer software. Place the devices at the appropriate levels of the Cisco three-layer hierarchical model design, including:

a. One Cisco 2911 series router

b. One Cisco 3560 switch

c. One Cisco 2960 switch

d. Four user workstations (PCs or laptops)

e. One printer

Step 2: Using Packet Tracer's drawing tool and indicate the hierarchical layers with different color coding and labels:

a. Access layer

b. Distribution layer

c. Core layer

Step 3: Configure the network and user devices. Check for end-to-end connectivity.

Step 4: Share your configuration and hierarchical network design Packet Tracer file with another student, group, the class, or the instructor.

Chapter 2 — LAN Redundancy

2.0.1.2 Class Activity – Stormy Traffic

Objective

Explain the purpose of the Spanning Tree Protocol (STP) in a switched LAN environment with redundant switch links.

Scenario

It is your first day on the job as a network administrator for a small- to medium-sized business. The previous network administrator left suddenly after a network upgrade took place for the business.

During the upgrade, a new switch was added. Since the upgrade, many employees complain that they are having trouble accessing the Internet and servers on your network. In fact, most of them cannot access the network at all. Your corporate manager asks you to immediately research what could be causing these connectivity problems and delays.

So you take a look at the equipment operating on your network at your main distribution facility in the building. You notice that the network topology seems to be visually correct and that cables have been connected correctly, routers and switches are powered on and operational, and switches are connected together to provide backup or redundancy.

However, one thing you do notice is that all of your switches' status lights are constantly blinking at a very fast pace to the point that they almost appear solid. You think you have found the problem with the connectivity issues your employees are experiencing.

Use the Internet to research STP. As you research, take notes and describe:

- Broadcast storm

- Switching loops

- The purpose of STP

- Variations of STP

Complete the reflection questions that accompany the PDF file for this activity. Save your work and be prepared to share your answers with the class.

Resources

- Internet access to the World Wide Web

Reflection

1. What is a definition of a broadcast storm? How does a broadcast storm develop?

   _____

2. What is a definition of a switching loop? What causes a switching loop?

   _____

3. How can you mitigate broadcast storms and switching loops caused by introducing redundant switches to your network?

   _____

4. What is the IEEE standard for STP and some other STP variations, as mentioned in the hyperlinks provided?

   _____

5. In answer to this scenario, what would be your first step (after visually checking your network) to correcting the described network problem?

   _____

2.1.2.10 Lab – Building a Switched Network with Redundant Links

Topology

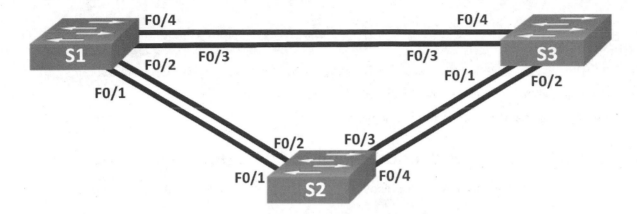

Addressing Table

Device	Interface	IP Address	Subnet Mask
S1	VLAN 1	192.168.1.1	255.255.255.0
S2	VLAN 1	192.168.1.2	255.255.255.0
S3	VLAN 1	192.168.1.3	255.255.255.0

Objectives

Part 1: Build the Network and Configure Basic Device Settings

Part 2: Determine the Root Bridge

Part 3: Observe STP Port Selection Based on Port Cost

Part 4: Observe STP Port Selection Based on Port Priority

Background / Scenario

Redundancy increases the availability of devices in the network topology by protecting the network from a single point of failure. Redundancy in a switched network is accomplished through the use of multiple switches or multiple links between switches. When physical redundancy is introduced into a network design, loops and duplicate frames can occur.

The Spanning Tree Protocol (STP) was developed as a Layer 2 loop-avoidance mechanism for redundant links in a switched network. STP ensures that there is only one logical path between all destinations on the network by intentionally blocking redundant paths that could cause a loop.

In this lab, you will use the **show spanning-tree** command to observe the STP election process of the root bridge. You will also observe the port selection process based on cost and priority.

Note: The switches used are Cisco Catalyst 2960s with Cisco IOS Release 15.0(2) (lanbasek9 image). Other switches and Cisco IOS versions can be used. Depending on the model and Cisco IOS version, the commands available and output produced might vary from what is shown in the labs.

Note: Make sure that the switches have been erased and have no startup configurations. If you are unsure, contact your instructor.

Required Resources

- 3 Switches (Cisco 2960 with Cisco IOS Release 15.0(2) lanbasek9 image or comparable)
- Console cables to configure the Cisco IOS devices via the console ports
- Ethernet cables as shown in the topology

Part 1: Build the Network and Configure Basic Device Settings

In Part 1, you will set up the network topology and configure basic settings on the switches.

Step 1: Cable the network as shown in the topology.

Attach the devices as shown in the topology diagram, and cable as necessary.

Step 2: Initialize and reload the switches as necessary.

Step 3: Configure basic settings for each switch.

a. Disable DNS lookup.

b. Configure the device name as shown in the topology.

c. Assign **class** as the encrypted privileged EXEC mode password.

d. Assign **cisco** as the console and vty passwords and enable login for console and vty lines.

e. Configure logging synchronous for the console line.

f. Configure a message of the day (MOTD) banner to warn users that unauthorized access is prohibited.

g. Configure the IP address listed in the Addressing Table for VLAN 1 on all switches.

h. Copy the running configuration to the startup configuration.

Step 4: Test connectivity.

Verify that the switches can ping one another.

Can S1 ping S2?   _____

Can S1 ping S3?   _____

Can S2 ping S3?   _____

Troubleshoot until you are able to answer yes to all questions.

Part 2: Determine the Root Bridge

Every spanning-tree instance (switched LAN or broadcast domain) has a switch designated as the root bridge. The root bridge serves as a reference point for all spanning-tree calculations to determine which redundant paths to block.

An election process determines which switch becomes the root bridge. The switch with the lowest bridge identifier (BID) becomes the root bridge. The BID is made up of a bridge priority value, an extended system ID, and the MAC address of the switch. The priority value can range from 0 to 65,535, in increments of 4,096, with a default value of 32,768.

Step 1: Deactivate all ports on the switches.

Step 2: Configure connected ports as trunks.

Step 3: Activate ports F0/2 and F0/4 on all switches.

Step 4: Display spanning tree information.

Issue the **show spanning-tree** command on all three switches. The Bridge ID Priority is calculated by adding the priority value and the extended system ID. The extended system ID is always the VLAN number. In the example below, all three switches have equal Bridge ID Priority values (32769 = 32768 + 1, where default priority = 32768, VLAN number = 1); therefore, the switch with the lowest MAC address becomes the root bridge (S2 in the example).

```
S1# show spanning-tree


VLAN0001
  Spanning tree enabled protocol ieee
  Root ID    Priority    32769
             Address     0cd9.96d2.4000
             Cost        19
             Port        2 (FastEthernet0/2)
             Hello Time   2 sec  Max Age 20 sec  Forward Delay 15 sec

  Bridge ID  Priority    32769  (priority 32768 sys-id-ext 1)
             Address     0cd9.96e8.8a00
             Hello Time   2 sec  Max Age 20 sec  Forward Delay 15 sec
             Aging Time  300 sec


Interface           Role Sts Cost      Prio.Nbr Type
------------------- ---- --- --------- -------- --------------------------------
Fa0/2               Root FWD 19        128.2    P2p
Fa0/4               Altn BLK 19        128.4    P2p
```

```
S2# show spanning-tree


VLAN0001
  Spanning tree enabled protocol ieee
  Root ID    Priority    32769
             Address     0cd9.96d2.4000
             This bridge is the root
             Hello Time   2 sec  Max Age 20 sec  Forward Delay 15 sec


  Bridge ID  Priority    32769  (priority 32768 sys-id-ext 1)
             Address     0cd9.96d2.4000
             Hello Time   2 sec  Max Age 20 sec  Forward Delay 15 sec
             Aging Time  300 sec


Interface          Role Sts Cost      Prio.Nbr Type
------------------- ---- --- --------- -------- -------------------------------
Fa0/2              Desg FWD 19        128.2    P2p
Fa0/4              Desg FWD 19        128.4    P2p


S3# show spanning-tree


VLAN0001
  Spanning tree enabled protocol ieee
  Root ID    Priority    32769
             Address     0cd9.96d2.4000
             Cost        19
             Port        2 (FastEthernet0/2)
             Hello Time   2 sec  Max Age 20 sec  Forward Delay 15 sec


  Bridge ID  Priority    32769  (priority 32768 sys-id-ext 1)
             Address     0cd9.96e8.7400
             Hello Time   2 sec  Max Age 20 sec  Forward Delay 15 sec
             Aging Time  300 sec


Interface          Role Sts Cost      Prio.Nbr Type
------------------- ---- --- --------- -------- -------------------------------
Fa0/2              Root FWD 19        128.2    P2p
Fa0/4              Desg FWD 19        128.4    P2p
```

Note: The default STP mode on the 2960 switch is Per VLAN Spanning Tree (PVST).

In the diagram below, record the Role and Status (Sts) of the active ports on each switch in the Topology.

S1 MAC: _____   **S3 MAC:** _____

S1 F0/4: _____   **S3 F0/4:** _____

S1 F0/3: _____   **S3 F0/3:** _____

S1 F0/1: _____   **S3 F0/2:** _____

S1 F0/2: _____   **S3 F0/1:** _____

S2 F0/2: _____   **S2 F0/3:** _____

S2 F0/1: _____   **S2 F0/4:** _____

S2 MAC: _____

Based on the output from your switches, answer the following questions.

Which switch is the root bridge? _____

Why did spanning tree select this switch as the root bridge?

_____

Which ports are the root ports on the switches? _____

Which ports are the designated ports on the switches? _____

What port is showing as an alternate port and is currently being blocked? _____

Why did spanning tree select this port as the non-designated (blocked) port?

_____

_____

_____

_____

Part 3: Observe STP Port Selection Based on Port Cost

The spanning tree algorithm (STA) uses the root bridge as the reference point and then determines which ports to block, based on path cost. The port with the lower path cost is preferred. If port costs are equal, then spanning tree compares BIDs. If the BIDs are equal, then the port priorities are used to break the tie. Lower values are always preferred. In Part 3, you will change the port cost to control which port is blocked by spanning tree.

Step 1: Locate the switch with the blocked port.

With the current configuration, only one switch should have a port that is blocked by STP. Issue the **show spanning-tree** command on both non-root switches. In the example below, spanning tree is blocking port F0/4 on the switch with the highest BID (S1).

```
S1# show spanning-tree


VLAN0001
  Spanning tree enabled protocol ieee
  Root ID    Priority    32769
             Address     0cd9.96d2.4000
             Cost        19
             Port        2 (FastEthernet0/2)
             Hello Time  2 sec  Max Age 20 sec  Forward Delay 15 sec


  Bridge ID  Priority    32769  (priority 32768 sys-id-ext 1)
             Address     0cd9.96e8.8a00
             Hello Time  2 sec  Max Age 20 sec  Forward Delay 15 sec
             Aging Time  300 sec


Interface           Role Sts Cost      Prio.Nbr Type
------------------- ---- --- --------- -------- -------------------------------
Fa0/2               Root FWD 19        128.2    P2p
Fa0/4               Altn BLK 19        128.4    P2p


S3# show spanning-tree


VLAN0001
  Spanning tree enabled protocol ieee
  Root ID    Priority    32769
             Address     0cd9.96d2.4000
             Cost        19
             Port        2 (FastEthernet0/2)
             Hello Time  2 sec  Max Age 20 sec  Forward Delay 15 sec


  Bridge ID  Priority    32769  (priority 32768 sys-id-ext 1)
```

```
              Address        0cd9.96e8.7400

              Hello Time    2 sec  Max Age 20 sec  Forward Delay 15 sec

              Aging Time    15   sec


Interface            Role Sts Cost      Prio.Nbr Type
------------------- ---- --- --------- -------- --------------------------------

Fa0/2                Root FWD 19        128.2    P2p
Fa0/4                Desg FWD 19        128.4    P2p
```

Note: Root bridge and port selection may differ in your topology.

Step 2: Change port cost.

In addition to the blocked port, the only other active port on this switch is the port designated as the root port. Lower the cost of this root port to 18 by issuing the **spanning-tree cost 18** interface configuration mode command.

```
S1(config)# interface f0/2
S1(config-if)# spanning-tree cost 18
```

Step 3: Observe spanning tree changes.

Re-issue the **show spanning-tree** command on both non-root switches. Observe that the previously blocked port (S1 - F0/4) is now a designated port and spanning tree is now blocking a port on the other non-root switch (S3 - F0/4).

```
S1# show spanning-tree


VLAN0001
  Spanning tree enabled protocol ieee
  Root ID    Priority    32769
             Address     0cd9.96d2.4000
             Cost        18
             Port        2 (FastEthernet0/2)
             Hello Time    2 sec  Max Age 20 sec  Forward Delay 15 sec


  Bridge ID  Priority    32769  (priority 32768 sys-id-ext 1)
             Address     0cd9.96e8.8a00
             Hello Time    2 sec  Max Age 20 sec  Forward Delay 15 sec
             Aging Time    300 sec


Interface            Role Sts Cost      Prio.Nbr Type
------------------- ---- --- --------- -------- --------------------------------

Fa0/2                Root FWD 18        128.2    P2p
Fa0/4                Desg FWD 19        128.4    P2p
```

```
S3# show spanning-tree


VLAN0001
  Spanning tree enabled protocol ieee
  Root ID    Priority    32769
             Address     0cd9.96d2.4000
             Cost        19
             Port        2 (FastEthernet0/2)
             Hello Time   2 sec  Max Age 20 sec  Forward Delay 15 sec

  Bridge ID  Priority    32769   (priority 32768 sys-id-ext 1)
             Address     0cd9.96e8.7400
             Hello Time   2 sec  Max Age 20 sec  Forward Delay 15 sec
             Aging Time  300 sec


Interface           Role Sts Cost      Prio.Nbr Type
------------------- ---- --- --------- -------- --------------------------------
Fa0/2               Root FWD 19        128.2    P2p
Fa0/4               Altn BLK 19        128.4    P2p
```

Why did spanning tree change the previously blocked port to a designated port, and block the port that was a designated port on the other switch?

_____

Step 4:   Remove port cost changes.

a. Issue the **no spanning-tree cost 18** interface configuration mode command to remove the cost statement that you created earlier.

   S1(config)# **interface f0/2**

   S1(config-if)# **no spanning-tree cost 18**

b. Re-issue the **show spanning-tree** command to verify that STP has reset the port on the non-root switches back to the original port settings. It takes approximately 30 seconds for STP to complete the port transition process.

Part 4:   Observe STP Port Selection Based on Port Priority

If port costs are equal, then spanning tree compares BIDs. If the BIDs are equal, then the port priorities are used to break the tie. The default port priority value is 128. STP aggregates the port priority with the port number to break ties. Lower values are always preferred. In Part 4, you will activate redundant paths to each switch to observe how STP selects a port using the port priority.

a. Activate ports F0/1 and F0/3 on all switches.

b. Wait 30 seconds for STP to complete the port transition process, and then issue the **show spanning-tree** command on the non-root switches. Observe that the root port has moved to the lower numbered port linked to the root switch, and blocked the previous root port.

```
S1# show spanning-tree


VLAN0001
  Spanning tree enabled protocol ieee
  Root ID    Priority    32769
             Address     0cd9.96d2.4000
             Cost        19
             Port        1 (FastEthernet0/1)
             Hello Time   2 sec  Max Age 20 sec  Forward Delay 15 sec


  Bridge ID  Priority    32769  (priority 32768 sys-id-ext 1)
             Address     0cd9.96e8.8a00
             Hello Time   2 sec  Max Age 20 sec  Forward Delay 15 sec
             Aging Time  15  sec


Interface           Role Sts Cost      Prio.Nbr Type
------------------- ---- --- --------- -------- --------------------------------
Fa0/1               Root FWD 19        128.1    P2p
Fa0/2               Altn BLK 19        128.2    P2p
Fa0/3               Altn BLK 19        128.3    P2p
Fa0/4               Altn BLK 19        128.4    P2p


S3# show spanning-tree


VLAN0001
  Spanning tree enabled protocol ieee
  Root ID    Priority    32769
             Address     0cd9.96d2.4000
             Cost        19
             Port        1 (FastEthernet0/1)
             Hello Time   2 sec  Max Age 20 sec  Forward Delay 15 sec


  Bridge ID  Priority    32769  (priority 32768 sys-id-ext 1)
             Address     0cd9.96e8.7400
             Hello Time   2 sec  Max Age 20 sec  Forward Delay 15 sec
             Aging Time  15  sec
```

```
Interface              Role Sts Cost      Prio.Nbr Type
-------------------    ---- --- --------- -------- --------------------------------
Fa0/1                  Root FWD 19        128.1    P2p
Fa0/2                  Altn BLK 19        128.2    P2p
Fa0/3                  Desg FWD 19        128.3    P2p
Fa0/4                  Desg FWD 19        128.4    P2p
```

What port did STP select as the root port on each non-root switch? _____

Why did STP select these ports as the root port on these switches?

_____

_____

Reflection

1. After a root bridge has been selected, what is the first value STP uses to determine port selection?

    _____

2. If the first value is equal on the two ports, what is the next value that STP uses to determine port selection?

    _____

3. If both values are equal on the two ports, what is the next value that STP uses to determine port selection?

    _____

2.3.2.3 Lab – Configuring Rapid PVST+, PortFast, and BPDU Guard

Topology

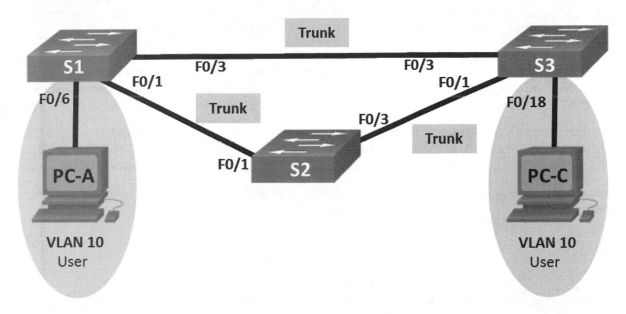

Addressing Table

Device	Interface	IP Address	Subnet Mask
S1	VLAN 99	192.168.1.11	255.255.255.0
S2	VLAN 99	192.168.1.12	255.255.255.0
S3	VLAN 99	192.168.1.13	255.255.255.0
PC-A	NIC	192.168.0.2	255.255.255.0
PC-C	NIC	192.168.0.3	255.255.255.0

VLAN Assignments

VLAN	Name
10	User
99	Management

Objectives

Part 1: Build the Network and Configure Basic Device Settings

Part 2: Configure VLANs, Native VLAN, and Trunks

Part 3: Configure the Root Bridge and Examine PVST+ Convergence

Part 4: Configure Rapid PVST+, PortFast, BPDU Guard, and Examine Convergence

Background / Scenario

The Per-VLAN Spanning Tree (PVST) protocol is Cisco proprietary. Cisco switches default to PVST. Rapid PVST+ (IEEE 802.1w) is an enhanced version of PVST+ and allows for faster spanning-tree calculations and convergence in response to Layer 2 topology changes. Rapid PVST+ defines three port states: discarding, learning, and forwarding, and provides multiple enhancements to optimize network performance.

In this lab, you will configure the primary and secondary root bridge, examine PVST+ convergence, configure Rapid PVST+ and compare its convergence to PVST+. In addition, you will configure edge ports to transition immediately to a forwarding state using PortFast and prevent the edge ports from forwarding BDPUs using BDPU guard.

Note: This lab provides minimal assistance with the actual commands necessary for configuration. However, the required commands are provided in Appendix A. Test your knowledge by trying to configure the devices without referring to the appendix.

Note: The switches used with CCNA hands-on labs are Cisco Catalyst 2960s with Cisco IOS Release 15.0(2) (lanbasek9 image). Other switches and Cisco IOS versions can be used. Depending on the model and Cisco IOS version, the commands available and output produced might vary from what is shown in the labs.

Note: Make sure that the switches have been erased and have no startup configurations. If you are unsure, contact your instructor.

Required Resources

- 3 Switches (Cisco 2960 with Cisco IOS Release 15.0(2) lanbasek9 image or comparable)
- 2 PCs (Windows 7, Vista, or XP with terminal emulation program, such as Tera Term)
- Console cables to configure the Cisco IOS devices via the console ports
- Ethernet cables as shown in the topology

Part 1: Build the Network and Configure Basic Device Settings

In Part 1, you will set up the network topology and configure basic settings, such as the interface IP addresses, device access, and passwords.

Step 1: Cable the network as shown in the topology.

Step 2: Configure PC hosts.

Step 3: Initialize and reload the switches as necessary.

Step 4: Configure basic settings for each switch.

a. Disable DNS lookup.

b. Configure the device name as shown in the Topology.

c. Assign **cisco** as the console and vty passwords and enable login.

d. Assign **class** as the encrypted privileged EXEC mode password.

e. Configure **logging synchronous** to prevent console messages from interrupting command entry.

f. Shut down all switch ports.

g. Copy the running configuration to startup configuration.

Part 2:   Configure VLANs, Native VLAN, and Trunks

In Part 2, you will create VLANs, assign switch ports to VLANs, configure trunk ports, and change the native VLAN for all switches.

Note: The required commands for Part 2 are provided in Appendix A. Test your knowledge by trying to configure the VLANs, native VLAN, and trunks without referring to the appendix.

Step 1:   Create VLANs.

Use the appropriate commands to create VLANs 10 and 99 on all of the switches. Name VLAN 10 as **User** and VLAN 99 as **Management**.

```
S1(config)# vlan 10
S1(config-vlan)# name User
S1(config-vlan)# vlan 99
S1(config-vlan)# name Management

S2(config)# vlan 10
S2(config-vlan)# name User
S2(config-vlan)# vlan 99
S2(config-vlan)# name Management

S3(config)# vlan 10
S3(config-vlan)# name User
S3(config-vlan)# vlan 99
S3(config-vlan)# name Management
```

Step 2:   Enable user ports in access mode and assign VLANs.

For S1 F0/6 and S3 F0/18, enable the ports, configure them as access ports, and assign them to VLAN 10.

Step 3:   Configure trunk ports and assign to native VLAN 99.

For ports F0/1 and F0/3 on all switches, enable the ports, configure them as trunk ports, and assign them to native VLAN 99.

Step 4:   Configure the management interface on all switches.

Using the Addressing Table, configure the management interface on all switches with the appropriate IP address.

Step 5:   Verify configurations and connectivity.

Use the **show vlan brief** command on all switches to verify that all VLANs are registered in the VLAN table and that the correct ports are assigned.

Use the **show interfaces trunk** command on all switches to verify trunk interfaces.

What is the default setting for spanning-tree mode on Cisco switches?

_____

Verify connectivity between PC-A and PC-C. Was your ping successful? _____

If your ping was unsuccessful, troubleshoot the configurations until the issue is resolved.

Note: It may be necessary to disable the PC firewall to successfully ping between PCs.

Part 3:   Configure the Root Bridge and Examine PVST+ Convergence

In Part 3, you will determine the default root in the network, assign the primary and secondary root, and use the **debug** command to examine convergence of PVST+.

Note: The required commands for Part 3 are provided in Appendix A. Test your knowledge by trying to configure the root bridge without referring to the appendix.

Step 1:   Determine the current root bridge.

Which command allows a user to determine the spanning-tree status of a Cisco Catalyst switch for all VLANs? Write the command in the space provided.

_____

Use the command on all three switches to determine the answers to the following questions:

Note: There are three instances of the spanning tree on each switch. The default STP configuration on Cisco switches is PVST+, which creates a separate spanning tree instance for each VLAN (VLAN 1 and any user-configured VLANs).

What is the bridge priority of switch S1 for VLAN 1? _____

What is the bridge priority of switch S2 for VLAN 1? _____

What is the bridge priority of switch S3 for VLAN 1? _____

Which switch is the root bridge? _____

Why was this switch elected as the root bridge?

_____

Step 2:   Configure a primary and secondary root bridge for all existing VLANs.

Having a root bridge (switch) elected by MAC address may lead to a suboptimal configuration. In this lab, you will configure switch S2 as the root bridge and S1 as the secondary root bridge.

a.   Configure switch S2 to be the primary root bridge for all existing VLANs. Write the command in the space provided.

_____

b. Configure switch S1 to be the secondary root bridge for all existing VLANs. Write the command in the space provided.

_____

Use the **show spanning-tree** command to answer the following questions:

What is the bridge priority of S1 for VLAN 1? _____

What is the bridge priority of S2 for VLAN 1? _____ .

Which interface in the network is in a blocking state? _____

Step 3: Change the Layer 2 topology and examine convergence.

To examine PVST+ convergence, you will create a Layer 2 topology change while using the **debug** command to monitor spanning-tree events.

a. Enter the **debug spanning-tree events** command in privileged EXEC mode on switch S3.

```
S3# debug spanning-tree events
Spanning Tree event debugging is on
```

b. Create a topology change by disabling interface F0/1 on S3.

```
S3(config)# interface f0/1

S3(config-if)# shutdown

*Mar  1 00:58:56.225: STP: VLAN0001 new root port Fa0/3, cost 38

*Mar  1 00:58:56.225: STP: VLAN0001 Fa0/3 -> listening

*Mar  1 00:58:56.225: STP[1]: Generating TC trap for port FastEthernet0/1

*Mar  1 00:58:56.225: STP: VLAN0010 new root port Fa0/3, cost 38

*Mar  1 00:58:56.225: STP: VLAN0010 Fa0/3 -> listening

*Mar  1 00:58:56.225: STP[10]: Generating TC trap for port FastEthernet0/1

*Mar  1 00:58:56.225: STP: VLAN0099 new root port Fa0/3, cost 38

*Mar  1 00:58:56.225: STP: VLAN0099 Fa0/3 -> listening

*Mar  1 00:58:56.225: STP[99]: Generating TC trap for port FastEthernet0/1

*Mar  1 00:58:56.242: %LINEPROTO-5-UPDOWN: Line protocol on Interface Vlan1, changed
state to down

*Mar  1 00:58:56.242: %LINEPROTO-5-UPDOWN: Line protocol on Interface Vlan99, changed
state to down

*Mar  1 00:58:58.214: %LINK-5-CHANGED: Interface FastEthernet0/1, changed state to ad-
ministratively down

*Mar  1 00:58:58.230: STP: VLAN0001 sent Topology Change Notice on Fa0/3

*Mar  1 00:58:58.230: STP: VLAN0010 sent Topology Change Notice on Fa0/3

*Mar  1 00:58:58.230: STP: VLAN0099 sent Topology Change Notice on Fa0/3

*Mar  1 00:58:59.220: %LINEPROTO-5-UPDOWN: Line protocol on Interface FastEthernet0/1,
changed state to down

*Mar  1 00:59:11.233: STP: VLAN0001 Fa0/3 -> learning

*Mar  1 00:59:11.233: STP: VLAN0010 Fa0/3 -> learning

*Mar  1 00:59:11.233: STP: VLAN0099 Fa0/3 -> learning
```

```
*Mar  1 00:59:26.240: STP[1]: Generating TC trap for port FastEthernet0/3
*Mar  1 00:59:26.240: STP: VLAN0001 Fa0/3 -> forwarding
*Mar  1 00:59:26.240: STP[10]: Generating TC trap for port FastEthernet0/3
*Mar  1 00:59:26.240: STP: VLAN0010 sent Topology Change Notice on Fa0/3
*Mar  1 00:59:26.240: STP: VLAN0010 Fa0/3 -> forwarding
*Mar  1 00:59:26.240: STP[99]: Generating TC trap for port FastEthernet0/3
*Mar  1 00:59:26.240: STP: VLAN0099 Fa0/3 -> forwarding
*Mar  1 00:59:26.248: %LINEPROTO-5-UPDOWN: Line protocol on Interface Vlan1, changed
state to up
*Mar  1 00:59:26.248: %LINEPROTO-5-UPDOWN: Line protocol on Interface Vlan99, changed
state to up
```

Note: Before proceeding, use the **debug** output to verify that all VLANs on F0/3 have reached a forwarding state then use the command **no debug spanning-tree events** to stop the **debug** output.

Through which port states do each VLAN on F0/3 proceed during network convergence?

_____

_____

Using the time stamp from the first and last STP debug message, calculate the time (to the nearest second) that it took for the network to converge. **Hint**: The debug timestamp format is date hh.mm.ss:msec.

_____

Part 4:   Configure Rapid PVST+, PortFast, BPDU Guard, and Examine Convergence

In Part 4, you will configure Rapid PVST+ on all switches. You will configure PortFast and BPDU guard on all access ports, and then use the **debug** command to examine Rapid PVST+ convergence.

Note: The required commands for Part 4 are provided in Appendix A. Test your knowledge by trying to configure the Rapid PVST+, PortFast, and BPDU guard without referring to the appendix.

Step 1:   Configure Rapid PVST+.

a.   Configure S1 for Rapid PVST+. Write the command in the space provided.

_____

b.   Configure S2 and S3 for Rapid PVST+.

c.   Verify configurations with the **show running-config | include spanning-tree mode** command.

```
S1# show running-config | include spanning-tree mode
spanning-tree mode rapid-pvst


S2# show running-config | include spanning-tree mode
spanning-tree mode rapid-pvst


S3# show running-config | include spanning-tree mode
spanning-tree mode rapid-pvst
```

Step 2: Configure PortFast and BPDU Guard on access ports.

PortFast is a feature of spanning tree that transitions a port immediately to a forwarding state as soon as it is turned on. This is useful in connecting hosts so that they can start communicating on the VLAN instantly, rather than waiting on spanning tree. To prevent ports that are configured with PortFast from forwarding BP-DUs, which could change the spanning tree topology, BPDU guard can be enabled. At the receipt of a BPDU, BPDU guard disables a port configured with PortFast.

a. Configure interface F0/6 on S1 with PortFast. Write the command in the space provided.

_____

b. Configure interface F0/6 on S1 with BPDU guard. Write the command in the space provided.

_____

c. Globally configure all non-trunking ports on switch S3 with PortFast. Write the command in the space provided.

_____

d. Globally configure all non-trunking PortFast ports on switch S3 with BPDU guard. Write the command in the space provided.

_____

Step 3: Examine Rapid PVST+ convergence.

a. Enter the **debug spanning-tree events** command in privileged EXEC mode on switch S3.

b. Create a topology change by enabling interface F0/1 on switch S3.

```
S3(config)# interface f0/1
S3(config-if)# no shutdown
*Mar  1 01:28:34.946: %LINK-3-UPDOWN: Interface FastEthernet0/1, changed state to up
*Mar  1 01:28:37.588: RSTP(1): initializing port Fa0/1
*Mar  1 01:28:37.588: RSTP(1): Fa0/1 is now designated
*Mar  1 01:28:37.588: RSTP(10): initializing port Fa0/1
*Mar  1 01:28:37.588: RSTP(10): Fa0/1 is now designated
*Mar  1 01:28:37.588: RSTP(99): initializing port Fa0/1
*Mar  1 01:28:37.588: RSTP(99): Fa0/1 is now designated
*Mar  1 01:28:37.597: RSTP(1): transmitting a proposal on Fa0/1
*Mar  1 01:28:37.597: RSTP(10): transmitting a proposal on Fa0/1
*Mar  1 01:28:37.597: RSTP(99): transmitting a proposal on Fa0/1
*Mar  1 01:28:37.597: RSTP(1): updt roles, received superior bpdu on Fa0/1
*Mar  1 01:28:37.597: RSTP(1): Fa0/1 is now root port
*Mar  1 01:28:37.597: RSTP(1): Fa0/3 blocked by re-root
```

```
*Mar  1 01:28:37.597: RSTP(1): synced Fa0/1

*Mar  1 01:28:37.597: RSTP(1): Fa0/3 is now alternate

*Mar  1 01:28:37.597: RSTP(10): updt roles, received superior bpdu on Fa0/1

*Mar  1 01:28:37.597: RSTP(10): Fa0/1 is now root port

*Mar  1 01:28:37.597: RSTP(10): Fa0/3 blocked by re-root

*Mar  1 01:28:37.597: RSTP(10): synced Fa0/1

*Mar  1 01:28:37.597: RSTP(10): Fa0/3 is now alternate

*Mar  1 01:28:37.597: RSTP(99): updt roles, received superior bpdu on Fa0/1

*Mar  1 01:28:37.605: RSTP(99): Fa0/1 is now root port

*Mar  1 01:28:37.605: RSTP(99): Fa0/3 blocked by re-root

*Mar  1 01:28:37.605: RSTP(99): synced Fa0/1

*Mar  1 01:28:37.605: RSTP(99): Fa0/3 is now alternate

*Mar  1 01:28:37.605: STP[1]: Generating TC trap for port FastEthernet0/1

*Mar  1 01:28:37.605: STP[10]: Generating TC trap for port FastEthernet0/1

*Mar  1 01:28:37.605: STP[99]: Generating TC trap for port FastEthernet0/1

*Mar  1 01:28:37.622: RSTP(1): transmitting an agreement on Fa0/1 as a response to a
proposal

*Mar  1 01:28:37.622: RSTP(10): transmitting an agreement on Fa0/1 as a response to a
proposal

*Mar  1 01:28:37.622: RSTP(99): transmitting an agreement on Fa0/1 as a response to a
proposal

*Mar  1 01:28:38.595: %LINEPROTO-5-UPDOWN: Line protocol on Interface FastEthernet0/1,
changed state to up
```

Using the time stamp from the first and last RSTP debug message, calculate the time that it took for the network to converge.

_____

Reflection

1. What is the main benefit of using Rapid PVST+?

_____

_____

2. How does configuring a port with PortFast allow for faster convergence?

_____

_____

3. What protection does BPDU guard provide?

_____

_____

Appendix A – Switch Configuration Commands

Switch S1

```
S1(config)# vlan 10
S1(config-vlan)# name User
S1(config-vlan)# vlan 99
S1(config-vlan)# name Management
S1(config-vlan)# exit
S1(config)# interface f0/6
S1(config-if)# no shutdown
S1(config-if)# switchport mode access
S1(config-if)# switchport access vlan 10
S1(config-if)# interface f0/1
S1(config-if)# no shutdown
S1(config-if)# switchport mode trunk
S1(config-if)# switchport trunk native vlan 99
S1(config-if)# interface f0/3
S1(config-if)# no shutdown
S1(config-if)# switchport mode trunk
S1(config-if)# switchport trunk native vlan 99
S1(config-if)# interface vlan 99
S1(config-if)# ip address 192.168.1.11 255.255.255.0
S1(config-if)# exit
S1(config)# spanning-tree vlan 1,10,99 root secondary
S1(config)# spanning-tree mode rapid-pvst
S1(config)# interface f0/6
S1(config-if)# spanning-tree portfast
S1(config-if)# spanning-tree bpduguard enable
```

Switch S2

```
S2(config)# vlan 10
S2(config-vlan)# name User
S2(config-vlan)# vlan 99
S2(config-vlan)# name Management
S2(config-vlan)# exit
S2(config)# interface f0/1
S2(config-if)# no shutdown
S2(config-if)# switchport mode trunk
S2(config-if)# switchport trunk native vlan 99
```

```
S2(config-if)# interface f0/3

S2(config-if)# no shutdown

S2(config-if)# switchport mode trunk

S2(config-if)# switchport trunk native vlan 99

S2(config-if)# interface vlan 99

S2(config-if)# ip address 192.168.1.12 255.255.255.0

S2(config-if)# exit

S2(config)# spanning-tree vlan 1,10,99 root primary

S2(config)# spanning-tree mode rapid-pvst
```

Switch S3

```
S3(config)# vlan 10

S3(config-vlan)# name User

S3(config-vlan)# vlan 99

S3(config-vlan)# name Management

S3(config-vlan)# exit

S3(config)# interface f0/18

S3(config-if)# no shutdown

S3(config-if)# switchport mode access

S3(config-if)# switchport access vlan 10

S3(config-if)# spanning-tree portfast

S3(config-if)# spanning-tree bpduguard enable

S3(config-if)# interface f0/1

S3(config-if)# no shutdown

S3(config-if)# switchport mode trunk

S3(config-if)# switchport trunk native vlan 99

S3(config-if)# interface f0/3

S3(config-if)# no shutdown

S3(config-if)# switchport mode trunk

S3(config-if)# switchport trunk native vlan 99

S3(config-if)# interface vlan 99

S3(config-if)# ip address 192.168.1.13 255.255.255.0

S3(config-if)# exit

S3(config)# spanning-tree mode rapid-pvst
```

2.4.3.4 Lab – Configuring HSRP and GLBP

Topology

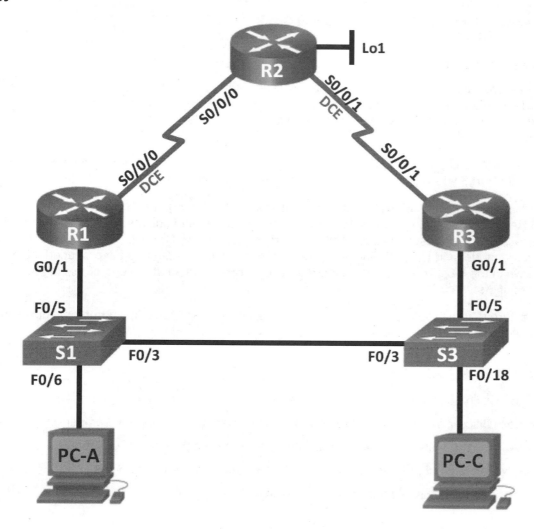

Addressing Table

Device	Interface	IP Address	Subnet Mask	Default Gateway
R1	G0/1	192.168.1.1	255.255.255.0	N/A
	S0/0/0 (DCE)	10.1.1.1	255.255.255.252	N/A
R2	S0/0/0	10.1.1.2	255.255.255.252	N/A
	S0/0/1 (DCE)	10.2.2.2	255.255.255.252	N/A
	Lo1	209.165.200.225	255.255.255.224	N/A
R3	G0/1	192.168.1.3	255.255.255.0	N/A
	S0/0/1	10.2.2.1	255.255.255.252	N/A
S1	VLAN 1	192.168.1.11	255.255.255.0	192.168.1.1
S3	VLAN 1	192.168.1.13	255.255.255.0	192.168.1.3
PC-A	NIC	192.168.1.31	255.255.255.0	192.168.1.1
PC-C	NIC	192.168.1.33	255.255.255.0	192.168.1.3

Objectives

Part 1: Build the Network and Verify Connectivity

Part 2: Configure First Hop Redundancy using HSRP

Part 3: Configure First Hop Redundancy using GLBP

Background / Scenario

Spanning tree provides loop-free redundancy between switches within your LAN. However, it does not provide redundant default gateways for end-user devices within your network if one of your routers fails. First Hop Redundancy Protocols (FHRPs) provide redundant default gateways for end devices with no end-user configuration necessary.

In this lab, you will configure two FHRPs. In Part 2, you will configure Cisco's Hot Standby Routing Protocol (HSRP), and in Part 3 you will configure Cisco's Gateway Load Balancing Protocol (GLBP).

Note: The routers used with CCNA hands-on labs are Cisco 1941 Integrated Services Routers (ISRs) with Cisco IOS Release 15.2(4)M3 (universalk9 image). The switches used are Cisco Catalyst 2960s with Cisco IOS Release 15.0(2) (lanbasek9 image). Other routers, switches, and Cisco IOS versions can be used. Depending on the model and Cisco IOS version, the commands available and output produced might vary from what is shown in the labs. Refer to the Router Interface Summary Table at the end of this lab for the correct interface identifiers.

Note: Make sure that the routers and switches have been erased and have no startup configurations. If you are unsure, contact your instructor.

Required Resources

- 3 Routers (Cisco 1941 with Cisco IOS Release 15.2(4)M3 universal image or comparable)
- 2 Switches (Cisco 2960 with Cisco IOS Release 15.0(2) lanbasek9 image or comparable)
- 2 PCs (Windows 7, Vista, or XP with terminal emulation program, such as Tera Term)
- Console cables to configure the Cisco IOS devices via the console ports
- Ethernet and serial cables as shown in the topology

Part 1: Build the Network and Verify Connectivity

In Part 1, you will set up the network topology and configure basic settings, such as the interface IP addresses, static routing, device access, and passwords.

Step 1: Cable the network as shown in the topology.

Attach the devices as shown in the topology diagram, and cable as necessary.

Step 2: Configure PC hosts.

Step 3: Initialize and reload the routers and switches as necessary.

Step 4: Configure basic settings for each router.

a. Disable DNS lookup.

b. Configure the device name as shown in the topology.

c. Configure IP addresses for the routers as listed in the Addressing Table.

d. Set clock rate to **128000** for all DCE serial interfaces.

e. Assign **class** as the encrypted privileged EXEC mode password.

f. Assign **cisco** for the console and vty password and enable login.

g. Configure **logging synchronous** to prevent console messages from interrupting command entry.

h. Copy the running configuration to the startup configuration.

Step 5: Configure basic settings for each switch.

a. Disable DNS lookup.

b. Configure the device name as shown in the topology.

c. Assign **class** as the encrypted privileged EXEC mode password.

d. Configure IP addresses for the switches as listed in the Addressing Table.

e. Configure the default gateway on each switch.

f. Assign **cisco** for the console and vty password and enable login.

g. Configure **logging synchronous** to prevent console messages from interrupting command entry.

h. Copy the running configuration to the startup configuration.

Step 6: Verify connectivity between PC-A and PC-C.

Ping from PC-A to PC-C. Were the ping results successful? _____

If the pings are not successful, troubleshoot the basic device configurations before continuing.

Note: It may be necessary to disable the PC firewall to successfully ping between PCs.

Step 7: Configure routing.

a. Configure EIGRP on the routers and use AS of 1. Add all the networks, except 209.165.200.224/27 into the EIGRP process.

b. Configure a default route on R2 using Lo1 as the exit interface to 209.165.200.224/27 network and redistribute this route into the EIGRP process.

Step 8: Verify connectivity.

a. From PC-A, you should be able to ping every interface on R1, R2, R3, and PC-C. Were all pings successful? _____

b. From PC-C, you should be able to ping every interface on R1, R2, R3, and PC-A. Were all pings successful? _____

Part 2: Configure First Hop Redundancy Using HSRP

Even though the topology has been designed with some redundancy (two routers and two switches on the same LAN network), both PC-A and PC-C are configured with only one gateway address. PC-A is using R1 and PC-C is using R3. If either of these routers or the interfaces on the routers went down, the PC could lose its connection to the Internet.

In Part 2, you will test how the network behaves both before and after configuring HSRP. To do this, you will determine the path that packets take to the loopback address on R2.

Step 1: Determine the path for Internet traffic for PC-A and PC-C.

a. From a command prompt on PC-A, issue a **tracert** command to the 209.165.200.225 loopback address of R2.

```
C:\ tracert 209.165.200.225

Tracing route to 209.165.200.225 over a maximum of 30 hops


   1    1 ms     1 ms     1 ms   192.168.1.1
   2   13 ms    13 ms    13 ms   209.165.200.225


Trace complete.
```

What path did the packets take from PC-A to 209.165.200.225? _____

b. From a command prompt on PC-C, issue a **tracert** command to the 209.165.200.225 loopback address of R2.

What path did the packets take from PC-C to 209.165.200.225? _____

Step 2: Start a ping session on PC-A, and break the connection between S1 and R1.

a. From a command prompt on PC-A, issue a **ping –t** command to the **209.165.200.225** address on R2. Make sure you leave the command prompt window open.

Note: The pings continue until you press **Ctrl+C**, or until you close the command prompt window.

```
C:\ ping -t 209.165.200.225

Pinging 209.165.200.225 with 32 bytes of data:
Reply from 209.165.200.225: bytes=32 time=9ms TTL=254
Reply from 209.165.200.225: bytes=32 time=9ms TTL=254
Reply from 209.165.200.225: bytes=32 time=9ms TTL=254
Reply from 209.165.200.225: bytes=32 time=9ms TTL=254
Reply from 209.165.200.225: bytes=32 time=9ms TTL=254
Reply from 209.165.200.225: bytes=32 time=9ms TTL=254
Reply from 209.165.200.225: bytes=32 time=9ms TTL=254
Reply from 209.165.200.225: bytes=32 time=9ms TTL=254
Reply from 209.165.200.225: bytes=32 time=9ms TTL=254
Reply from 209.165.200.225: bytes=32 time=9ms TTL=254
Reply from 209.165.200.225: bytes=32 time=9ms TTL=254
```

```
Reply from 209.165.200.225: bytes=32 time=9ms TTL=254

Reply from 209.165.200.225: bytes=32 time=9ms TTL=254

<output omitted>
```

b. As the ping continues, disconnect the Ethernet cable from F0/5 on S1. You can also shut down the S1 F0/5 interface, which creates the same result.

   What happened to the ping traffic?

   _____

c. Repeat Steps 2a and 2b on PC-C and S3. Disconnect cable from F0/5 on S3.

   What were your results?

   _____

d. Reconnect the Ethernet cables to F0/5 or enable the F0/5 interface on both S1 and S3, respectively. Re-issue pings to 209.165.200.225 from both PC-A and PC-C to make sure connectivity is re-established.

Step 3:   Configure HSRP on R1 and R3.

In this step, you will configure HSRP and change the default gateway address on PC-A, PC-C, S1, and S2 to the virtual IP address for HSRP. R1 becomes the active router via configuration of the HSRP priority command.

a. Configure HSRP on R1.

```
R1(config)# interface g0/1

R1(config-if)# standby 1 ip 192.168.1.254

R1(config-if)# standby 1 priority 150

R1(config-if)# standby 1 preempt
```

b. Configure HSRP on R3.

```
R3(config)# interface g0/1

R3(config-if)# standby 1 ip 192.168.1.254
```

c. Verify HSRP by issuing the **show standby** command on R1 and R3.

```
R1# show standby

GigabitEthernet0/1 - Group 1

  State is Active

    1 state change, last state change 00:02:11

  Virtual IP address is 192.168.1.254

  Active virtual MAC address is 0000.0c07.ac01

    Local virtual MAC address is 0000.0c07.ac01 (v1 default)

  Hello time 3 sec, hold time 10 sec

    Next hello sent in 0.784 secs

  Preemption enabled

  Active router is local

  Standby router is 192.168.1.3, priority 100 (expires in 9.568 sec)

  Priority 150 (configured 150)

  Group name is "hsrp-Gi0/1-1" (default)
```

```
R3# show standby
GigabitEthernet0/1 - Group 1
  State is Standby
    4 state changes, last state change 00:02:20
  Virtual IP address is 192.168.1.254
  Active virtual MAC address is 0000.0c07.ac01
    Local virtual MAC address is 0000.0c07.ac01 (v1 default)
  Hello time 3 sec, hold time 10 sec
    Next hello sent in 2.128 secs
  Preemption disabled
  Active router is 192.168.1.1, priority 150 (expires in 10.592 sec)
  Standby router is local
  Priority 100 (default 100)
  Group name is "hsrp-Gi0/1-1" (default)
```

Using the output shown above, answer the following questions:

Which router is the active router? _____

What is the MAC address for the virtual IP address? _____

What is the IP address and priority of the standby router?

_____

_____

d. Use the **show standby brief** command on R1 and R3 to view an HSRP status summary. Sample output is shown below.

```
R1# show standby brief
                     P indicates configured to preempt.
                     |
Interface   Grp  Pri P State    Active         Standby        Virtual IP
Gi0/1       1    150 P Active   local          192.168.1.3    192.168.1.254


R3# show standby brief
                     P indicates configured to preempt.
                     |
Interface   Grp  Pri P State    Active         Standby        Virtual IP
Gi0/1       1    100   Standby 192.168.1.1     local          192.168.1.254
```

e. Change the default gateway address for PC-A, PC-C, S1, and S3. Which address should you use?

_____

Verify the new settings. Issue a ping from both PC-A and PC-C to the loopback address of R2. Are the pings successful? _____

Step 4:   Start a ping session on PC-A and break the connection between the switch that is connected to the Active HSRP router (R1).

a. From a command prompt on PC-A, issue a **ping –t** command to the 209.165.200.225 address on R2. Ensure that you leave the command prompt window open.

b. As the ping continues, disconnect the Ethernet cable from F0/5 on S1 or shut down the F0/5 interface.

What happened to the ping traffic?

_____

_____

_____

Step 5:   Verify HSRP settings on R1 and R3.

a. Issue the **show standby brief** command on R1 and R3.

Which router is the active router? _____

b. Reconnect the cable between the switch and the router or enable interface F0/5.

c. Disable the HSRP configuration commands on R1 and R3.

```
R1(config)# interface g0/1
R1(config-if)# no standby 1


R3(config)# interface g0/1
R3(config-if)# no standby 1
```

Part 3:   Configure First Hop Redundancy Using GLBP

By default, HSRP does NOT do load balancing. The active router always handles all of the traffic, while the standby router sits unused, unless there is a link failure. This is not an efficient use of resources. GLBP provides nonstop path redundancy for IP by sharing protocol and MAC addresses between redundant gateways. GLBP also allows a group of routers to share the load of the default gateway on a LAN. Configuring GLBP is very similar to HSRP. Load balancing can be done in a variety of ways using GLBP. In this lab, you will use the round-robin method.

Step 1:   Configure GLBP on R1 and R3.

a. Configure GLBP on R1.

```
R1(config)# interface g0/1
R1(config-if)# glbp 1 ip 192.168.1.254
R1(config-if)# glbp 1 preempt
R1(config-if)# glbp 1 priority 150
R1(config-if)# glbp 1 load-balancing round-robin
```

b. Configure GLBP on R3.

```
R3(config)# interface g0/1
R3(config-if)# glbp 1 ip 192.168.1.254
R3(config-if)# glbp 1 load-balancing round-robin
```

Step 2: Verify GLBP on R1 and R3.

a. Issue the **show glbp brief** command on R1 and R3.

```
R1# show glbp brief
Interface   Grp  Fwd Pri State     Address          Active router    Standby router
Gi0/1       1    -   150 Active    192.168.1.254    local            192.168.1.3
Gi0/1       1    1   -   Active    0007.b400.0101   local            -
Gi0/1       1    2   -   Listen    0007.b400.0102   192.168.1.3      -
```

```
R3# show glbp brief
Interface   Grp  Fwd Pri State     Address          Active router    Standby router
Gi0/1       1    -   100 Standby   192.168.1.254    192.168.1.1      local
Gi0/1       1    1   -   Listen    0007.b400.0101   192.168.1.1      -
Gi0/1       1    2   -   Active    0007.b400.0102   local            -
```

Step 3: Generate traffic from PC-A and PC-C to the R2 loopback interface.

a. From a command prompt on PC-A, ping the 209.165.200.225 address of R2.

```
C:\> ping 209.165.200.225
```

b. Issue an **arp –a** command on PC-A. Which MAC address is used for the 192.168.1.254 address?

_____

c. Generate more traffic to the loopback interface of R2. Issue another **arp –a** command. Did the MAC address change for the default gateway address of 192.168.1.254?

_____

As you can see, both R1 and R3 play a role in forwarding traffic to the loopback interface of R2. Neither router remains idle.

Step 4: Start a ping session on PC-A, and break the connection between the switch that is connected to R1.

a. From a command prompt on PC-A, issue a **ping –t** command to the 209.165.200.225 address on R2. Make sure you leave the command prompt window open.

b. As the ping continues, disconnect the Ethernet cable from F0/5 on S1 or shut down the F0/5 interface.

What happened to the ping traffic?

_____

Reflection

1. Why would there be a need for redundancy in a LAN?

_____

2. If you had a choice, which protocol would you implement in your network, HSRP or GLBP? Explain your choice.

_____

Router Interface Summary Table

Router Interface Summary				
Router Model	**Ethernet Interface #1**	**Ethernet Interface #2**	**Serial Interface #1**	**Serial Interface #2**
1800	Fast Ethernet 0/0 (F0/0)	Fast Ethernet 0/1 (F0/1)	Serial 0/0/0 (S0/0/0)	Serial 0/0/1 (S0/0/1)
1900	Gigabit Ethernet 0/0 (G0/0)	Gigabit Ethernet 0/1 (G0/1)	Serial 0/0/0 (S0/0/0)	Serial 0/0/1 (S0/0/1)
2801	Fast Ethernet 0/0 (F0/0)	Fast Ethernet 0/1 (F0/1)	Serial 0/1/0 (S0/1/0)	Serial 0/1/1 (S0/1/1)
2811	Fast Ethernet 0/0 (F0/0)	Fast Ethernet 0/1 (F0/1)	Serial 0/0/0 (S0/0/0)	Serial 0/0/1 (S0/0/1)
2900	Gigabit Ethernet 0/0 (G0/0)	Gigabit Ethernet 0/1 (G0/1)	Serial 0/0/0 (S0/0/0)	Serial 0/0/1 (S0/0/1)

Note: To find out how the router is configured, look at the interfaces to identify the type of router and how many interfaces the router has. There is no way to effectively list all the combinations of configurations for each router class. This table includes identifiers for the possible combinations of Ethernet and Serial interfaces in the device. The table does not include any other type of interface, even though a specific router may contain one. An example of this might be an ISDN BRI interface. The string in parenthesis is the legal abbreviation that can be used in Cisco IOS commands to represent the interface.

2.5.1.1 Class Activity– Documentation Tree

Objective

Identify common STP configuration issues.

Scenario

The employees in your building are having difficulty accessing a web server on the network. You look for the network documentation that the previous network engineer used before he transitioned to a new job; however, you cannot find any network documentation whatsoever.

Therefore, you decide create your own network recordkeeping system. You decide to start at the access layer of your network hierarchy. This is where redundant switches are located, as well as the company servers, printers, and local hosts.

You create a matrix to record your documentation and include access layer switches on the list. You also decide to document switch names, ports in use, cabling connections, and root ports, designated ports, and alternate ports.

For more detailed instructions on how to design your model, use the student PDF that accompanies this activity.

Resources

- Packet Tracer software
- Word processing software

Directions

Step 1:   Create the topology diagram with three redundant switches.

Step 2:   Connect host devices to the switches.

Step 3:   Create the switch documentation matrix.

   a.   Name and switch location

   b.   General switch description

   c.   Model, IOS version, and image name

   d.   Switch serial number

   e.   MAC address

   f.   Ports currently in use

   g.   Cable connections

   h.   Root ports

   i.   Designated ports, status, and cost

   j.   Alternate ports, status, and cost

Step 4:   Use show commands to locate Layer 2 switch information.

   a.   show version

   b.   show cdp neighbors detail

   c.   show spanning-tree

Chapter 3 — Link Aggregation

3.0.1.2 Class Activity – Imagine This

Objective

Explain the operation of link aggregation in a switched LAN environment.

Scenario

It is the end of the work day. In your small- to medium-sized business, you are trying to explain to the network engineers about EtherChannel and how it looks when it is physically set up. The network engineers have difficulties envisioning how two switches could possibly be connected via several links that collectively act as one channel or connection. Your company is definitely considering implementing an EtherChannel network.

Therefore, you end the meeting with an assignment for the engineers. To prepare for the next day's meeting, they are to perform some research and bring to the meeting one graphic representation of an EtherChannel network connection. They are tasked with explaining how an EtherChannel network operates to the other engineers.

When researching EtherChannel, a good question to search for is "What does EtherChannel look like?" Prepare a few slides to demonstrate your research that will be presented to the network engineering group. These slides should provide a solid grasp of how EtherChannels are physically created within a network topology. Your goal is to ensure that everyone leaving the next meeting will have a good idea as to why they would consider moving to a network topology using EtherChannel as an option.

Required Resources

- Internet connectivity for research
- Software program for presentation model

Step 1: Use the Internet to research graphics depicting EtherChannel.

Step 2: Prepare a three-slide presentation to share with the class.

a. The first slide should show a very short, concise definition of a switch-to-switch EtherChannel.

b. The second slide should show a graphic of how a switch-to-switch EtherChannel physical topology would look if used in a small- to medium-sized business.

c. The third slide should list three advantages of using EtherChannel.

3.2.1.4 Lab – Configuring EtherChannel

Topology

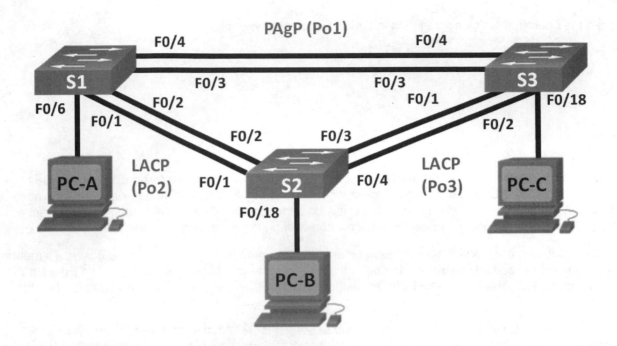

Addressing Table

Device	Interface	IP Address	Subnet Mask
S1	VLAN 99	192.168.99.11	255.255.255.0
S2	VLAN 99	192.168.99.12	255.255.255.0
S3	VLAN 99	192.168.99.13	255.255.255.0
PC-A	NIC	192.168.10.1	255.255.255.0
PC-B	NIC	192.168.10.2	255.255.255.0
PC-C	NIC	192.168.10.3	255.255.255.0

Objectives

Part 1: Configure Basic Switch Settings

Part 2: Configure PAgP

Part 3: Configure LACP

Background / Scenario

Link aggregation allows the creation of logical links that are comprised of two or more physical links. This provides increased throughput beyond using only one physical link. Link aggregation also provides redundancy if one of the links fails.

In this lab, you will configure EtherChannel, a form of link aggregation used in switched networks. You will configure EtherChannel using Port Aggregation Protocol (PAgP) and Link Aggregation Control Protocol (LACP).

Note: PAgP is a Cisco-proprietary protocol that you can only run on Cisco switches and on switches that are licensed vendors to support PAgP. LACP is a link aggregation protocol that is defined by IEEE 802.3ad, and it is not associated with any specific vendor.

LACP allows Cisco switches to manage Ethernet channels between switches that conform to the 802.3ad protocol. You can configure up to 16 ports to form a channel. Eight of the ports are in active mode and the other eight are in standby mode. When any of the active ports fail, a standby port becomes active. Standby mode works only for LACP, not for PAgP.

Note: The switches used with CCNA hands-on labs are Cisco Catalyst 2960s with Cisco IOS Release 15.0(2) (lanbasek9 image). Other switches and Cisco IOS versions can be used. Depending on the model and Cisco IOS version, the commands available and output produced might vary from what is shown in the labs.

Note: Make sure that the switches have been erased and have no startup configurations. If you are unsure, contact your instructor.

Required Resources

- 3 Switches (Cisco 2960 with Cisco IOS Release 15.0(2) lanbasek9 image or comparable)
- 3 PCs (Windows 7, Vista, or XP with terminal emulation program, such as Tera Term)
- Console cables to configure the Cisco IOS devices via the console ports
- Ethernet cables as shown in the topology

Part 1: Configure Basic Switch Settings

In Part 1, you will set up the network topology and configure basic settings, such as the interface IP addresses, device access, and passwords.

Step 1: Cable the network as shown in the topology.

Attach the devices as shown in the topology diagram, and cable as necessary.

Step 2: Initialize and reload the switches.

Step 3: Configure basic settings for each switch.

a. Disable DNS lookup.

b. Configure the device name as displayed in the topology.

c. Encrypt plain text passwords.

d. Create a MOTD banner warning users that unauthorized access is prohibited.

e. Assign **class** as the encrypted privileged EXEC mode password.

f. Assign **cisco** as the console and vty password and enable login.

g. Configure logging synchronous to prevent console message from interrupting command entry.

h. Shut down all switchports except the ports connected to PCs.

i. Configure VLAN 99 and name it **Management**.

j. Configure VLAN 10 and name it **Staff**.

k. Configure the switch ports with attached hosts as access ports in VLAN 10.

l. Assign the IP addresses according to the Addressing Table.

m. Copy the running configuration to startup configuration.

Step 4: Configure the PCs.

Assign IP addresses to the PCs according to the Addressing Table.

Part 2: Configure PAgP

PAgP is a Cisco proprietary protocol for link aggregation. In Part 2, a link between S1 and S3 will be configured using PAgP.

Step 1: Configure PAgP on S1 and S3.

For a link between S1 and S3, configure the ports on S1 with PAgP desirable mode and the ports on S3 with PAgP auto mode. Enable the ports after PAgP modes have been configured.

```
S1(config)# interface range f0/3-4
S1(config-if-range)# channel-group 1 mode desirable
Creating a port-channel interface Port-channel 1


S1(config-if-range)# no shutdown


S3(config)# interface range f0/3-4
S3(config-if-range)# channel-group 1 mode auto
Creating a port-channel interface Port-channel 1


S3(config-if-range)# no shutdown
*Mar  1 00:09:12.792: %LINK-3-UPDOWN: Interface FastEthernet0/3, changed state to up
*Mar  1 00:09:12.792: %LINK-3-UPDOWN: Interface FastEthernet0/4, changed state to up
S3(config-if-range)#
*Mar  1 00:09:15.384: %LINEPROTO-5-UPDOWN: Line protocol on Interface FastEthernet0/3,
changed state to up
*Mar  1 00:09:16.265: %LINEPROTO-5-UPDOWN: Line protocol on Interface FastEthernet0/4,
changed state to up
S3(config-if-range)#
*Mar  1 00:09:16.357: %LINK-3-UPDOWN: Interface Port-channel1, changed state to up
*Mar  1 00:09:17.364: %LINEPROTO-5-UPDOWN: Line protocol on Interface Port-channel1,
changed state to up
*Mar  1 00:09:44.383: %LINEPROTO-5-UPDOWN: Line protocol on Interface Vlan1, changed
state to up
```

Step 2: Examine the configuration on the ports.

Currently the F0/3, F0/4, and Po1 (Port-channel1) interfaces on both S1 and S3 are in access operational mode with the administrative mode in dynamic auto. Verify the configuration using the **show run interface** *interface-id* and **show interfaces** *interface-id* **switchport** commands, respectively. The example configuration outputs for F0/3 on S1 are as follows:

```
S1# show run interface f0/3
Building configuration...

Current configuration : 103 bytes
!
interface FastEthernet0/3
 channel-group 1 mode desirable

S1# show interfaces f0/3 switchport
Name: Fa0/3
Switchport: Enabled
Administrative Mode: dynamic auto
Operational Mode: static access (member of bundle Po1)
Administrative Trunking Encapsulation: dot1q
Operational Trunking Encapsulation: native
Negotiation of Trunking: On
Access Mode VLAN: 1 (default)
Trunking Native Mode VLAN: 1 (default)
Administrative Native VLAN tagging: enabled
Voice VLAN: none
Administrative private-vlan host-association: none
Administrative private-vlan mapping: none
Administrative private-vlan trunk native VLAN: none
Administrative private-vlan trunk Native VLAN tagging: enabled
Administrative private-vlan trunk encapsulation: dot1q
Administrative private-vlan trunk normal VLANs: none
Administrative private-vlan trunk associations: none
Administrative private-vlan trunk mappings: none
Operational private-vlan: none
Trunking VLANs Enabled: ALL
Pruning VLANs Enabled: 2-1001
Capture Mode Disabled
Capture VLANs Allowed: ALL

Protected: false
Unknown unicast blocked: disabled
```

```
Unknown multicast blocked: disabled

Appliance trust: none
```

Step 3:   Verify that the ports have been aggregated.

```
S1# show etherchannel summary

Flags:  D - down         P - bundled in port-channel

        I - stand-alone s - suspended

        H - Hot-standby (LACP only)

        R - Layer3       S - Layer2

        U - in use       f - failed to allocate aggregator


        M - not in use, minimum links not met

        u - unsuitable for bundling

        w - waiting to be aggregated

        d - default port



Number of channel-groups in use: 1

Number of aggregators:           1


Group  Port-channel  Protocol    Ports
------+-------------+-----------+-------------------------------------------
1      Po1(SU)        PAgP        Fa0/3(P)    Fa0/4(P)


S3# show etherchannel summary

Flags:  D - down         P - bundled in port-channel

        I - stand-alone s - suspended

        H - Hot-standby (LACP only)

        R - Layer3       S - Layer2

        U - in use       f - failed to allocate aggregator


        M - not in use, minimum links not met

        u - unsuitable for bundling

        w - waiting to be aggregated

        d - default port



Number of channel-groups in use: 1

Number of aggregators:           1
```

```
Group  Port-channel  Protocol    Ports
------+-------------+-----------+-------------------------------------------------
1       Po1(SU)         PAgP      Fa0/3(P)    Fa0/4(P)
```

What do the flags, SU and P, indicate in the Ethernet summary?

_____

_____

Step 4: Configure trunk ports.

After the ports have been aggregated, commands applied at the port channel interface affect all the links that were bundled together. Manually configure the Po1 ports on S1 and S3 as trunk ports and assign them to native VLAN 99.

```
S1(config)# interface port-channel 1
S1(config-if)# switchport mode trunk
S1(config-if)# switchport trunk native vlan 99

S3(config)# interface port-channel 1
S3(config-if)# switchport mode trunk
S3(config-if)# switchport trunk native vlan 99
```

Step 5: Verify that the ports are configured as trunk ports.

a. Issue the **show run interface** *interface-id* commands on S1 and S3. What commands are listed for F0/3 and F0/4 on both switches? Compare the results to the running configuration for the Po1 interface? Record your observation.

_____

_____

b. Issue the **show interfaces trunk** and **show spanning-tree** commands on S1 and S3. What trunk port is listed? What is the native VLAN? What is concluding result from the output?

_____

From the **show spanning-tree** output, what is port cost and port priority for the aggregated link?

_____

Part 3: Configure LACP

LACP is an open source protocol for link aggregation developed by the IEEE. In Part 3, the link between S1 and S2, and the link between S2 and S3 will be configured using LACP. Also, the individual links will be configured as trunks before they are bundled together as EtherChannels.

Step 1: Configure LACP between S1 and S2.

```
S1(config)# interface range f0/1-2
S1(config-if-range)# switchport mode trunk
S1(config-if-range)# switchport trunk native vlan 99
S1(config-if-range)# channel-group 2 mode active
Creating a port-channel interface Port-channel 2

S1(config-if-range)# no shutdown


S2(config)# interface range f0/1-2
S2(config-if-range)# switchport mode trunk
S2(config-if-range)# switchport trunk native vlan 99
S2(config-if-range)# channel-group 2 mode passive
Creating a port-channel interface Port-channel 2


S2(config-if-range)# no shutdown
```

Step 2: Verify that the ports have been aggregated.

What protocol is Po2 using for link aggregation? Which ports are aggregated to form Po2? Record the command used to verify.

_____

_____

Step 3: Configure LACP between S2 and S3.

a. Configure the link between S2 and S3 as Po3 and use LACP as the link aggregation protocol.

```
S2(config)# interface range f0/3-4
S2(config-if-range)# switchport mode trunk
S2(config-if-range)# switchport trunk native vlan 99
S2(config-if-range)# channel-group 3 mode active
Creating a port-channel interface Port-channel 3
S2(config-if-range)# no shutdown


S3(config)# interface range f0/1-2
S3(config-if-range)# switchport mode trunk
S3(config-if-range)# switchport trunk native vlan 99
S3(config-if-range)# channel-group 3 mode passive
Creating a port-channel interface Port-channel 3


S3(config-if-range)# no shutdown
```

b. Verify that the EtherChannel has formed.

Step 4: Verify end-to-end connectivity.

Verify that all devices can ping each other within the same VLAN. If not, troubleshoot until there is end-to-end connectivity.

Note: It may be necessary to disable the PC firewall to ping between PCs.

Reflection

What could prevent EtherChannels from forming?

_____

3.2.2.4 Lab – Troubleshooting EtherChannel

Topology

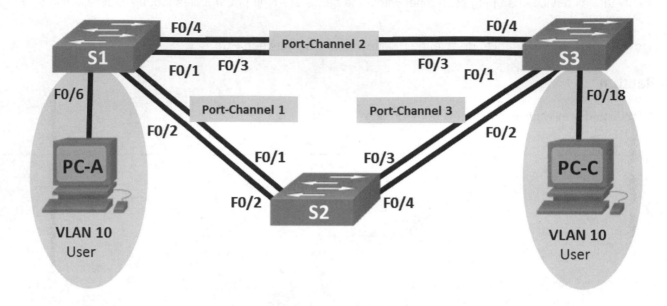

Addressing Table

Device	Interface	IP Address	Subnet Mask
S1	VLAN 99	192.168.1.11	255.255.255.0
S2	VLAN 99	192.168.1.12	255.255.255.0
S3	VLAN 99	192.168.1.13	255.255.255.0
PC-A	NIC	192.168.0.2	255.255.255.0
PC-C	NIC	192.168.0.3	255.255.255.0

VLAN Assignments

VLAN	Name
10	User
99	Management

Objectives

Part 1: Build the Network and Load Device Configurations

Part 2: Troubleshoot EtherChannel

Background / Scenario

The switches at your company were configured by an inexperienced network administrator. Several errors in the configuration have resulted in speed and connectivity issues. Your manager has asked you to trouble-shoot and correct the configuration errors and document your work. Using your knowledge of EtherChannel and standard testing methods, find and correct the errors. Ensure that all of the EtherChannels use Port Aggregation Protocol (PAgP), and that all hosts are reachable.

Note: The switches used are Cisco Catalyst 2960s with Cisco IOS Release 15.0(2) (lanbasek9 image). Other switches and Cisco IOS versions can be used. Depending on the model and Cisco IOS version, the commands available and output produced might vary from what is shown in the labs.

Note: Make sure that the switches have been erased and have no startup configurations. If you are unsure, contact your instructor.

Required Resources

- 3 Switches (Cisco 2960 with Cisco IOS Release 15.0(2) lanbasek9 image or comparable)
- 2 PCs (Windows 7, Vista, or XP with a terminal emulation program, such as Tera Term)
- Console cables to configure the Cisco IOS devices via the console ports
- Ethernet cables as shown in the topology

Part 1: Build the Network and Load Device Configurations

In Part 1, you will set up the network topology, configure basic settings on the PC hosts, and load configurations on the switches.

Step 1:   Cable the network as shown in the topology.

Step 2:   Configure the PC hosts.

Step 3:   Erase the startup and VLAN configurations and reload the switches.

Step 4:   Load switch configurations.

Load the following configurations into the appropriate switch. All switches have the same passwords. The privileged EXEC password is **class**. The password for console and vty access is **cisco**. As all switches are Cisco devices, the network administrator decided to use Cisco's PAgP on all port channels configured with EtherChannel. Switch S2 is the root bridge for all VLANs in the topology.

Switch S1 Configuration:

```
hostname S1
interface range f0/1-24, g0/1-2
shutdown
exit
enable secret class
no ip domain lookup
line vty 0 15
password cisco
```

```
login
line con 0
 password cisco
 logging synchronous
 login
 exit
vlan 10
 name User
vlan 99
 Name Management
interface range f0/1-2
 switchport mode trunk

 channel-group 1 mode active
 switchport trunk native vlan 99
 no shutdown
interface range f0/3-4
 channel-group 2 mode desirable
 switchport trunk native vlan 99

 no shutdown
interface f0/6
 switchport mode access
 switchport access vlan 10
 no shutdown
interface vlan 99
 ip address 192.168.1.11 255.255.255.0
interface port-channel 1
 switchport trunk native vlan 99
 switchport mode trunk
interface port-channel 2
 switchport trunk native vlan 99
 switchport mode access
```

Switch S2 Configuration:

```
hostname S2
interface range f0/1-24, g0/1-2
 shutdown
 exit
```

```
enable secret class
no ip domain lookup
line vty 0 15
 password cisco
 login
line con 0
 password cisco
 logging synchronous
 login
 exit
vlan 10
 name User
vlan 99
 name Management
spanning-tree vlan 1,10,99 root primary
interface range f0/1-2
 switchport mode trunk
 channel-group 1 mode desirable
 switchport trunk native vlan 99
 no shutdown
interface range f0/3-4
 switchport mode trunk
 channel-group 3 mode desirable
 switchport trunk native vlan 99

interface vlan 99
 ip address 192.168.1.12 255.255.255.0
interface port-channel 1
 switchport trunk native vlan 99
 switchport trunk allowed vlan 1,99

interface port-channel 3
 switchport trunk native vlan 99
 switchport trunk allowed vlan 1,10,99
 switchport mode trunk
```

Switch S3 Configuration:

```
hostname S3
interface range f0/1-24, g0/1-2
```

```
  shutdown
  exit
enable secret class
no ip domain lookup
line vty 0 15
  password cisco
  login
line con 0
  password cisco
  logging synchronous
  login
  exit
vlan 10
  name User
vlan 99
  name Management
interface range f0/1-2



interface range f0/3-4
  switchport mode trunk

  channel-group 3 mode desirable
  switchport trunk native vlan 99
  no shutdown
interface f0/18
  switchport mode access
  switchport access vlan 10
  no shutdown
interface vlan 99
  ip address 192.168.1.13 255.255.255.0
interface port-channel 3
  switchport trunk native vlan 99
  switchport mode trunk
```

Step 5:   Save your configuration.

Part 2: Troubleshoot EtherChannel

In Part 2, you must examine the configurations on all switches, make corrections if needed, and verify full functionality.

Step 1: Troubleshoot S1.

a. Use the **show interfaces trunk** command to verify that the port channels are functioning as trunk ports.

Do port channels 1 and 2 appear as trunked ports? _____

b. Use the **show etherchannel summary** command to verify that interfaces are configured in the correct port channel, the proper protocol is configured, and the interfaces are in use.

Based on the output, are there any EtherChannel issues? If issues are found, record them in the space provided below.

_____

_____

c. Use the command **show run | begin interface Port-channel** command to view the running configuration beginning with the first port channel interface.

d. Resolve all problems found in the outputs from the previous **show** commands. Record the commands used to correct the configurations.

_____

_____

_____

_____

_____

e. Use the **show interfaces trunk** command to verify trunk settings.

f. Use the **show etherchannel summary** command to verify that the port channels are up and in use.

Step 2: Troubleshoot S2.

a. Issue the command to verify that the port channels are functioning as trunk ports. Record the command used in the space provided below.

_____

Based on the output, are there any issues with the configurations? If issues are found, record them in the space provided below.

_____

_____

b. Issue the command to verify that interfaces are configured in the correct port channel and the proper protocol is configured.

Based on the output, are there any EtherChannel issues? If issues are found, record them in the space provided below.

_____

c. Use the command **show run | begin interface Port-channel** to view the running configuration beginning with the first port-channel interface.

d. Resolve all problems found in the outputs from the previous **show** commands. Record the commands used to correct the configuration.

_____

_____

_____

_____

_____

e. Issue the command to verify trunk settings.

f. Issue the command to verify that the port channels are functioning. Remember that port channel issues can be caused by either end of the link.

Step 3:   Troubleshoot S3.

a. Issue the command to verify that the port channels are functioning as trunk ports.

Based on the output, are there any issues with the configurations? If issues are found, record them in the space provided below.

_____

_____

b. Issue the command to verify that the interfaces are configured in the correct port channel and that the proper protocol is configured.

Based on the output, are there any EtherChannel issues? If issues are found, record them in the space provided below.

_____

_____

c. Use the command **show run | begin interface Port-channel** command to view the running configuration beginning with the first port channel interface.

d. Resolve all problems found. Record the commands used to correct the configuration.

_____

_____

_____

_____

_____

_____

_____

_____

e. Issue the command to verify trunk settings. Record the command used in the space provided below.

_____

f. Issue the command to verify that the port channels are functioning. Record the command used in the space provided below.

_____

Step 4: Verify EtherChannel and Connectivity.

a. Use the **show interfaces etherchannel** command to verify full functionality of the port channels.

b. Verify connectivity of the management VLAN.

Can S1 ping S2? _____

Can S1 ping S3? _____

Can S2 ping S3? _____

c. Verify connectivity of PCs.

Can PC-A ping PC-C? _____

If EtherChannels are not fully functional, connectivity between switches does not exist, or connectivity between hosts does not exist. Troubleshoot to resolve any remaining issues.

Note: It may be necessary to disable the PC firewall for pings between the PCs to succeed.

3.3.1.1 Class Activity – Linking Up

Objective

Describe link aggregation.

Scenario

Many bottlenecks occur on your small- to medium-sized business network, even though you have configured VLANs, STP, and other network traffic options on the company's switches.

Instead of keeping the switches as they are currently configured, you would like to try EtherChannel as an option for, at least, part of the network to see if it will lesson traffic congestion between your access and distribution layer switches.

Your company uses Catalyst 3560 switches at the distribution layer and Catalyst 2960 and 2950 switches at the access layer of the network. To verify if these switches can perform EtherChannel, you visit the *System Requirements to Implement EtherChannel on Catalyst Switches*. This site allows you to gather more information to determine if EtherChannel is a good option for the equipment and network currently in place.

After researching the models, you decide to use a simulation software program to practice configuring Ether-Channel before implementing it live on your network. As a part of this procedure, you ensure that the equipment simulated in Packet Tracer will support these practice configurations.

Resources

- World Wide Web connectivity
- Packet Tracer software
- Word processing or spreadsheet software

Directions

Step 1:   Visit *System Requirements to Implement EtherChannel on Catalyst Switches*.

- a. Pay particular attention to the Catalyst 3560, 2960, and 2950 model information.
- b. Record any information you feel would be useful to deciding whether to use EtherChannel in your company.

Step 2:   Create a matrix to record the information you recorded in Step 1b, including:

- a. Number of ports allowed to bundled for an EtherChannel group
- b. Maximum group bandwidth supported by bundling the ports
- c. IOS version needed to support EtherChannel on the switch model
- d. Load balancing availability
- e. Load balancing configuration options
- f. Network layers supported for EtherChannel operation

Step 3:   Open Packet Tracer.

- a. Notice how many ports are available to bundle for EtherChannel on all three switch models.
- b. Check all three models to see how many EtherChannel groups you could create on each model.
- c. Make sure the IOS version is recent enough to support all EtherChannel configurations.
- d. Do not configure your simulated network, but do check the models available in the Packet Tracer to make sure they will support all the EtherChannel configuration options.

Step 4:   Share your matrix with another group or the class.

Chapter 4 — Wireless LANs

4.0.1.2 Class Activity – Make Mine Wireless

Objective

Explain how wireless LAN components are deployed in a small- to medium-sized business.

Scenario

As the network administrator for your small- to medium-sized business, you realize that your wireless network needs updating, both inside and outside of your building. Therefore, you decide to research how other businesses and educational and community groups set up their WLANs for better access to their employees and clients.

To research this topic, you visit the Customer Case Studies and Research website to see how other businesses use wireless technology. After viewing a few of the videos, or reading some of the case study PDFs, you decide to select two to show to your CEO to support upgrading to a more robust wireless solution for your company.

To complete this class modeling activity, open the accompanying PDF for further instructions on how to proceed.

Resources

Internet access to the WWW

Step 1:   Open your browser and the URL specified for this activity.

a.   Choose two case studies about wireless LAN upgrades from the list to read, located on the Customer Case Studies and Research website.

b.   As you view the media or read the PDFs, write notes for the following categories:

  1)   The WLAN *challenge* that the company sought to mitigate

  2)   The *solution* that was found to the challenge

  3)   The *results* that were gained by WLAN updates

Step 2:   Share your findings.

a.   Share your findings with the class or a classmate.

b.   Play the media or show the PDF for one of the case studies you chose from the URL page.

c.   In your own words, explain the challenge, solution, and results learned from the media or PDF.

d.   Explain how the results you found could be applied to improve your company's network.

4.1.2.10 Lab – Investigating Wireless Implementations

Objectives

Part 1: Explore Integrated Wireless Routers

Part 2: Explore Wireless Access Points

Background / Scenario

The number of mobile devices, such as smart phones, tablets, and laptops, continues to increase. These mobile devices can connect via integrated wireless routers or wireless access points (WAPs) to access the Internet and other network resources. Wireless routers are typically employed in home and small business networks. WAPs are more common in larger, more complex networks.

In this lab, you will explore some integrated wireless routers and Cisco WAPs. You will access online emulators for some of Linksys routers and Cisco WAPs. The emulators imitate the configuration screens for the Linksys routers and Cisco WAPs.

Required Resources

Device with Internet access

Part 1:   Explore Integrated Wireless Routers

Integrated wireless routers usually perform the functions of the following devices:

- a switch by connecting wired devices

- an access point by connecting wireless devices

- a router/gateway by providing access to the Internet through a modem to the ISP

Currently there are many different broadcast standards for wireless routers:

- 802.11b

- 802.11g

- 802.11n

- 802.11ac

The differences between these standards are speed and signal strength. In addition to the standards, each integrated wireless router may have features that meet your network requirement, such as content filtering, QoS, IPv6 support, and wireless security.

In Part 1, you will search the Internet for three different wireless routers and create a list of the important router feature by recording them in the following table. During your search, you can also record additional features that are important to you in the **Other Features** column in the table.

To explore emulators for some of the Linksys routers, go to http://ui.linksys.com/files/.

Note: The Linksys emulators may not provide the most current version of the firmware.

Brand/Model	Price	IPv6-Enabled	Wireless Security	Band	Other Features
Linksys/EA4500	$129.99 USD	Yes	WPA2	Dual-band N (2.4 GHz and 5 GHz)	Separate Guest Network, 4 Gigabit Ethernet Ports, QoS, remote administration from mobile devices, such as smart phones

After you have completed the table above, determine which integrated wireless router you would choose for your home. Explain your choice.

_____

_____

_____

Part 2:   Explore Wireless Access Points

Unlike integrated wireless routers, a WAP does not have integrated switch and router functions. A WAP only allows users to access the network wirelessly using mobile devices and provides a connection to the main wired network infrastructure. With the correct user credentials, wireless users can access resources on the network.

In this part, you will explore two Cisco WAPs, WAP321 and AP541N. Cisco's website (http://www.cisco.com) can provide you with technical specifications regarding these WAPs. Furthermore, online emulators are also available at the following links:

To access an online WAP321 emulator, go to http://www.cisco.com/assets/sol/sb/wap321_sps/main.html.

To access an online AP541N emulator, go to https://www.cisco.com/assets/sol/sb/AP541N_GUI/ AP541N_1_9_2/Getting_Started.htm.

Model	Security	Band	Other Features / Comments
WAP321			
AP541N			

Reflection

What features on the wireless routers or WAPs are important for your network? Why?

_____

_____

4.4.2.3 Lab – Configuring a Wireless Router and Client

Topology

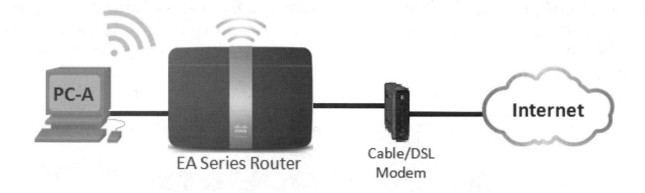

EA Series Router   Cable/DSL Modem

Linksys Router Settings

Network Name (SSID)	CCNA-Net
Network Password	cisconet
Router Password	cisco123

Objectives

Part 1: Configure Basic Settings on a Linksys EA Series Router

Part 2: Secure the Wireless Network

Part 3: Review Additional Features on a Linksys EA Series Router

Part 4: Connect a Wireless Client

Background / Scenario

Surfing the web from anywhere in the home or office has become common. Without wireless connectivity, users would be limited to connect only where there is a wired connection. Users have embraced the flexibility that wireless routers provide for accessing the network and the Internet.

In this lab, you will configure a Linksys Smart Wi-Fi router, which includes applying WPA2 security settings and activating DHCP services. You will review some added features available on these routers, such as USB storage, parental controls, and time restrictions. You will also configure a wireless PC client.

Required Resources

- 1 Linksys EA Series Router (EA4500 with firmware version 2.1.39.145204 or comparable)
- 1 Cable or DSL modem (Optional - needed for Internet service and normally supplied by ISP)
- 1 PC with a Wireless NIC (Windows 7, Vista, or XP)
- Ethernet cables as shown in the topology

Part 1:   Configure Basic Settings on a Linksys EA Series Router

The most efficient way to configure basic settings on an EA Series router is to run the Linksys EA Series Setup CD that came with the router. If the Setup CD is unavailable, download the Setup program from http://Linksys.com/support.

Step 1:   Insert the Linksys EA-Series Setup CD into the PC.

When prompted, select **Set up your Linksys Router**. You will be asked to read and accept the License Terms for using the software. Click **Next >** after accepting the license terms.

Step 2:   Cable the network as shown in the topology.

Follow the directions in the next window for connecting the power cable and Ethernet cable from your cable modem or DSL modem. You may connect the PC to one of the four unused Ethernet ports on the back of the router. After you have connected everything, click **Next >**.

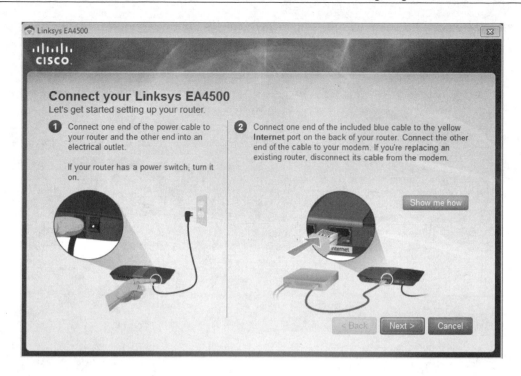

Step 3: Configure Linksys router settings.

a.   Allow time for the **Linksys router settings** window to display. Use the **Linksys Router Settings** table at the beginning of this lab to fill in the fields in this window. Click **Next** to display the summary router settings screen. Click **Next**.

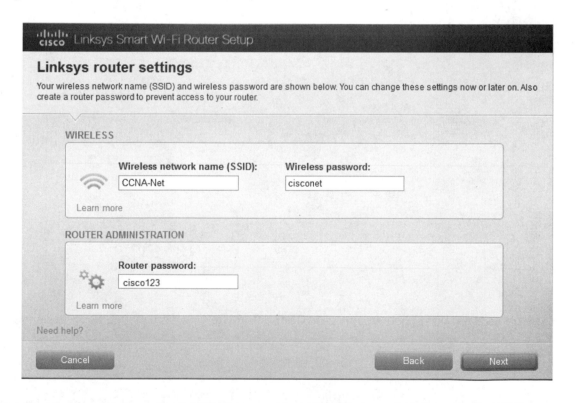

b.   The **Create your Linksys Smart Wi-Fi account** window displays. A Linksys Smart Wi-Fi account associates your router to the account, allowing you to remotely manage the router using a browser or mobile device running the Smart Wi-Fi app. For this lab, bypass the account setup process. Click the **No thanks** box and press **Continue**.

Note: An account can be setup by browsing to www.linksyssmartwifi.com.

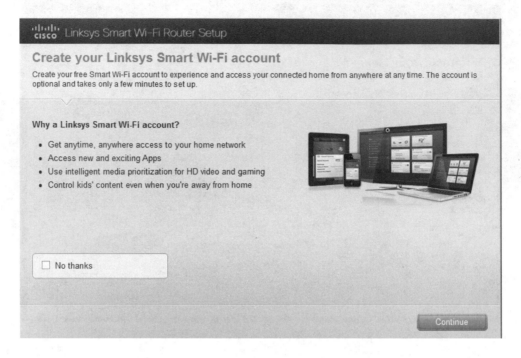

c. A **Sign In** window displays. In the **Access Router** field, enter **cisco123,** and click **Sign In**.

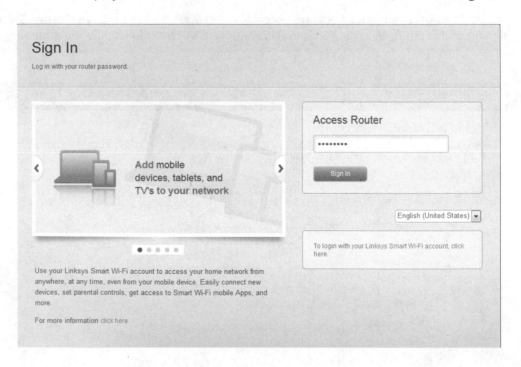

d. On the Linksys Smart Wi-Fi home page, click **Connectivity** to view and change basic router settings.

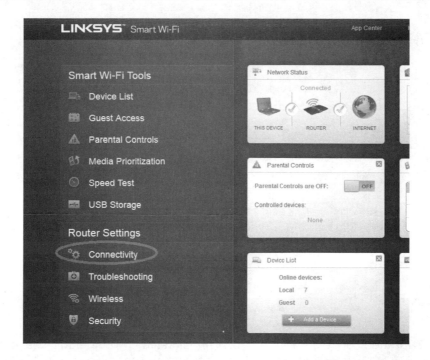

e. On the **Basic** tab, you can edit the SSID name and password, change the router password, perform firm-
    ware updates, and set the time zone for your router. (The router password and SSID information was set
    in Step 3a.) Select the correct time zone for your router from the drop-down box and click **Apply**.

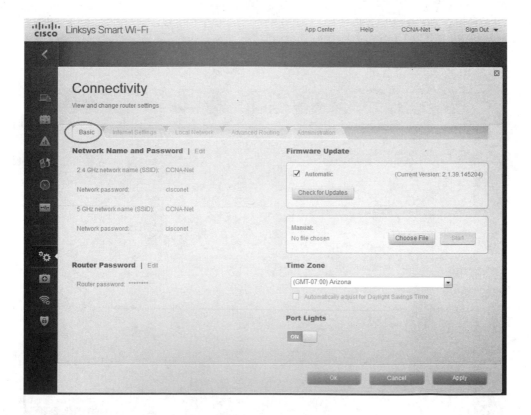

f. The **Internet Settings** tab provides information about the Internet connection. In the example, the router
    automatically configured the connection for DHCP. Both IPv4 and IPv6 information can be displayed from
    this screen.

g. The **Local Network** tab controls the local DHCP server settings. The default local network settings specify the 192.168.1.0/24 network and the local IP address of the default router is 192.168.1.1. This can be changed by clicking **Edit** next to **Router Details**. DHCP Server settings can be changed on this screen. You can set the DHCP starting address, maximum number of DHCP users, client lease time, and static DNS servers. Click **Apply** to accept all changes made on this screen.

Note: If DHCP is used to obtain ISP connection information, these DNS addresses will most likely be populated with the ISP's DNS server information.

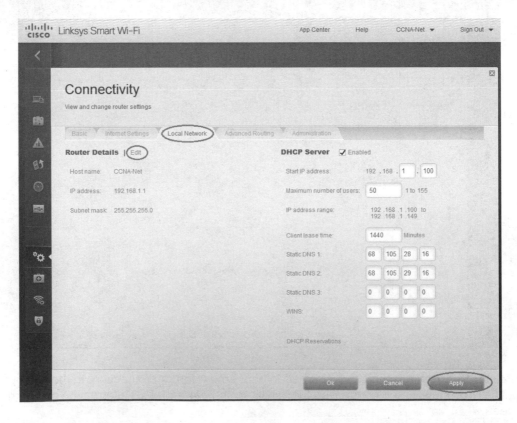

h. The **Advanced Routing** tab allows you to disable Network Address translation (NAT), which is enabled by default. This screen also allows you to add static routes. Click **Apply** to accept any desired changes made on this screen.

i.   The **Administration** tab provides controls for the management of the Smart Wi-Fi software. By chicking the appropriate box, you can activate remote management access to the router. You can also activate HTTPS access and restrict wireless management. Universal Plug and Play (UPnP) and Application Layer Gateway controls are also available on this screen. Click **Apply** to accept any desired changes made on this screen.

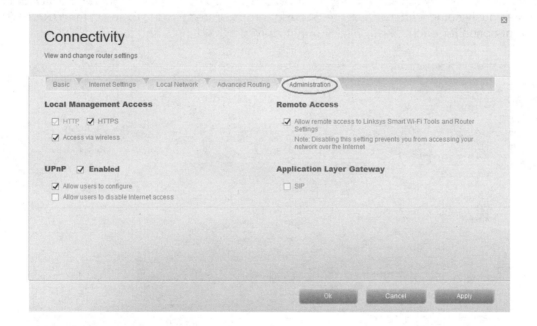

Part 2:   Secure the Wireless Network

In Part 2, you will secure the Linksys EA series router wireless network and review firewall and port forwarding options on a Linksys Smart Wi-Fi router.

Step 1:   Add WPA security on the wireless routers.

a.   From the Linksys Smart Wi-Fi home page, click **Wireless**.

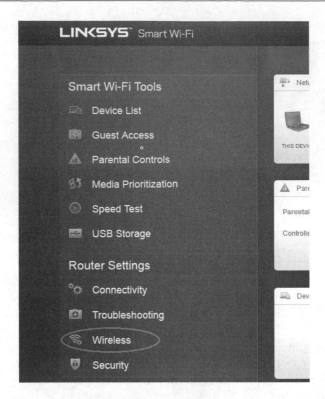

b. The **Wireless** window displays the settings for both the 2.4 and 5 GHz radios. Use the **Edit** button next to each column to modify the security setting on each wireless frequency range. (The SSID and password were previously set in Part 1.) Click the **Security mode** drop-down list to select the **WPA2/WPA Mixed Personal** option for each range. Click **Apply** to save your settings, and then click **OK**.

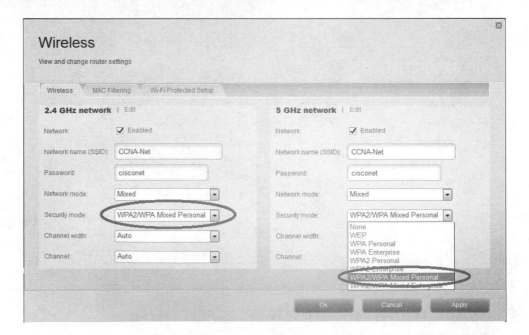

Step 2:   Apply firewall and port forwarding settings.

a. From the Linksys Smart Wi-Fi home page, click **Security**. In the **Security** windows, the **Firewall**, **DMZ**, and **Apps and Gaming** tabs are available to view and change router security settings.

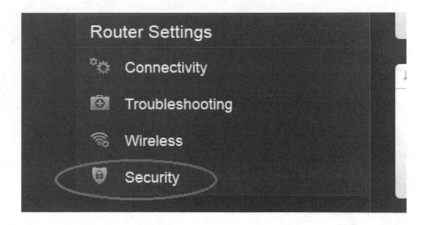

b. The **Firewall** tab displays firewall settings, where you can enable or disable IPv4 and IPv6 Stateful Packet Inspection (SPI) firewall protection, Virtual Private Network (VPN) Passthrough options, and Internet filters. Click **Apply** to accept any desired changes made on this screen.

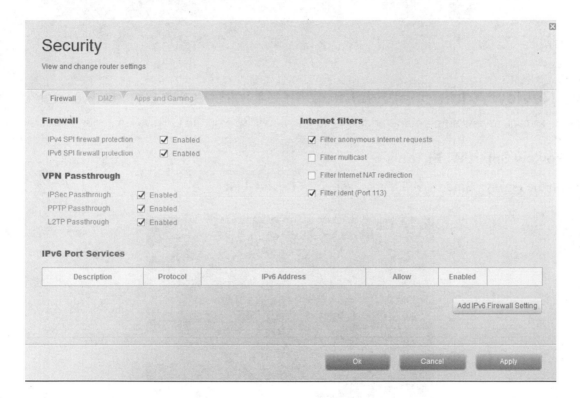

c. The **Apps and Gaming** tab provides port forwarding capabilities. In the example, ports 5060 and 5061 have been opened for a VoIP Softphone application running on a local device at IP address 192.168.1.126. Click **Apply** to accept any desired changes made on this screen.

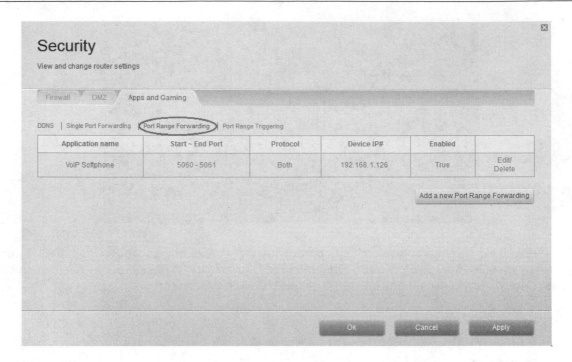

Part 3:   Review Additional Features on a Linksys EA Series Router

In Part 3, you will review some of the additional features available on the Linksys EA series router.

Step 1:   Review Smart Wi-Fi Tools.

a.   From the Linksys Smart Wi-Fi home page, click **Device List**.

The **Device List** window displays the list of clients on the local network. Notice that there is a tab for the **Guest Network**. If the Guest network was activated, clients on that network would be displayed in the **Guest Network** tab.

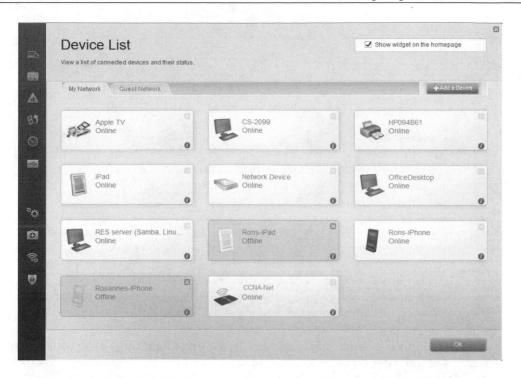

b. From the Linksys Smart Wi-Fi home page, click **Guest Access**. Clients on the guest network only have access to the Internet and are unable to access other clients on the local network. To allow guest access, click on the **Allow guest access** toggle button. Click **Edit** link (next to the Guest network name and password) to change the Guest network password and click **OK** to accept the changes.

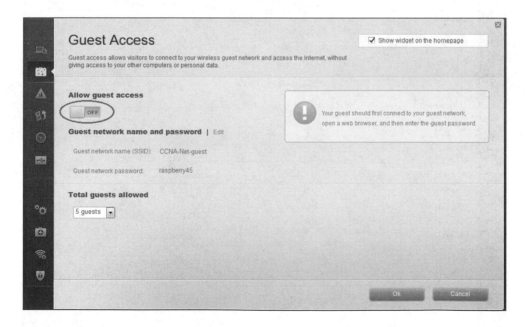

c. From the Linksys Smart Wi-Fi home page, click **Parental Controls**. Use these settings to restrict Internet access on selected devices and to restrict time and websites. Click **OK** to save the settings.

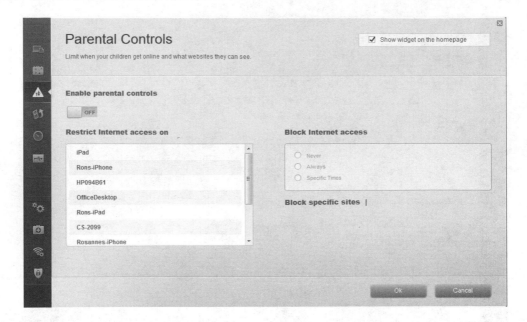

d. From the Linksys Smart Wi-Fi home page, click on **Media Prioritization**. These settings allows you to assign network bandwidth prioritization to selected devices on the local network. In the example, the device labeled Apple TV has been given the highest priority for network resources. To make prioritization changes, just drag and drop the listed devices, and click **OK** to save your settings.

e. From the Linksys Smart Wi-Fi home page, click **Speed Test**. Use this utility to test your Internet access speeds. The example shows the results of the speed test. The router stores the results of each speed tests and allows you to display that history.

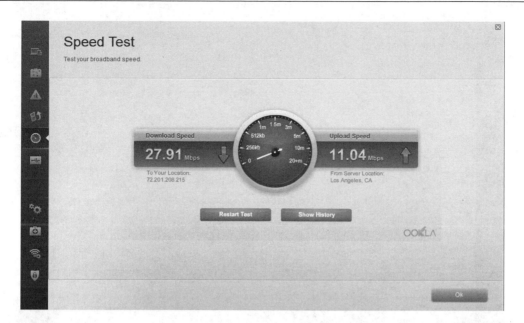

f. From the Linksys Smart Wi-Fi home page, click **USB Storage**. Use this screen to review your USB drive settings. From here, you can click on the appropriate tab to set up FTP and Media Servers. You can also set up individual user accounts for access to these servers by clicking the tabs at the top of this screen. A USB storage device is plugged into the back of the router to use this option. Click **OK** to save any desired changes.

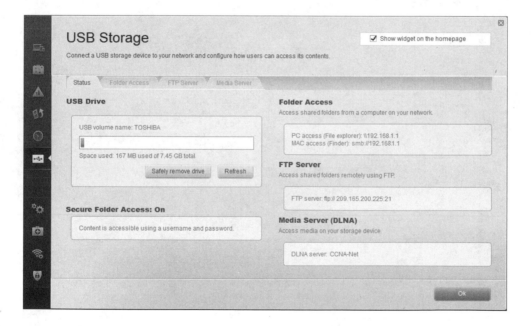

Step 2:   Troubleshoot the router.

From the Linksys Smart Wi-Fi home page, click **Troubleshooting**.

a. The **Status** tab provides a list of clients on the local network along with their NIC MAC and IP addresses. It also displays how they are connected to the network. Click **OK** to save any desired changes.

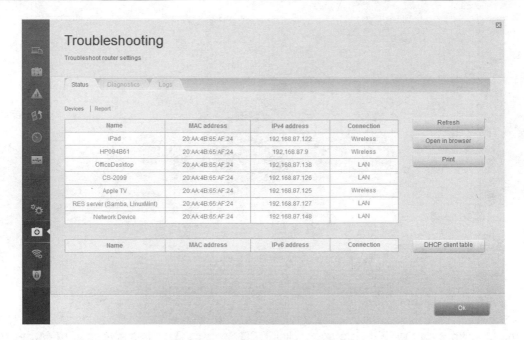

b. The **Diagnostics** tab provides the ping and traceroute utilities. It also allows you to reboot the router, backup and restore the router configuration, restore a previous firmware version, release and renew the Internet addresses on your router, and reset to factory default settings. Click **OK** to save any desired changes.

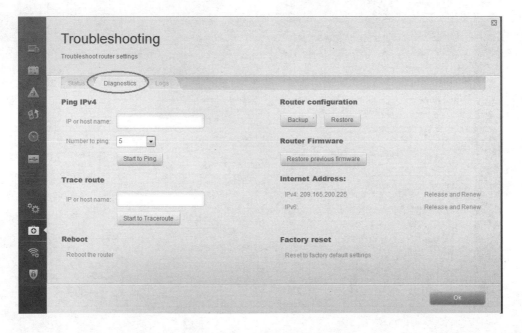

c. The **Logs** tab provides Incoming and Outgoing, Security, and DHCP logs. You can print and clear these logs from this screen. Click **OK** to save any desired changes.

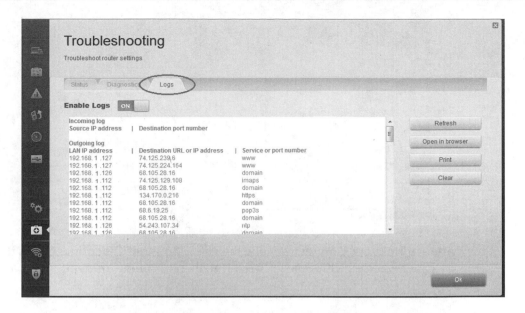

Part 4:   Connect a Wireless Client

In Part 4, you will configure the PC's wireless NIC to connect to the Linksys EA Series Router.

Note: This lab was performed using a PC running the Windows 7 operating system. You should be able to perform the lab with other Windows operating systems listed; however, menu selections and screens may vary.

Step 1:   Use the Network and Sharing Center.

a. Open the **Network and Sharing Center** by clicking the Windows **Start** button > **Control Panel** > **View network status and tasks** under Network and Internet heading in the Category View.

b. In the left pane, click the **Change adapter settings** link.

The **Network Connections** window provides the list of NICs available on this PC. Look for your **Local Area Connection** and **Wireless Network Connection** adapters in this window.

Note: VPN adapters and other types of network connections may also be displayed in this window.

Step 2:   Work with your wireless NIC.

a. Select and right-click the **Wireless Network Connection** option to display a drop-down list. If your wireless NIC is disabled, you must **Enable** it.

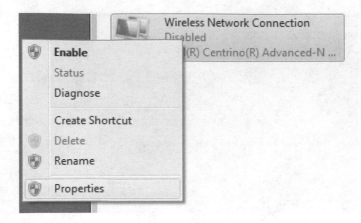

b. Right-click the **Wireless Network Connection**, and then click **Connect/Disconnect**. This displays a list of SSIDs in range of your wireless NIC. Select **CCNA-Net**, then click the **Connect**.

c. When prompted, enter **cisconet** to supply the network security key, and then click **OK**.

d. The wireless icon should display in your taskbar when you have a wireless connection. Click this icon to display the list of SSIDs in range of your PC.

e.   The SSID **CCNA-Ne**t should now show that you are connected to the CCNA-Net wireless network.

Reflection

Why would you not want to use WEP security for your wireless network?

_____

4.5.1.1 Class Activity – Inside and Outside Control

Objective

Explain how wireless LAN components are deployed in a small- to medium-sized business.

Scenario

An assessment has been completed to validate the need for an upgrade to your small- to medium-sized wireless network. Approved for purchase are indoor and outdoor access points and one wireless controller. You must compare equipment models and their specifications before you purchase.

Therefore, you visit the Wireless Compare Products and Services web site and see a features chart for indoor and outdoor wireless access points and controller devices. After reviewing the chart, you note there is some terminology with which you are unfamiliar:

- Federal Information Processing Standard (FIPS)
- MIMO
- Cisco CleanAir Technology
- Cisco FlexConnect
- Band Select

Research the above terms. Prepare your own chart with your company's most important requirements listed for purchasing the indoor and outdoor wireless access points and wireless controller. This chart will assist in validating your purchase order to your accounting manager and CEO.

Resources

Internet access to the World Wide Web

Part 1:   Secure Background Knowledge of Wireless Terminology

Step 1:   Define unfamiliar wireless terms.

a. FIPS

b. MIMO

c. Cisco CleanAir Technology

d. Cisco FlexConnect

e. Band Select

Step 2:   Visit the Wireless Compare Products and Services web site.

a. Compare the devices in each category based on their feature sets.

b. Choose one model from each category: indoor, outdoor, and controller categories for the upgrades for your business.

Step 3:   Create a chart for each device chosen in Step 2b to include:

a. The main type of selected device (indoor access point, outdoor access point, or controller).

b. A graphic of each selected device.

c. Five of the most beneficial features that the selected models would provide your business.

Step 4:   After research is complete, explain, and justify your choices with another student, class group, or entire class.

Chapter 5 — Adjust and Troublshoot Single-Area OSPF

5.0.1.2 Class Activity – DR and BDR Elections

Objectives

Modify the OSPF interface priority to influence the Designated Router (DR) and Backup Designated Router (BDR) election.

Scenario

You are trying to decide how to influence the selection of the designated router and backup designated router for your OSPF network. This activity simulates that process.

Three separate designated-router election scenarios will be presented. The focus is on electing a DR and BDR for your group. Refer to the PDF for this activity for the remaining instructions.

If additional time is available, two groups can be combined to simulate DR and BDR elections.

Required Resources

- Router priorities paper sign example (student developed)
- Router ID paper sign example (student developed)

Directions

This is a group activity with four classmates comprising each group. Before reporting to the group, each student will prepare router priority and router ID signs to bring to the group.

Step 1:   Decide the router priority.

a. Prior to joining your group, use a clean sheet of paper. On one side of the paper, write DEFAULT ROUTER PRIORITY = 1.

b. On the other side of the same sheet of paper, write ROUTER PRIORITY = (choose a number between 0 and 255).

Step 2:   Decide the router ID.

a. On a second clean sheet of paper, on one side, write ROUTER ID = (any IPv4 number).

b. On the other side, write ROUTER ID = Loopback (any IPv4) number.

Step 3:   Begin DR and BDR elections.

a. Start the first election process.

   1) Students within the group will show each other the router priority numbers they selected for Step 1b.

   2) After comparing their priority numbers, the student with the highest priority number is elected the DR and the student with the second-highest priority number is elected the BDR. Any student, who wrote 0 as their priority number, cannot participate in the election.

   3) The elected DR student will announce the elections by saying "I am the DR for all of you in this group. Please send me any changes to your networks or interfaces to IP address 224.0.0.6. I will then forward those changes to all of you at IP address 224.0.0.5. Stay tuned for future updates."

> 4) The BDR's elected student will say, "I am your BDR. Please send all changes to your router interfaces or networks to the DR. If the DR does not announce your changes, I will step in and do that from that point onward."

b. Start the second election process.

> 1) Students will hold up their DEFAULT ROUTER PRIORITY = 1 sign first. When it is agreed that all of the students have the same router priority, they will put that paper down.

> 2) Next, students will display their ROUTER ID = Loopback (IPv4) address signs.

> 3) The student with the highest loopback IPv4 address wins the election and repeats "I am the DR for all of you in this group. Our priorities are the same, but I have the highest loopback address on my router as compared to all of you; therefore, you have elected me as your DR. Please send all changes to your network addresses or interfaces to 224.0.0.6. I will then report any changes to all of you via 224.0.0.5."

> 4) The BDR will repeat his/her respective phrase from Step 3a,4).

c. Start the third election process, but this time, all students can choose which sides of their papers to display. The DR/BDR election process uses the highest router priority first, highest loopback router ID second, and highest IPv4 router ID third, and elects a DR and BDR.

> 1) Elect a DR and BDR.

> 2) Justify your elections.

> 3) If you have time, get together with another group and go through the scenario processes again to solidify DR and BDR elections.

5.1.1.9 Lab - Configuring Basic Single-Area OSPFv2

Topology

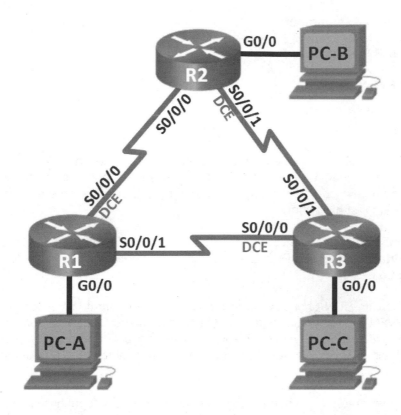

Addressing Table

Device	Interface	IP Address	Subnet Mask	Default Gateway
R1	G0/0	192.168.1.1	255.255.255.0	N/A
	S0/0/0 (DCE)	192.168.12.1	255.255.255.252	N/A
	S0/0/1	192.168.13.1	255.255.255.252	N/A
R2	G0/0	192.168.2.1	255.255.255.0	N/A
	S0/0/0	192.168.12.2	255.255.255.252	N/A
	S0/0/1 (DCE)	192.168.23.1	255.255.255.252	N/A
R3	G0/0	192.168.3.1	255.255.255.0	N/A
	S0/0/0 (DCE)	192.168.13.2	255.255.255.252	N/A
	S0/0/1	192.168.23.2	255.255.255.252	N/A
PC-A	NIC	192.168.1.3	255.255.255.0	192.168.1.1
PC-B	NIC	192.168.2.3	255.255.255.0	192.168.2.1
PC-C	NIC	192.168.3.3	255.255.255.0	192.168.3.1

Objectives

Part 1: Build the Network and Configure Basic Device Settings

Part 2: Configure and Verify OSPF Routing

Part 3: Change Router ID Assignments

Part 4: Configure OSPF Passive Interfaces

Part 5: Change OSPF Metrics

Background / Scenario

Open Shortest Path First (OSPF) is a link-state routing protocol for IP networks. OSPFv2 is defined for IPv4 networks, and OSPFv3 is defined for IPv6 networks. OSPF detects changes in the topology, such as link failures, and converges on a new loop-free routing structure very quickly. It computes each route using Dijkstra's algorithm, a shortest path first algorithm.

In this lab, you will configure the network topology with OSPFv2 routing, change the router ID assignments, configure passive interfaces, adjust OSPF metrics, and use a number of CLI commands to display and verify OSPF routing information.

Note: The routers used with CCNA hands-on labs are Cisco 1941 Integrated Services Routers (ISRs) with Cisco IOS Release 15.2(4)M3 (universalk9 image). Other routers and Cisco IOS versions can be used. Depending on the model and Cisco IOS version, the commands available and output produced might vary from what is shown in the labs. Refer to the Router Interface Summary Table at the end of this lab for the correct interface identifiers.

Note: Make sure that the routers have been erased and have no startup configurations. If you are unsure, contact your instructor.

Required Resources

- 3 Routers (Cisco 1941 with Cisco IOS Release 15.2(4)M3 universal image or comparable)
- 3 PCs (Windows 7, Vista, or XP with terminal emulation program, such as Tera Term)
- Console cables to configure the Cisco IOS devices via the console ports
- Ethernet and serial cables as shown in the topology

Part 1: Build the Network and Configure Basic Device Settings

In Part 1, you set up the network topology and configure basic settings on the PC hosts and routers.

Step 1: Cable the network as shown in the topology.

Step 2: Initialize and reload the routers as necessary.

Step 3:   Configure basic settings for each router.

    a.   Disable DNS lookup.

    b.   Configure device name as shown in the topology.

    c.   Assign **class** as the privileged EXEC password.

    d.   Assign **cisco** as the console and vty passwords.

    e.   Configure a message of the day (MOTD) banner to warn users that unauthorized access is prohibited.

    f.   Configure **logging synchronous** for the console line.

    g.   Configure the IP address listed in the Addressing Table for all interfaces.

    h.   Set the clock rate for all DCE serial interfaces at **128000**.

    i.   Copy the running configuration to the startup configuration.

Step 4:   Configure PC hosts.

Step 5:   Test connectivity.

The routers should be able to ping one another, and each PC should be able to ping its default gateway. The PCs are unable to ping other PCs until OSPF routing is configured. Verify and troubleshoot if necessary.

Part 2:   Configure and Verify OSPF Routing

In Part 2, you will configure OSPFv2 routing on all routers in the network and then verify that routing tables are updated correctly. After OSPF has been verified, you will configure OSPF authentication on the links for added security.

Step 1:   Configure OSPF on R1.

    a.   Use the **router ospf** command in global configuration mode to enable OSPF on R1.

```
R1(config)# router ospf 1
```

    Note: The OSPF process id is kept locally and has no meaning to other routers on the network.

    b.   Configure the **network** statements for the networks on R1. Use an area ID of 0.

```
R1(config-router)# network 192.168.1.0 0.0.0.255 area 0
R1(config-router)# network 192.168.12.0 0.0.0.3 area 0
R1(config-router)# network 192.168.13.0 0.0.0.3 area 0
```

Step 2:   Configure OSPF on R2 and R3.

Use the **router ospf** command and add the **network** statements for the networks on R2 and R3. Neighbor adjacency messages display on R1 when OSPF routing is configured on R2 and R3.

```
R1#

00:22:29: %OSPF-5-ADJCHG: Process 1, Nbr 192.168.23.1 on Serial0/0/0 from LOADING to
FULL, Loading Done

R1#

00:23:14: %OSPF-5-ADJCHG: Process 1, Nbr 192.168.23.2 on Serial0/0/1 from LOADING to
FULL, Loading Done

R1#
```

Step 3: Verify OSPF neighbors and routing information.

a. Issue the **show ip ospf neighbor** command to verify that each router lists the other routers in the network as neighbors.

R1# **show ip ospf neighbor**

Neighbor ID	Pri	State	Dead Time	Address	Interface
192.168.23.2	0	FULL/ -	00:00:33	192.168.13.2	Serial0/0/1
192.168.23.1	0	FULL/ -	00:00:30	192.168.12.2	Serial0/0/0

b. Issue the **show ip route** command to verify that all networks display in the routing table on all routers.

R1# **show ip route**
```
Codes: L - local, C - connected, S - static, R - RIP, M - mobile, B - BGP
       D - EIGRP, EX - EIGRP external, O - OSPF, IA - OSPF inter area
       N1 - OSPF NSSA external type 1, N2 - OSPF NSSA external type 2
       E1 - OSPF external type 1, E2 - OSPF external type 2, E - EGP
       i - IS-IS, L1 - IS-IS level-1, L2 - IS-IS level-2, ia - IS-IS inter area
       * - candidate default, U - per-user static route, o - ODR
       P - periodic downloaded static route


Gateway of last resort is not set


      192.168.1.0/24 is variably subnetted, 2 subnets, 2 masks
C        192.168.1.0/24 is directly connected, GigabitEthernet0/0
L        192.168.1.1/32 is directly connected, GigabitEthernet0/0
O     192.168.2.0/24 [110/65] via 192.168.12.2, 00:32:33, Serial0/0/0
O     192.168.3.0/24 [110/65] via 192.168.13.2, 00:31:48, Serial0/0/1
      192.168.12.0/24 is variably subnetted, 2 subnets, 2 masks
C        192.168.12.0/30 is directly connected, Serial0/0/0
L        192.168.12.1/32 is directly connected, Serial0/0/0
      192.168.13.0/24 is variably subnetted, 2 subnets, 2 masks
C        192.168.13.0/30 is directly connected, Serial0/0/1
L        192.168.13.1/32 is directly connected, Serial0/0/1
      192.168.23.0/30 is subnetted, 1 subnets
O        192.168.23.0/30 [110/128] via 192.168.12.2, 00:31:38, Serial0/0/0
                         [110/128] via 192.168.13.2, 00:31:38, Serial0/0/1
```

What command would you use to only see the OSPF routes in the routing table?

Step 4:   Verify OSPF protocol settings.

The **show ip protocols** command is a quick way to verify vital OSPF configuration information. This information includes the OSPF process ID, the router ID, networks the router is advertising, the neighbors the router is receiving updates from, and the default administrative distance, which is 110 for OSPF.

```
R1# show ip protocols
*** IP Routing is NSF aware ***


Routing Protocol is "ospf 1"
  Outgoing update filter list for all interfaces is not set
  Incoming update filter list for all interfaces is not set
  Router ID 192.168.13.1
  Number of areas in this router is 1. 1 normal 0 stub 0 nssa
  Maximum path: 4
  Routing for Networks:
    192.168.1.0 0.0.0.255 area 0
    192.168.12.0 0.0.0.3 area 0
    192.168.13.0 0.0.0.3 area 0
  Routing Information Sources:
    Gateway         Distance      Last Update
    192.168.23.2         110      00:19:16
    192.168.23.1         110      00:20:03
  Distance: (default is 110)
```

Step 5:   Verify OSPF process information.

Use the **show ip ospf** command to examine the OSPF process ID and router ID. This command displays the OSPF area information, as well as the last time the SPF algorithm was calculated.

```
R1# show ip ospf
Routing Process "ospf 1" with ID 192.168.13.1
Start time: 00:20:23.260, Time elapsed: 00:25:08.296
Supports only single TOS(TOS0) routes
Supports opaque LSA
Supports Link-local Signaling (LLS)
Supports area transit capability
Supports NSSA (compatible with RFC 3101)
Event-log enabled, Maximum number of events: 1000, Mode: cyclic
Router is not originating router-LSAs with maximum metric
Initial SPF schedule delay 5000 msecs
Minimum hold time between two consecutive SPFs 10000 msecs
Maximum wait time between two consecutive SPFs 10000 msecs
Incremental-SPF disabled
Minimum LSA interval 5 secs
```

```
Minimum LSA arrival 1000 msecs
LSA group pacing timer 240 secs
Interface flood pacing timer 33 msecs
Retransmission pacing timer 66 msecs
Number of external LSA 0. Checksum Sum 0x000000
Number of opaque AS LSA 0. Checksum Sum 0x000000
Number of DCbitless external and opaque AS LSA 0
Number of DoNotAge external and opaque AS LSA 0
Number of areas in this router is 1. 1 normal 0 stub 0 nssa
Number of areas transit capable is 0
External flood list length 0
IETF NSF helper support enabled
Cisco NSF helper support enabled
Reference bandwidth unit is 100 mbps
    Area BACKBONE(0)
        Number of interfaces in this area is 3
        Area has no authentication
        SPF algorithm last executed 00:22:53.756 ago
        SPF algorithm executed 7 times
        Area ranges are
        Number of LSA 3. Checksum Sum 0x019A61
        Number of opaque link LSA 0. Checksum Sum 0x000000
        Number of DCbitless LSA 0
        Number of indication LSA 0
        Number of DoNotAge LSA 0
        Flood list length 0
```

Step 6: Verify OSPF interface settings.

a. Issue the **show ip ospf interface brief** command to display a summary of OSPF-enabled interfaces.

```
R1# show ip ospf interface brief
Interface     PID   Area              IP Address/Mask    Cost   State Nbrs F/C
Se0/0/1       1     0                 192.168.13.1/30    64     P2P   1/1
Se0/0/0       1     0                 192.168.12.1/30    64     P2P   1/1
Gi0/0         1     0                 192.168.1.1/24     1      DR    0/0
```

b. For a more detailed list of every OSPF-enabled interface, issue the **show ip ospf interface** command.

```
R1# show ip ospf interface
Serial0/0/1 is up, line protocol is up
  Internet Address 192.168.13.1/30, Area 0, Attached via Network Statement
  Process ID 1, Router ID 192.168.13.1, Network Type POINT_TO_POINT, Cost: 64
  Topology-MTID    Cost    Disabled    Shutdown       Topology Name
        0           64       no          no              Base
```

```
    Transmit Delay is 1 sec, State POINT_TO_POINT
    Timer intervals configured, Hello 10, Dead 40, Wait 40, Retransmit 5
      oob-resync timeout 40
      Hello due in 00:00:01
    Supports Link-local Signaling (LLS)
    Cisco NSF helper support enabled
    IETF NSF helper support enabled
    Index 3/3, flood queue length 0
    Next 0x0(0)/0x0(0)
    Last flood scan length is 1, maximum is 1
    Last flood scan time is 0 msec, maximum is 0 msec
    Neighbor Count is 1, Adjacent neighbor count is 1
      Adjacent with neighbor 192.168.23.2
    Suppress hello for 0 neighbor(s)
  Serial0/0/0 is up, line protocol is up
    Internet Address 192.168.12.1/30, Area 0, Attached via Network Statement
    Process ID 1, Router ID 192.168.13.1, Network Type POINT_TO_POINT, Cost: 64
    Topology-MTID    Cost    Disabled    Shutdown      Topology Name
          0           64       no          no            Base
    Transmit Delay is 1 sec, State POINT_TO_POINT
    Timer intervals configured, Hello 10, Dead 40, Wait 40, Retransmit 5
      oob-resync timeout 40
      Hello due in 00:00:03
    Supports Link-local Signaling (LLS)
    Cisco NSF helper support enabled
    IETF NSF helper support enabled
    Index 2/2, flood queue length 0
    Next 0x0(0)/0x0(0)
    Last flood scan length is 1, maximum is 1
    Last flood scan time is 0 msec, maximum is 0 msec
    Neighbor Count is 1, Adjacent neighbor count is 1
      Adjacent with neighbor 192.168.23.1
    Suppress hello for 0 neighbor(s)
  GigabitEthernet0/0 is up, line protocol is up
    Internet Address 192.168.1.1/24, Area 0, Attached via Network Statement
    Process ID 1, Router ID 192.168.13.1, Network Type BROADCAST, Cost: 1
    Topology-MTID    Cost    Disabled    Shutdown      Topology Name
          0           1        no          no            Base
    Transmit Delay is 1 sec, State DR, Priority 1
    Designated Router (ID) 192.168.13.1, Interface address 192.168.1.1
    No backup designated router on this network
```

```
    Timer intervals configured, Hello 10, Dead 40, Wait 40, Retransmit 5
      oob-resync timeout 40
      Hello due in 00:00:01
    Supports Link-local Signaling (LLS)
    Cisco NSF helper support enabled
    IETF NSF helper support enabled
    Index 1/1, flood queue length 0
    Next 0x0(0)/0x0(0)
    Last flood scan length is 0, maximum is 0
    Last flood scan time is 0 msec, maximum is 0 msec
    Neighbor Count is 0, Adjacent neighbor count is 0
    Suppress hello for 0 neighbor(s)
```

Step 7: Verify end-to-end connectivity.

Each PC should be able to ping the other PCs in the topology. Verify and troubleshoot if necessary.

Note: It may be necessary to disable the PC firewall to ping between PCs.

Part 3: Change Router ID Assignments

The OSPF router ID is used to uniquely identify the router in the OSPF routing domain. Cisco routers derive the router ID in one of three ways and with the following precedence:

1) IP address configured with the OSPF **router-id** command, if present

2) Highest IP address of any of the router's loopback addresses, if present

3) Highest active IP address on any of the router's physical interfaces

Because no router IDs or loopback interfaces have been configured on the three routers, the router ID for each router is determined by the highest IP address of any active interface.

In Part 3, you will change the OSPF router ID assignment using loopback addresses. You will also use the **router-id** command to change the router ID.

Step 1: Change router IDs using loopback addresses.

a. Assign an IP address to loopback 0 on R1.

```
R1(config)# interface lo0
R1(config-if)# ip address 1.1.1.1 255.255.255.255
R1(config-if)# end
```

b. Assign IP addresses to Loopback 0 on R2 and R3. Use IP address 2.2.2.2/32 for R2 and 3.3.3.3/32 for R3.

c. Save the running configuration to the startup configuration on all three routers.

d. You must reload the routers in order to reset the router ID to the loopback address. Issue the **reload** command on all three routers. Press Enter to confirm the reload.

e. After the router completes the reload process, issue the **show ip protocols** command to view the new router ID.

```
R1# show ip protocols
*** IP Routing is NSF aware ***


Routing Protocol is "ospf 1"
  Outgoing update filter list for all interfaces is not set
  Incoming update filter list for all interfaces is not set
  Router ID 1.1.1.1
  Number of areas in this router is 1. 1 normal 0 stub 0 nssa
  Maximum path: 4
  Routing for Networks:
    192.168.1.0 0.0.0.255 area 0
    192.168.12.0 0.0.0.3 area 0
    192.168.13.0 0.0.0.3 area 0
  Routing Information Sources:
    Gateway         Distance      Last Update
    3.3.3.3              110      00:01:00
    2.2.2.2              110      00:01:14
  Distance: (default is 110)
```

f. Issue the **show ip ospf neighbor** command to display the router ID changes for the neighboring routers.

```
R1# show ip ospf neighbor


Neighbor ID     Pri   State         Dead Time   Address         Interface
3.3.3.3           0   FULL/  -      00:00:35    192.168.13.2    Serial0/0/1
2.2.2.2           0   FULL/  -      00:00:32    192.168.12.2    Serial0/0/0
R1#
```

Step 2:   Change the router ID on R1 using the router-id command.

The preferred method for setting the router ID is with the **router-id** command.

a. Issue the **router-id 11.11.11.11** command on R1 to reassign the router ID. Notice the informational message that appears when issuing the **router-id** command.

```
R1(config)# router ospf 1
R1(config-router)# router-id 11.11.11.11
Reload or use "clear ip ospf process" command, for this to take effect
R1(config)# end
```

b. You will receive an informational message telling you that you must either reload the router or use the **clear ip ospf process** command for the change to take effect. Issue the **clear ip ospf process** command on all three routers. Type **yes** to reply to the reset verification message, and press ENTER.

c. Set the router ID for R2 to **22.22.22.22** and the router ID for R3 to **33.33.33.33**. Then use **clear ip ospf process** command to reset ospf routing process.

d. Issue the **show ip protocols** command to verify that the router ID changed on R1.

```
R1# show ip protocols
*** IP Routing is NSF aware ***


Routing Protocol is "ospf 1"
  Outgoing update filter list for all interfaces is not set
  Incoming update filter list for all interfaces is not set
  Router ID 11.11.11.11
  Number of areas in this router is 1. 1 normal 0 stub 0 nssa
  Maximum path: 4
  Routing for Networks:
    192.168.1.0 0.0.0.255 area 0
    192.168.12.0 0.0.0.3 area 0
    192.168.13.0 0.0.0.3 area 0
  Passive Interface(s):
    GigabitEthernet0/1
  Routing Information Sources:
    Gateway         Distance      Last Update
    33.33.33.33         110        00:00:19
    22.22.22.22         110        00:00:31
    3.3.3.3             110        00:00:41
    2.2.2.2             110        00:00:41
  Distance: (default is 110)
```

e. Issue the **show ip ospf neighbor** command on R1 to verify that new router ID for R2 and R3 is listed.

```
R1# show ip ospf neighbor


Neighbor ID     Pri   State        Dead Time   Address         Interface
33.33.33.33       0   FULL/  -     00:00:36    192.168.13.2    Serial0/0/1
22.22.22.22       0   FULL/  -     00:00:32    192.168.12.2    Serial0/0/0
```

Part 4: Configure OSPF Passive Interfaces

The **passive-interface** command prevents routing updates from being sent through the specified router interface. This is commonly done to reduce traffic on the LANs as they do not need to receive dynamic routing protocol communication. In Part 4, you will use the **passive-interface** command to configure a single interface as passive. You will also configure OSPF so that all interfaces on the router are passive by default, and then enable OSPF routing advertisements on selected interfaces.

Step 1: Configure a passive interface.

a. Issue the **show ip ospf interface g0/0** command on R1. Notice the timer indicating when the next Hello packet is expected. Hello packets are sent every 10 seconds and are used between OSPF routers to verify that their neighbors are up.

```
R1# show ip ospf interface g0/0
GigabitEthernet0/0 is up, line protocol is up
  Internet Address 192.168.1.1/24, Area 0, Attached via Network Statement
```

```
   Process ID 1, Router ID 11.11.11.11, Network Type BROADCAST, Cost: 1
   Topology-MTID    Cost    Disabled    Shutdown     Topology Name
        0            1         no         no            Base
   Transmit Delay is 1 sec, State DR, Priority 1
   Designated Router (ID) 11.11.11.11, Interface address 192.168.1.1
   No backup designated router on this network
   Timer intervals configured, Hello 10, Dead 40, Wait 40, Retransmit 5
     oob-resync timeout 40
     Hello due in 00:00:02
   Supports Link-local Signaling (LLS)
   Cisco NSF helper support enabled
   IETF NSF helper support enabled
   Index 1/1, flood queue length 0
   Next 0x0(0)/0x0(0)
   Last flood scan length is 0, maximum is 0
   Last flood scan time is 0 msec, maximum is 0 msec
   Neighbor Count is 0, Adjacent neighbor count is 0
   Suppress hello for 0 neighbor(s)
```

b. Issue the **passive-interface** command to change the G0/0 interface on R1 to passive.

```
R1(config)# router ospf 1
R1(config-router)# passive-interface g0/0
```

c. Re-issue the **show ip ospf interface g0/0** command to verify that G0/0 is now passive.

```
R1# show ip ospf interface g0/0
GigabitEthernet0/0 is up, line protocol is up
   Internet Address 192.168.1.1/24, Area 0, Attached via Network Statement
   Process ID 1, Router ID 11.11.11.11, Network Type BROADCAST, Cost: 1
   Topology-MTID    Cost    Disabled    Shutdown     Topology Name
        0            1         no         no            Base
   Transmit Delay is 1 sec, State DR, Priority 1
   Designated Router (ID) 11.11.11.11, Interface address 192.168.1.1
   No backup designated router on this network
   Timer intervals configured, Hello 10, Dead 40, Wait 40, Retransmit 5
     oob-resync timeout 40
     No Hellos (Passive interface)
   Supports Link-local Signaling (LLS)
   Cisco NSF helper support enabled
   IETF NSF helper support enabled
   Index 1/1, flood queue length 0
   Next 0x0(0)/0x0(0)
   Last flood scan length is 0, maximum is 0
   Last flood scan time is 0 msec, maximum is 0 msec
```

```
        Neighbor Count is 0, Adjacent neighbor count is 0
        Suppress hello for 0 neighbor(s)
```

d. Issue the **show ip route** command on R2 and R3 to verify that a route to the 192.168.1.0/24 network is still available.

```
R2# show ip route
Codes: L - local, C - connected, S - static, R - RIP, M - mobile, B - BGP
       D - EIGRP, EX - EIGRP external, O - OSPF, IA - OSPF inter area
       N1 - OSPF NSSA external type 1, N2 - OSPF NSSA external type 2
       E1 - OSPF external type 1, E2 - OSPF external type 2
       i - IS-IS, su - IS-IS summary, L1 - IS-IS level-1, L2 - IS-IS level-2
       ia - IS-IS inter area, * - candidate default, U - per-user static route
       o - ODR, P - periodic downloaded static route, H - NHRP, l - LISP
       + - replicated route, % - next hop override


Gateway of last resort is not set


        2.0.0.0/32 is subnetted, 1 subnets
C          2.2.2.2 is directly connected, Loopback0
O       192.168.1.0/24 [110/65] via 192.168.12.1, 00:58:32, Serial0/0/0
        192.168.2.0/24 is variably subnetted, 2 subnets, 2 masks
C          192.168.2.0/24 is directly connected, GigabitEthernet0/0
L          192.168.2.1/32 is directly connected, GigabitEthernet0/0
O       192.168.3.0/24 [110/65] via 192.168.23.2, 00:58:19, Serial0/0/1
        192.168.12.0/24 is variably subnetted, 2 subnets, 2 masks
C          192.168.12.0/30 is directly connected, Serial0/0/0
L          192.168.12.2/32 is directly connected, Serial0/0/0
        192.168.13.0/30 is subnetted, 1 subnets
O          192.168.13.0 [110/128] via 192.168.23.2, 00:58:19, Serial0/0/1
                       [110/128] via 192.168.12.1, 00:58:32, Serial0/0/0
        192.168.23.0/24 is variably subnetted, 2 subnets, 2 masks
C          192.168.23.0/30 is directly connected, Serial0/0/1
L          192.168.23.1/32 is directly connected, Serial0/0/1
```

Step 2: Set passive interface as the default on a router.

a. Issue the **show ip ospf neighbor** command on R1 to verify that R2 is listed as an OSPF neighbor.

```
R1# show ip ospf neighbor
```

Neighbor ID	Pri	State	Dead Time	Address	Interface
33.33.33.33	0	FULL/ -	00:00:31	192.168.13.2	Serial0/0/1
22.22.22.22	0	FULL/ -	00:00:32	192.168.12.2	Serial0/0/0

b. Issue the **passive-interface default** command on R2 to set the default for all OSPF interfaces as passive.

```
R2(config)# router ospf 1

R2(config-router)# passive-interface default

R2(config-router)#

*Apr  3 00:03:00.979: %OSPF-5-ADJCHG: Process 1, Nbr 11.11.11.11 on Serial0/0/0 from
FULL to DOWN, Neighbor Down: Interface down or detached

*Apr  3 00:03:00.979: %OSPF-5-ADJCHG: Process 1, Nbr 33.33.33.33 on Serial0/0/1 from
FULL to DOWN, Neighbor Down: Interface down or detached
```

c. Re-issue the **show ip ospf neighbor** command on R1. After the dead timer expires, R2 will no longer be listed as an OSPF neighbor.

```
R1# show ip ospf neighbor


Neighbor ID     Pri   State         Dead Time   Address        Interface
33.33.33.33       0   FULL/  -      00:00:34    192.168.13.2   Serial0/0/1
```

d. Issue the **show ip ospf interface S0/0/0** command on R2 to view the OSPF status of interface S0/0/0.

```
R2# show ip ospf interface s0/0/0

Serial0/0/0 is up, line protocol is up

  Internet Address 192.168.12.2/30, Area 0, Attached via Network Statement

  Process ID 1, Router ID 22.22.22.22, Network Type POINT_TO_POINT, Cost: 64

  Topology-MTID    Cost    Disabled    Shutdown    Topology Name
       0            64        no          no           Base

  Transmit Delay is 1 sec, State POINT_TO_POINT

  Timer intervals configured, Hello 10, Dead 40, Wait 40, Retransmit 5

    oob-resync timeout 40

    No Hellos (Passive interface)

  Supports Link-local Signaling (LLS)

  Cisco NSF helper support enabled

  IETF NSF helper support enabled

  Index 2/2, flood queue length 0

  Next 0x0(0)/0x0(0)

  Last flood scan length is 0, maximum is 0

  Last flood scan time is 0 msec, maximum is 0 msec

  Neighbor Count is 0, Adjacent neighbor count is 0

  Suppress hello for 0 neighbor(s)
```

e. If all interfaces on R2 are passive, then no routing information is being advertised. In this case, R1 and R3 should no longer have a route to the 192.168.2.0/24 network. You can verify this by using the **show ip route** command.

f. On R2, issue the **no passive-interface** command so the router will send and receive OSPF routing updates. After entering this command, you will see an informational message that a neighbor adjacency has been established with R1.

```
R2(config)# router ospf 1

R2(config-router)# no passive-interface s0/0/0
```

```
R2(config-router)#
*Apr  3 00:18:03.463: %OSPF-5-ADJCHG: Process 1, Nbr 11.11.11.11 on Serial0/0/0 from
LOADING to FULL, Loading Done
```

g. Re-issue the **show ip route** and **show ip ospf neighbor** commands on R1 and R3, and look for a route to the 192.168.2.0/24 network.

What interface is R3 using to route to the 192.168.2.0/24 network? _____

What is the accumulated cost metric for the 192.168.2.0/24 network on R3? _____

Does R2 show up as an OSPF neighbor on R1? _____

Does R2 show up as an OSPF neighbor on R3? _____

What does this information tell you?

_____

_____

_____

_____

h. Change interface S0/0/1 on R2 to allow it to advertise OSPF routes. Record the commands used below.

_____

_____

i. Re-issue the **show ip route** command on R3.

What interface is R3 using to route to the 192.168.2.0/24 network? _____

What is the accumulated cost metric for the 192.168.2.0/24 network on R3 now and how is this calculated?

_____

Is R2 listed as an OSPF neighbor to R3? _____

Part 5: Change OSPF Metrics

In Part 5, you will change OSPF metrics using the **auto-cost reference-bandwidth** command, the **bandwidth** command, and the **ip ospf cost** command.

Note: All DCE interfaces should have been configured with a clocking rate of 128000 in Part 1.

Step 1:   Change the reference bandwidth on the routers.

The default reference-bandwidth for OSPF is 100Mb/s (Fast Ethernet speed). However, most modern infrastructure devices have links that are faster than 100Mb/s. Because the OSPF cost metric must be an integer, all links with transmission speeds of 100Mb/s or higher have a cost of 1. This results in Fast Ethernet, Gigabit Ethernet, and 10G Ethernet interfaces all having the same cost. Therefore, the reference-bandwidth must be changed to a higher value to accommodate networks with links faster that 100Mb/s.

a. Issue the **show interface** command on R1 to view the default bandwidth setting for the G0/0 interface.

```
R1# show interface g0/0
GigabitEthernet0/0 is up, line protocol is up
   Hardware is CN Gigabit Ethernet, address is c471.fe45.7520 (bia c471.fe45.7520)
   MTU 1500 bytes, BW 1000000 Kbit/sec, DLY 100 usec,
      reliability 255/255, txload 1/255, rxload 1/255
   Encapsulation ARPA, loopback not set
   Keepalive set (10 sec)
   Full Duplex, 100Mbps, media type is RJ45
   output flow-control is unsupported, input flow-control is unsupported
   ARP type: ARPA, ARP Timeout 04:00:00
   Last input never, output 00:17:31, output hang never
   Last clearing of "show interface" counters never
   Input queue: 0/75/0/0 (size/max/drops/flushes); Total output drops: 0
   Queueing strategy: fifo
   Output queue: 0/40 (size/max)
   5 minute input rate 0 bits/sec, 0 packets/sec
   5 minute output rate 0 bits/sec, 0 packets/sec
      0 packets input, 0 bytes, 0 no buffer
      Received 0 broadcasts (0 IP multicasts)
      0 runts, 0 giants, 0 throttles
      0 input errors, 0 CRC, 0 frame, 0 overrun, 0 ignored
      0 watchdog, 0 multicast, 0 pause input
      279 packets output, 89865 bytes, 0 underruns
      0 output errors, 0 collisions, 1 interface resets
      0 unknown protocol drops
      0 babbles, 0 late collision, 0 deferred
      1 lost carrier, 0 no carrier, 0 pause output
      0 output buffer failures, 0 output buffers swapped out
```

Note: The bandwidth setting on G0/0 may differ from what is shown above if the PC host interface can only support Fast Ethernet speed. If the PC host interface is not capable of supporting gigabit speed, then the bandwidth will most likely be displayed as 100000 Kbit/sec.

b.   Issue the **show ip route ospf** command on R1 to determine the route to the 192.168.3.0/24 network.

```
R1# show ip route ospf
Codes: L - local, C - connected, S - static, R - RIP, M - mobile, B - BGP
       D - EIGRP, EX - EIGRP external, O - OSPF, IA - OSPF inter area
       N1 - OSPF NSSA external type 1, N2 - OSPF NSSA external type 2
       E1 - OSPF external type 1, E2 - OSPF external type 2
       i - IS-IS, su - IS-IS summary, L1 - IS-IS level-1, L2 - IS-IS level-2
       ia - IS-IS inter area, * - candidate default, U - per-user static route
       o - ODR, P - periodic downloaded static route, H - NHRP, l - LISP
       + - replicated route, % - next hop override


Gateway of last resort is not set


O      192.168.2.0/24 [110/65] via 192.168.12.2, 00:01:08, Serial0/0/0
O      192.168.3.0/24 [110/65] via 192.168.13.2, 00:00:57, Serial0/0/1
       192.168.23.0/30 is subnetted, 1 subnets
O         192.168.23.0 [110/128] via 192.168.13.2, 00:00:57, Serial0/0/1
                       [110/128] via 192.168.12.2, 00:01:08, Serial0/0/0
```

Note: The accumulated cost to the 192.168.3.0/24 network from R1 is 65.

c.   Issue the **show ip ospf interface** command on R3 to determine the routing cost for G0/0.

```
R3# show ip ospf interface g0/0
GigabitEthernet0/0 is up, line protocol is up
   Internet Address 192.168.3.1/24, Area 0, Attached via Network Statement
   Process ID 1, Router ID 3.3.3.3, Network Type BROADCAST, Cost: 1
   Topology-MTID    Cost    Disabled    Shutdown       Topology Name
        0            1         no          no             Base
   Transmit Delay is 1 sec, State DR, Priority 1
   Designated Router (ID) 192.168.23.2, Interface address 192.168.3.1
   No backup designated router on this network
   Timer intervals configured, Hello 10, Dead 40, Wait 40, Retransmit 5
     oob-resync timeout 40
     Hello due in 00:00:05
   Supports Link-local Signaling (LLS)
   Cisco NSF helper support enabled
   IETF NSF helper support enabled
   Index 1/1, flood queue length 0
   Next 0x0(0)/0x0(0)
   Last flood scan length is 0, maximum is 0
   Last flood scan time is 0 msec, maximum is 0 msec
```

```
     Neighbor Count is 0, Adjacent neighbor count is 0

     Suppress hello for 0 neighbor(s)
```

d. Issue the **show ip ospf interface s0/0/1** command on R1 to view the routing cost for S0/0/1.

```
R1# show ip ospf interface s0/0/1
Serial0/0/1 is up, line protocol is up
  Internet Address 192.168.13.1/30, Area 0, Attached via Network Statement
  Process ID 1, Router ID 1.1.1.1, Network Type POINT_TO_POINT, Cost: 64
  Topology-MTID   Cost    Disabled    Shutdown      Topology Name
        0          64        no          no            Base
  Transmit Delay is 1 sec, State POINT_TO_POINT
  Timer intervals configured, Hello 10, Dead 40, Wait 40, Retransmit 5
    oob-resync timeout 40
    Hello due in 00:00:04
  Supports Link-local Signaling (LLS)
  Cisco NSF helper support enabled
  IETF NSF helper support enabled
  Index 3/3, flood queue length 0
  Next 0x0(0)/0x0(0)
  Last flood scan length is 1, maximum is 1
  Last flood scan time is 0 msec, maximum is 0 msec
  Neighbor Count is 1, Adjacent neighbor count is 1
    Adjacent with neighbor 192.168.23.2
  Suppress hello for 0 neighbor(s)
```

The sum of the costs of these two interfaces is the accumulated cost for the route to the 192.168.3.0/24 network on R3 (1 + 64 = 65), as can be seen in the output from the **show ip route** command.

e. Issue the **auto-cost reference-bandwidth 10000** command on R1 to change the default reference bandwidth setting. With this setting, 10Gb/s interfaces will have a cost of 1, 1 Gb/s interfaces will have a cost of 10, and 100Mb/s interfaces will have a cost of 100.

```
R1(config)# router ospf 1
R1(config-router)# auto-cost reference-bandwidth 10000
% OSPF: Reference bandwidth is changed.
        Please ensure reference bandwidth is consistent across all routers.
```

f. Issue the **auto-cost reference-bandwidth 10000** command on routers R2 and R3.

g. Re-issue the **show ip ospf interface** command to view the new cost of G0/0 on R3, and S0/0/1 on R1.

```
R3# show ip ospf interface g0/0
GigabitEthernet0/0 is up, line protocol is up
  Internet Address 192.168.3.1/24, Area 0, Attached via Network Statement
  Process ID 1, Router ID 3.3.3.3, Network Type BROADCAST, Cost: 10
  Topology-MTID   Cost    Disabled    Shutdown      Topology Name
        0          10        no          no            Base
  Transmit Delay is 1 sec, State DR, Priority 1
  Designated Router (ID) 192.168.23.2, Interface address 192.168.3.1
```

```
    No backup designated router on this network
    Timer intervals configured, Hello 10, Dead 40, Wait 40, Retransmit 5
      oob-resync timeout 40
      Hello due in 00:00:02
    Supports Link-local Signaling (LLS)
    Cisco NSF helper support enabled
    IETF NSF helper support enabled
    Index 1/1, flood queue length 0
    Next 0x0(0)/0x0(0)
    Last flood scan length is 0, maximum is 0
    Last flood scan time is 0 msec, maximum is 0 msec
    Neighbor Count is 0, Adjacent neighbor count is 0
    Suppress hello for 0 neighbor(s)
```

Note: If the device connected to the G0/0 interface does not support Gigabit Ethernet speed, the cost will be different than the output display. For example, the cost will be 100 for Fast Ethernet speed (100Mb/s).

```
R1# show ip ospf interface s0/0/1
Serial0/0/1 is up, line protocol is up
    Internet Address 192.168.13.1/30, Area 0, Attached via Network Statement
    Process ID 1, Router ID 1.1.1.1, Network Type POINT_TO_POINT, Cost: 6476
    Topology-MTID    Cost    Disabled    Shutdown    Topology Name
         0           6476      no          no          Base
    Transmit Delay is 1 sec, State POINT_TO_POINT
    Timer intervals configured, Hello 10, Dead 40, Wait 40, Retransmit 5
      oob-resync timeout 40
      Hello due in 00:00:05
    Supports Link-local Signaling (LLS)
    Cisco NSF helper support enabled
    IETF NSF helper support enabled
    Index 3/3, flood queue length 0
    Next 0x0(0)/0x0(0)
    Last flood scan length is 1, maximum is 1
    Last flood scan time is 0 msec, maximum is 0 msec
    Neighbor Count is 1, Adjacent neighbor count is 1
      Adjacent with neighbor 192.168.23.2
    Suppress hello for 0 neighbor(s)
```

h. Re-issue the **show ip route ospf** command to view the new accumulated cost for the 192.168.3.0/24 route (10 + 6476 = 6486).

Note: If the device connected to the G0/0 interface does not support Gigabit Ethernet speed, the total cost will be different than the output display. For example, the accumulated cost will be 6576 if G0/0 is operating at Fast Ethernet speed (100Mb/s).

```
R1# show ip route ospf
Codes: L - local, C - connected, S - static, R - RIP, M - mobile, B - BGP
```

```
          D - EIGRP, EX - EIGRP external, O - OSPF, IA - OSPF inter area

          N1 - OSPF NSSA external type 1, N2 - OSPF NSSA external type 2

          E1 - OSPF external type 1, E2 - OSPF external type 2

          i - IS-IS, su - IS-IS summary, L1 - IS-IS level-1, L2 - IS-IS level-2

          ia - IS-IS inter area, * - candidate default, U - per-user static route

          o - ODR, P - periodic downloaded static route, H - NHRP, l - LISP

          + - replicated route, % - next hop override


Gateway of last resort is not set


O        192.168.2.0/24 [110/6486] via 192.168.12.2, 00:05:40, Serial0/0/0

O        192.168.3.0/24 [110/6486] via 192.168.13.2, 00:01:08, Serial0/0/1

          192.168.23.0/30 is subnetted, 1 subnets

O           192.168.23.0 [110/12952] via 192.168.13.2, 00:05:17, Serial0/0/1

                         [110/12952] via 192.168.12.2, 00:05:17, Serial0/0/
```

Note: Changing the default reference-bandwidth on the routers from 100 to 10,000 in effect changed the accumulated costs of all routes by a factor of 100, but the cost of each interface link and route is now more accurately reflected.

i. To reset the reference-bandwidth back to its default value, issue the **auto-cost reference-bandwidth 100** command on all three routers.

```
R1(config)# router ospf 1

R1(config-router)# auto-cost reference-bandwidth 100

% OSPF: Reference bandwidth is changed.

        Please ensure reference bandwidth is consistent across all routers.
```

Why would you want to change the OSPF default reference-bandwidth?

_____

_____

Step 2: Change the bandwidth for an interface.

On most serial links, the bandwidth metric will default to 1544 Kbits (that of a T1). If this is not the actual speed of the serial link, the bandwidth setting will need to be changed to match the actual speed to allow the route cost to be calculated correctly in OSPF. Use the **bandwidth** command to adjust the bandwidth setting on an interface.

Note: A common misconception is to assume that the **bandwidth** command will change the physical bandwidth, or speed, of the link. The command modifies the bandwidth metric used by OSPF to calculate routing costs, and does not modify the actual bandwidth (speed) of the link.

a. Issue the **show interface s0/0/0** command on R1 to view the current bandwidth setting on S0/0/0. Even though the clock rate, link speed on this interface was set to 128Kb/s, the bandwidth is still showing 1544Kb/s.

```
R1# show interface s0/0/0

Serial0/0/0 is up, line protocol is up

  Hardware is WIC MBRD Serial

  Internet address is 192.168.12.1/30

  MTU 1500 bytes, BW 1544 Kbit/sec, DLY 20000 usec,

     reliability 255/255, txload 1/255, rxload 1/255

  Encapsulation HDLC, loopback not set

  Keepalive set (10 sec)

<Output omitted>
```

b. Issue the **show ip route ospf** command on R1 to view the accumulated cost for the route to network 192.168.23.0/24 using S0/0/0. Note that there are two equal-cost (128) routes to the 192.168.23.0/24 network, one via S0/0/0 and one via S0/0/1.

```
R1# show ip route ospf

Codes: L - local, C - connected, S - static, R - RIP, M - mobile, B - BGP

       D - EIGRP, EX - EIGRP external, O - OSPF, IA - OSPF inter area

       N1 - OSPF NSSA external type 1, N2 - OSPF NSSA external type 2

       E1 - OSPF external type 1, E2 - OSPF external type 2

       i - IS-IS, su - IS-IS summary, L1 - IS-IS level-1, L2 - IS-IS level-2

       ia - IS-IS inter area, * - candidate default, U - per-user static route

       o - ODR, P - periodic downloaded static route, H - NHRP, l - LISP

       + - replicated route, % - next hop override


Gateway of last resort is not set


O     192.168.2.0/24 [110/65] via 192.168.12.2, 00:00:26, Serial0/0/0
O     192.168.3.0/24 [110/65] via 192.168.13.2, 00:00:26, Serial0/0/1
      192.168.23.0/30 is subnetted, 1 subnets
O        192.168.23.0 [110/128] via 192.168.13.2, 00:00:26, Serial0/0/1
                      [110/128] via 192.168.12.2, 00:00:26, Serial0/0/0
```

c. Issue the **bandwidth 128** command to set the bandwidth on S0/0/0 to 128Kb/s.

```
R1(config)# interface s0/0/0

R1(config-if)# bandwidth 128
```

d. Re-issue the **show ip route ospf** command. The routing table no longer displays the route to the 192.168.23.0/24 network over the S0/0/0 interface. This is because the best route, the one with the lowest cost, is now via S0/0/1.

```
R1# show ip route ospf

Codes: L - local, C - connected, S - static, R - RIP, M - mobile, B - BGP

        D - EIGRP, EX - EIGRP external, O - OSPF, IA - OSPF inter area

        N1 - OSPF NSSA external type 1, N2 - OSPF NSSA external type 2

        E1 - OSPF external type 1, E2 - OSPF external type 2

        i - IS-IS, su - IS-IS summary, L1 - IS-IS level-1, L2 - IS-IS level-2

        ia - IS-IS inter area, * - candidate default, U - per-user static route
```

```
           o - ODR, P - periodic downloaded static route, H - NHRP, l - LISP
           + - replicated route, % - next hop override


Gateway of last resort is not set


O       192.168.2.0/24 [110/129] via 192.168.12.2, 00:01:47, Serial0/0/0
O       192.168.3.0/24 [110/65] via 192.168.13.2, 00:04:51, Serial0/0/1
        192.168.23.0/30 is subnetted, 1 subnets
O          192.168.23.0 [110/128] via 192.168.13.2, 00:04:51, Serial0/0/1
```

e. Issue the **show ip ospf interface brief** command. The cost for S0/0/0 has changed from 64 to 781 which is an accurate cost representation of the link speed.

```
R1# show ip ospf interface brief

Interface    PID    Area              IP Address/Mask     Cost   State Nbrs F/C
Se0/0/1      1      0                 192.168.13.1/30     64     P2P   1/1
Se0/0/0      1      0                 192.168.12.1/30     781    P2P   1/1
Gi0/0        1      0                 192.168.1.1/24      1      DR    0/0
```

f. Change the bandwidth for interface S0/0/1 to the same setting as S0/0/0 on R1.

g. Re-issue the **show ip route ospf** command to view the accumulated cost of both routes to the 192.168.23.0/24 network. Note that there are again two equal-cost (845) routes to the 192.168.23.0/24 network, one via S0/0/0 and one via S0/0/1.

```
R1# show ip route ospf

Codes: L - local, C - connected, S - static, R - RIP, M - mobile, B - BGP
       D - EIGRP, EX - EIGRP external, O - OSPF, IA - OSPF inter area
       N1 - OSPF NSSA external type 1, N2 - OSPF NSSA external type 2
       E1 - OSPF external type 1, E2 - OSPF external type 2
       i - IS-IS, su - IS-IS summary, L1 - IS-IS level-1, L2 - IS-IS level-2
       ia - IS-IS inter area, * - candidate default, U - per-user static route
       o - ODR, P - periodic downloaded static route, H - NHRP, l - LISP
       + - replicated route, % - next hop override


Gateway of last resort is not set


O       192.168.2.0/24 [110/782] via 192.168.12.2, 00:00:09, Serial0/0/0
O       192.168.3.0/24 [110/782] via 192.168.13.2, 00:00:09, Serial0/0/1
        192.168.23.0/30 is subnetted, 1 subnets
O          192.168.23.0 [110/845] via 192.168.13.2, 00:00:09, Serial0/0/1
                        [110/845] via 192.168.12.2, 00:00:09, Serial0/0/0
```

Explain how the costs to the 192.168.3.0/24 and 192.168.23.0/30 networks from R1 were calculated.

_____

_____

_____

h. Issue the **show ip route ospf** command on R3. The accumulated cost of the 192.168.1.0/24 is still show-ing as 65. Unlike the **clock rate** command, the **bandwidth** command needs to be applied on each side of a serial link.

```
R3# show ip route ospf

Codes: L - local, C - connected, S - static, R - RIP, M - mobile, B - BGP
       D - EIGRP, EX - EIGRP external, O - OSPF, IA - OSPF inter area
       N1 - OSPF NSSA external type 1, N2 - OSPF NSSA external type 2
       E1 - OSPF external type 1, E2 - OSPF external type 2
       i - IS-IS, su - IS-IS summary, L1 - IS-IS level-1, L2 - IS-IS level-2
       ia - IS-IS inter area, * - candidate default, U - per-user static route
       o - ODR, P - periodic downloaded static route, H - NHRP, l - LISP
       + - replicated route, % - next hop override


Gateway of last resort is not set


O     192.168.1.0/24 [110/65] via 192.168.13.1, 00:30:58, Serial0/0/0
O     192.168.2.0/24 [110/65] via 192.168.23.1, 00:30:58, Serial0/0/1
      192.168.12.0/30 is subnetted, 1 subnets
O        192.168.12.0 [110/128] via 192.168.23.1, 00:30:58, Serial0/0/1
                      [110/128] via 192.168.13.1, 00:30:58, Serial0/0/0
```

i. Issue the **bandwidth 128** command on all remaining serial interfaces in the topology.

What is the new accumulated cost to the 192.168.23.0/24 network on R1? Why?

_____

_____

Step 3: Change the route cost.

OSPF uses the bandwidth setting to calculate the cost for a link by default. However, you can override this calculation by manually setting the cost of a link using the **ip ospf cost** command. Like the **bandwidth** com-mand, the **ip ospf cost** command only affects the side of the link where it was applied.

a. Issue the **show ip route ospf** on R1.

```
R1# show ip route ospf

Codes: L - local, C - connected, S - static, R - RIP, M - mobile, B - BGP
       D - EIGRP, EX - EIGRP external, O - OSPF, IA - OSPF inter area
```

```
        N1 - OSPF NSSA external type 1, N2 - OSPF NSSA external type 2
        E1 - OSPF external type 1, E2 - OSPF external type 2
        i - IS-IS, su - IS-IS summary, L1 - IS-IS level-1, L2 - IS-IS level-2
        ia - IS-IS inter area, * - candidate default, U - per-user static route
        o - ODR, P - periodic downloaded static route, H - NHRP, l - LISP
        + - replicated route, % - next hop override


Gateway of last resort is not set


O       192.168.2.0/24 [110/782] via 192.168.12.2, 00:00:26, Serial0/0/0
O       192.168.3.0/24 [110/782] via 192.168.13.2, 00:02:50, Serial0/0/1
        192.168.23.0/30 is subnetted, 1 subnets
O          192.168.23.0 [110/1562] via 192.168.13.2, 00:02:40, Serial0/0/1
                        [110/1562] via 192.168.12.2, 00:02:40, Serial0/0/0
```

b. Apply the **ip ospf cost 1565** command to the S0/0/1 interface on R1. A cost of 1565 is higher than the accumulated cost of the route through R2 which is 1562.

```
R1(config)# interface s0/0/1
R1(config-if)# ip ospf cost 1565
```

c. Re-issue the **show ip route ospf** command on R1 to display the effect this change has made on the routing table. All OSPF routes for R1 are now being routed through R2.

```
R1# show ip route ospf
Codes: L - local, C - connected, S - static, R - RIP, M - mobile, B - BGP
       D - EIGRP, EX - EIGRP external, O - OSPF, IA - OSPF inter area
       N1 - OSPF NSSA external type 1, N2 - OSPF NSSA external type 2
       E1 - OSPF external type 1, E2 - OSPF external type 2
       i - IS-IS, su - IS-IS summary, L1 - IS-IS level-1, L2 - IS-IS level-2
       ia - IS-IS inter area, * - candidate default, U - per-user static route
       o - ODR, P - periodic downloaded static route, H - NHRP, l - LISP
       + - replicated route, % - next hop override


Gateway of last resort is not set


O       192.168.2.0/24 [110/782] via 192.168.12.2, 00:02:06, Serial0/0/0
O       192.168.3.0/24 [110/1563] via 192.168.12.2, 00:05:31, Serial0/0/0
        192.168.23.0/30 is subnetted, 1 subnets
O          192.168.23.0 [110/1562] via 192.168.12.2, 01:14:02, Serial0/0/0
```

Note: Manipulating link costs using the **ip ospf cost** command is the easiest and preferred method for changing OSPF route costs. In addition to changing the cost based on bandwidth, a network administrator may have other reasons for changing the cost of a route, such as preference for a particular service provider or the actual monetary cost of a link or route.

Explain why the route to the 192.168.3.0/24 network on R1 is now going through R2?

_____

_____

_____

Reflection

1. Why is it important to control the router ID assignment when using the OSPF protocol?

    _____

    _____

    _____

2. Why is the DR/BDR election process not a concern in this lab?

    _____

    _____

    _____

3. Why would you want to set an OSPF interface to passive?

    _____

    _____

    _____

Router Interface Summary Table

Router Interface Summary				
Router Model	**Ethernet Interface #1**	**Ethernet Interface #2**	**Serial Interface #1**	**Serial Interface #2**
1800	Fast Ethernet 0/0 (F0/0)	Fast Ethernet 0/1 (F0/1)	Serial 0/0/0 (S0/0/0)	Serial 0/0/1 (S0/0/1)
1900	Gigabit Ethernet 0/0 (G0/0)	Gigabit Ethernet 0/1 (G0/1)	Serial 0/0/0 (S0/0/0)	Serial 0/0/1 (S0/0/1)
2801	Fast Ethernet 0/0 (F0/0)	Fast Ethernet 0/1 (F0/1)	Serial 0/1/0 (S0/1/0)	Serial 0/1/1 (S0/1/1)
2811	Fast Ethernet 0/0 (F0/0)	Fast Ethernet 0/1 (F0/1)	Serial 0/0/0 (S0/0/0)	Serial 0/0/1 (S0/0/1)
2900	Gigabit Ethernet 0/0 (G0/0)	Gigabit Ethernet 0/1 (G0/1)	Serial 0/0/0 (S0/0/0)	Serial 0/0/1 (S0/0/1)

Note: To find out how the router is configured, look at the interfaces to identify the type of router and how many interfaces the router has. There is no way to effectively list all the combinations of configurations for each router class. This table includes identifiers for the possible combinations of Ethernet and Serial interfaces in the device. The table does not include any other type of interface, even though a specific router may contain one. An example of this might be an ISDN BRI interface. The string in parenthesis is the legal abbreviation that can be used in Cisco IOS commands to represent the interface.

5.1.2.13 Lab - Configuring OSPFv2 on a Multiaccess Network

Topology

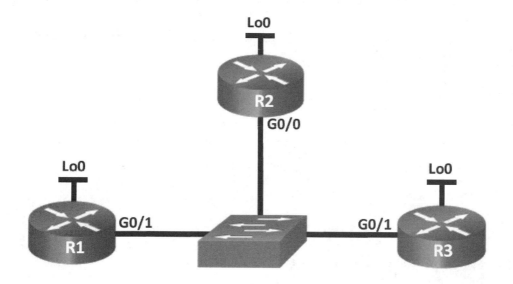

Addressing Table

Device	Interface	IP Address	Subnet Mask
R1	G0/1	192.168.1.1	255.255.255.0
	Lo0	192.168.31.11	255.255.255.255
R2	G0/0	192.168.1.2	255.255.255.0
	Lo0	192.168.31.22	255.255.255.255
R3	G0/1	192.168.1.3	255.255.255.0
	Lo0	192.168.31.33	255.255.255.255

Objectives

Part 1: Build the Network and Configure Basic Device Settings

Part 2: Configure and Verify OSPFv2 on the DR, BDR, and DROther

Part 3: Configure OSPFv2 Interface Priority to Determine the DR and BDR

Background / Scenario

A multiaccess network is a network with more than two devices on the same shared media. Examples include Ethernet and Frame Relay. On multiaccess networks, OSPFv2 elects a Designated Router (DR) to be the collection and distribution point for link-state advertisements (LSAs) that are sent and received. A Backup Designated Router (BDR) is also elected in case the DR fails. All other routers become DROthers as this indicates a router that is neither the DR nor the BDR.

Because the DR acts as a focal point for OSPF routing protocol communication, the router chosen should be capable of supporting a heavier traffic load than other routers in the network. A router with a powerful CPU and adequate DRAM is typically the best choice for the DR.

In this lab, you will configure OSPFv2 on the DR, BDR, and DROther. You will then modify the priority of routers to control the outcome of the DR/BDR election process and ensure that the desired router becomes the DR.

Note: The routers used with CCNA hands-on labs are Cisco 1941 Integrated Services Routers (ISRs) with Cisco IOS Release 15.2(4)M3 (universalk9 image). The switches used are Cisco Catalyst 2960s with Cisco IOS Release 15.0(2) (lanbasek9 image). Other routers, switches, and Cisco IOS versions can be used. Depending on the model and Cisco IOS version, the commands available and output produced might vary from what is shown in the labs. Refer to the Router Interface Summary Table at the end of this lab for the correct interface identifiers.

Note: Make sure that the routers and switches have been erased and have no startup configurations. If you are unsure, contact your instructor.

Required Resources

- 3 Routers (Cisco 1941 with Cisco IOS Release 15.2(4)M3 universal image or comparable)
- 1 Switch (Cisco 2960 with Cisco IOS Release 15.0(2) lanbasek9 image or comparable)
- Console cables to configure the Cisco IOS devices via the console ports
- Ethernet cables as shown in the topology

Part 1:   Build the Network and Configure Basic Device Settings

In Part 1, you will set up the network topology and configure basic settings on the routers.

Step 1:   Cable the network as shown in the topology.

Attach the devices as shown in the topology diagram, and cable as necessary.

Step 2:   Initialize and reload the routers.

Step 3:   Configure basic settings for each router.

a.   Disable DNS lookup.

b.   Configure device names as shown in the topology.

c.   Assign **class** as the privileged EXEC password.

d.   Assign **cisco** as the console and vty passwords.

e.   Encrypt the plain text passwords.

f.   Configure a MOTD banner to warn users that unauthorized access is prohibited.

g.   Configure **logging synchronous** for the console line.

h.   Configure the IP addresses listed in the Addressing Table for all interfaces.

i.   Use the **show ip interface brief** command to verify that the IP addressing is correct and that the interfaces are active.

j.   Copy the running configuration to the startup configuration.

Part 2:   Configure and Verify OSPFv2 on the DR, BDR, and DROther

In Part 2, you will configure OSPFv2 on the DR, BDR, and DROther. The DR and BDR election process takes place as soon as the first router has its interface enabled on the multiaccess network. This can happen as the routers are powered-on or when the OSPF **network** command for that interface is configured. If a new router enters the network after the DR and BDR have already been elected, it does not become the DR or BDR, even if it has a higher OSPF interface priority or router ID than the current DR or BDR. Configure the OSPF process on the router with the highest router ID first to ensure that this router becomes the DR.

Step 1:   Configure OSPF on R3.

Configure the OSPF process on R3 (the router with the highest router ID) to ensure that this router becomes the DR.

a.   Assign 1 as the process ID for the OSPF process. Configure the router to advertise the 192.168.1.0/24 network. Use an area ID of 0 for the OSPF *area-id* parameter in the **network** statement.

What factor determined that R3 has the highest router ID?

_____

b.   Verify that OSPF has been configured and R3 is the DR.

What command would you use to verify that OSPF has been configured correctly and R3 is the DR?

_____

Step 2:   Configure OSPF on R2.

Configure the OSPF process on R2 (the router with the second highest router ID) to ensure that this router becomes the BDR.

a.   Assign 1 as the process ID for the OSPF process. Configure the router to advertise the 192.168.1.0/24 network. Use an area ID of 0 for the OSPF *area-id* parameter in the **network** statement.

b.   Verify that the OSPF has been configured and that R2 is the BDR. Record the command used for verification.

_____

c.   Issue the **show ip ospf neighbor** command to view information about the other routers in the OSPF area.

```
R2# show ip ospf neighbor

Neighbor ID     Pri   State          Dead Time   Address       Interface
192.168.31.33    1    FULL/DR        00:00:33    192.168.1.3   GigabitEthernet0/0
```

Notice that R3 is the DR.

Step 3:   Configure OSPF on R1.

Configure the OSPF process on R1 (the router with the lowest router ID). This router will be designated as DROther instead of DR or BDR.

a.   Assign 1 as the process ID for the OSPF process. Configure the router to advertise the 192.168.1.0/24 network. Use an area ID of 0 for the OSPF *area-id* parameter in the **network** statement.

b.   Issue **show ip ospf interface brief** command to verify that OSPF has been configured and R1 is the DROther.

```
R1# show ip ospf interface brief

Interface    PID    Area           IP Address/Mask     Cost   State Nbrs F/C
Gi0/1         1      0             192.168.1.1/24       1     DROTH 2/2
```

c.   Issue the **show ip ospf neighbor** command to view information about the other routers in the OSPF area.

```
R1# show ip ospf neighbor

Neighbor ID     Pri   State        Dead Time    Address        Interface
192.168.31.22    1    FULL/BDR     00:00:35     192.168.1.2    GigabitEthernet0/1
192.168.31.33    1    FULL/DR      00:00:30     192.168.1.3    GigabitEthernet0/1
```

What priority are both the DR and BDR routers? _____

Part 3:   Configure OSPFv2 Interface Priority to Determine the DR and BDR

In Part 3, you will configure router interface priority to determine the DR/BDR election, reset the OSPFv2 process, and then verify that the DR and BDR routers have changed. OSPF interface priority overrides all other settings in determining which routers become the DR and BDR.

Step 1:   Configure R1 G0/1 with OSPF priority 255.

A value of 255 is the highest possible interface priority.

```
R1(config)# interface g0/1
R1(config-if)# ip ospf priority 255
R1(config-if)# end
```

Step 2:   Configure R3 G0/1 with OSPF priority 100.

```
R3(config)# interface g0/1
R3(config-if)# ip ospf priority 100
R3(config-if)# end
```

Step 3:   Configure R2 G0/0 with OSPF priority 0.

A priority of 0 causes the router to be ineligible to participate in an OSPF election and does not become a DR or BDR.

```
R2(config)# interface g0/0
R2(config-if)# ip ospf priority 0
R2(config-if)# end
```

Step 4:   Reset the OSPF process.

a.   Issue the **show ip ospf neighbor** command to determine the DR and BDR.

b.   Has the DR designation changed? _____   Which router is the DR? _____

Has the BDR designation changed? _____   Which router is the BDR? _____

What is the role of R2 now? _____

Explain the immediate effects caused by the **ip ospf priority** command.

_____

_____

_____

Note: If the DR and BDR designations did not change, issue the **clear ip ospf 1 process** command on all of the routers to reset the OSPF processes and force a new election.

If the **clear ip ospf process** command does not reset the DR and BDR, issue the **reload** command on all routers after saving the running configuration to the startup configuration.

c. Issue the **show ip ospf interface** command on R1 and R3 to confirm the priority settings and DR/BDR status on the routers.

```
R1# show ip ospf interface
GigabitEthernet0/1 is up, line protocol is up
  Internet Address 192.168.1.1/24, Area 0
  Process ID 1, Router ID 192.168.31.11, Network Type BROADCAST, Cost: 1
  Transmit Delay is 1 sec, State DR, Priority 255
  Designated Router (ID) 192.168.31.11, Interface address 192.168.1.1
  Backup Designated router (ID) 192.168.31.33, Interface address 192.168.1.3
  Timer intervals configured, Hello 10, Dead 40, Wait 40, Retransmit 5
    oob-resync timeout 40
    Hello due in 00:00:00
  Supports Link-local Signaling (LLS)
  Index 1/1, flood queue length 0
  Next 0x0(0)/0x0(0)
  Last flood scan length is 1, maximum is 2
  Last flood scan time is 0 msec, maximum is 0 msec
  Neighbor Count is 2, Adjacent neighbor count is 2
    Adjacent with neighbor 192.168.31.22
    Adjacent with neighbor 192.168.31.33   (Backup Designated Router)
  Suppress hello for 0 neighbor(s)


R3# show ip ospf interface
GigabitEthernet0/1 is up, line protocol is up
  Internet Address 192.168.1.3/24, Area 0
  Process ID 1, Router ID 192.168.31.33, Network Type BROADCAST, Cost: 1
  Transmit Delay is 1 sec, State BDR, Priority 100
  Designated Router (ID) 192.168.31.11, Interface address 192.168.1.1
  Backup Designated router (ID) 192.168.31.33, Interface address 192.168.1.3
  Timer intervals configured, Hello 10, Dead 40, Wait 40, Retransmit 5
    oob-resync timeout 40
    Hello due in 00:00:00
  Supports Link-local Signaling (LLS)
  Index 1/1, flood queue length 0
  Next 0x0(0)/0x0(0)
  Last flood scan length is 0, maximum is 2
  Last flood scan time is 0 msec, maximum is 0 msec
  Neighbor Count is 2, Adjacent neighbor count is 2
```

```
        Adjacent with neighbor 192.168.31.22

        Adjacent with neighbor 192.168.31.11   (Designated Router)

    Suppress hello for 0 neighbor(s)
```

Which router is now the DR? _____

Which router is now the BDR? _____

Did the interface priority override the router ID in determining the DR/BDR? _____

Reflection

1. List the criteria used from highest to lowest for determining the DR on an OSPF network.

    _____

    _____

    _____

2. What is the significance of a 255 interface priority?

    _____

Router Interface Summary Table

Router Interface Summary				
Router Model	**Ethernet Interface #1**	**Ethernet Interface #2**	**Serial Interface #1**	**Serial Interface #2**
1800	Fast Ethernet 0/0 (F0/0)	Fast Ethernet 0/1 (F0/1)	Serial 0/0/0 (S0/0/0)	Serial 0/0/1 (S0/0/1)
1900	Gigabit Ethernet 0/0 (G0/0)	Gigabit Ethernet 0/1 (G0/1)	Serial 0/0/0 (S0/0/0)	Serial 0/0/1 (S0/0/1)
2801	Fast Ethernet 0/0 (F0/0)	Fast Ethernet 0/1 (F0/1)	Serial 0/1/0 (S0/1/0)	Serial 0/1/1 (S0/1/1)
2811	Fast Ethernet 0/0 (F0/0)	Fast Ethernet 0/1 (F0/1)	Serial 0/0/0 (S0/0/0)	Serial 0/0/1 (S0/0/1)
2900	Gigabit Ethernet 0/0 (G0/0)	Gigabit Ethernet 0/1 (G0/1)	Serial 0/0/0 (S0/0/0)	Serial 0/0/1 (S0/0/1)

Note: To find out how the router is configured, look at the interfaces to identify the type of router and how many interfaces the router has. There is no way to effectively list all the combinations of configurations for each router class. This table includes identifiers for the possible combinations of Ethernet and Serial interfaces in the device. The table does not include any other type of interface, even though a specific router may contain one. An example of this might be an ISDN BRI interface. The string in parenthesis is the legal abbreviation that can be used in Cisco IOS commands to represent the interface.

5.1.5.8 Lab - Configuring OSFPv2 Advanced Features

Topology

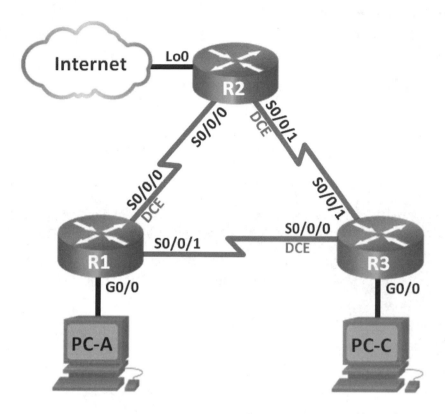

Addressing Table

Device	Interface	IP Address	Subnet Mask	Default Gateway
R1	G0/0	192.168.1.1	255.255.255.0	N/A
	S0/0/0 (DCE)	192.168.12.1	255.255.255.252	N/A
	S0/0/1	192.168.13.1	255.255.255.252	N/A
R2	Lo0	209.165.200.225	255.255.255.252	N/A
	S0/0/0	192.168.12.2	255.255.255.252	N/A
	S0/0/1 (DCE)	192.168.23.1	255.255.255.252	N/A
R3	G0/0	192.168.3.1	255.255.255.0	N/A
	S0/0/0 (DCE)	192.168.13.2	255.255.255.252	N/A
	S0/0/1	192.168.23.2	255.255.255.252	N/A
PC-A	NIC	192.168.1.3	255.255.255.0	192.168.1.1
PC-C	NIC	192.168.3.3	255.255.255.0	192.168.3.1

Objectives

Part 1: Build the Network and Configure Basic Device Settings

Part 2: Configure and Verify OSPF Routing

Part 3: Change OSPF Metrics

Part 4: Configure and Propagate a Static Default Route

Part 5: Configure OSPF Authentication

Background / Scenario

Open Shortest Path First (OSPF) has advanced features to allow changes to be made to control metrics, default route propagation, and security.

In this lab, you will adjust OSPF metrics on the router interfaces, configure OSPF route propagation, and use Message Digest 5 (MD5) authentication to secure OSPF routing information.

Note: The routers used with CCNA hands-on labs are Cisco 1941 Integrated Services Routers (ISRs) with Cisco IOS Release 15.2(4)M3 (universalk9 image). Other routers and Cisco IOS versions can be used. Depending on the model and Cisco IOS version, the commands available and output produced might vary from what is shown in the labs. Refer to the Router Interface Summary Table at the end of this lab for the correct interface identifiers.

Note: Make sure that the routers have been erased and have no startup configurations. If you are unsure, contact your instructor.

Required Resources

- 3 Routers (Cisco 1941 with Cisco IOS Release 15.2(4)M3 universal image or comparable)
- 2 PCs (Windows 7, Vista, or XP with terminal emulation program, such as Tera Term)
- Console cables to configure the Cisco IOS devices via the console ports
- Ethernet and serial cables as shown in the topology

Part 1: Build the Network and Configure Basic Device Settings

In Part 1, you will set up the network topology and configure basic settings on the PC hosts and routers.

Step 1:   Cable the network as shown in the topology.

Step 2:   Initialize and reload the routers as necessary.

Step 3:   Configure basic settings for each router.

a. Disable DNS lookup.

b. Configure device name as shown in the topology.

c. Assign **class** as the privileged EXEC password.

d. Assign **cisco** as the console and vty passwords.

e. Encrypt the clear text passwords.

f. Configure a MOTD banner to warn users that unauthorized access is prohibited.

g. Configure **logging synchronous** for the console line.

h. Configure the IP addresses listed in the Addressing Table for all interfaces.

i. Set the clock rate for all DCE serial interfaces at 128000.

j. Copy the running configuration to the startup configuration.

Step 4:   Configure PC hosts.

Refer to the Addressing Table for PC host address information.

Step 5:   Test connectivity.

At this point, the PCs are unable to ping each other. However, the routers should be able to ping the directly connected neighbor interfaces, and the PCs should be able to ping their default gateway. Verify and trouble-shoot if necessary.

Part 2:   Configure and Verify OSPF Routing

In Part 2, you will configure OSPFv2 routing on all routers in the network and then verify that routing tables are updated correctly.

Step 1:   Configure the router ID on all routers.

Assign 1 as the process ID for this OSPF process. Each router should be given the following router ID assignments:

- R1 Router ID: **1.1.1.1**
- R2 Router ID: **2.2.2.2**
- R3 Router ID: **3.3.3.3**

Step 2:   Configure OSPF network information on the routers.

Step 3:   Verify OSPF routing.

a. Issue the **show ip ospf neighbor** command to verify that each router is listing the other routers in the network.

b. Issue the **show ip route ospf** command to verify that all OSPF networks are present in the routing table on all routers.

Step 4:   Test end-to-end connectivity.

Ping PC-C from PC-A to verify end-to-end connectivity. The pings should be successful. If they are not, troubleshoot as necessary.

Note: It may be necessary to disable the PC firewall for the pings to be successful.

Part 3:   Change OSPF Metrics

In Part 3, you will change OSPF metrics using the **bandwidth** command, the **auto-cost reference-band-width** command, and the **ip ospf cost** command. Making these changes will provide more accurate metrics to OSPF.

Note: All DCE interfaces should have been configured with a clocking rate of 128000 in Part 1.

Step 1:   Change the bandwidth on all serial interfaces to 128Kb/s.

a.   Issue the **show ip ospf interface brief** command to view the default cost settings on the router interfaces.

```
R1# show ip ospf interface brief
Interface    PID    Area        IP Address/Mask    Cost    State   Nbrs F/C
Se0/0/1      1      0           192.168.13.1/30    64      P2P     1/1
Se0/0/0      1      0           192.168.12.1/30    64      P2P     1/1
Gi0/0        1      0           192.168.1.1/24     1       DR      0/0
```

b.   Use the **bandwidth 128** interface command on all serial interfaces.

c.   Issue the **show ip ospf interface brief** command to view the new cost settings.

```
R1# show ip ospf interface brief
Interface    PID    Area        IP Address/Mask    Cost    State   Nbrs F/C
Se0/0/1      1      0           192.168.13.1/30    781     P2P     1/1
Se0/0/0      1      0           192.168.12.1/30    781     P2P     1/1
Gi0/0        1      0           192.168.1.1/24     1       DR      0/0
```

Step 2:   Change the reference bandwidth on the routers.

a.   Issue the **auto-cost reference-bandwidth 1000** command on the routers to change the default reference bandwidth setting to account for Gigabit Ethernet Interfaces.

b.   Re-issue the **show ip ospf interface brief** command to view how this command has changed cost values.

```
R1# show ip ospf interface brief
Interface    PID    Area        IP Address/Mask    Cost    State   Nbrs F/C
Se0/0/1      1      0           192.168.13.1/30    7812    P2P     0/0
Se0/0/0      1      0           192.168.12.1/30    7812    P2P     0/0
Gi0/0        1      0           192.168.1.1/24     1       DR      0/0
```

Note: If the router had Fast Ethernet interfaces instead of Gigabit Ethernet interfaces, then the cost would now be 10 on those interfaces.

Step 3:   Change the route cost.

a.   Issue the **show ip route ospf** command to display the current OSPF routes on R1. Notice that there are currently two routes in the table that use the S0/0/1 interface.

```
R1# show ip route ospf
Codes: L - local, C - connected, S - static, R - RIP, M - mobile, B - BGP
       D - EIGRP, EX - EIGRP external, O - OSPF, IA - OSPF inter area
       N1 - OSPF NSSA external type 1, N2 - OSPF NSSA external type 2
       E1 - OSPF external type 1, E2 - OSPF external type 2
       i - IS-IS, su - IS-IS summary, L1 - IS-IS level-1, L2 - IS-IS level-2
       ia - IS-IS inter area, * - candidate default, U - per-user static route
       o - ODR, P - periodic downloaded static route, H - NHRP, l - LISP
       + - replicated route, % - next hop override
```

```
Gateway of last resort is not set


O       192.168.3.0/24 [110/7822] via 192.168.13.2, 00:00:12, Serial0/0/1
        192.168.23.0/30 is subnetted, 1 subnets
O          192.168.23.0 [110/15624] via 192.168.13.2, 00:00:12, Serial0/0/1
                        [110/15624] via 192.168.12.2, 00:20:03, Serial0/0/0
```

b. Apply the **ip ospf cost 16000** command to the S0/0/1 interface on R1. A cost of 16,000 is higher than the accumulated cost of the route through R2 which is 15,624.

c. Issue the **show ip ospf interface brief** command on R1 to view the cost change to S0/0/1.

```
R1# show ip ospf interface brief
```

Interface	PID	Area	IP Address/Mask	Cost	State	Nbrs F/C
Se0/0/1	1	0	192.168.13.1/30	16000	P2P	1/1
Se0/0/0	1	0	192.168.12.1/30	7812	P2P	1/1
Gi0/0	1	0	192.168.1.1/24	1	DR	0/0

d. Re-issue the **show ip route ospf** command on R1 to display the effect this change has made on the routing table. All OSPF routes for R1 are now being routed through R2.

```
R1# show ip route ospf
Codes: L - local, C - connected, S - static, R - RIP, M - mobile, B - BGP
       D - EIGRP, EX - EIGRP external, O - OSPF, IA - OSPF inter area
       N1 - OSPF NSSA external type 1, N2 - OSPF NSSA external type 2
       E1 - OSPF external type 1, E2 - OSPF external type 2
       i - IS-IS, su - IS-IS summary, L1 - IS-IS level-1, L2 - IS-IS level-2
       ia - IS-IS inter area, * - candidate default, U - per-user static route
       o - ODR, P - periodic downloaded static route, H - NHRP, l - LISP
       + - replicated route, % - next hop override


Gateway of last resort is not set


O       192.168.3.0/24 [110/15625] via 192.168.12.2, 00:05:31, Serial0/0/0
        192.168.23.0/30 is subnetted, 1 subnets
O          192.168.23.0 [110/15624] via 192.168.12.2, 01:14:02, Serial0/0/0
```

Explain why the route to the 192.168.3.0/24 network on R1 is now going through R2?

_____

_____

_____

Part 4: Configure and Propagate a Static Default Route

In Part 4, you will use a loopback interface on R2 to simulate an ISP connection to the Internet. You will create a static default route on R2, and then OSPF will propagate that route to the other two routers on the network.

Step 1: Configure a static default route on R2 to loopback 0.

Configure a default route using the loopback interface configured in Part 1, to simulate a connection to an ISP.

Step 2: Have OSPF propagate the default static route.

Issue the **default-information originate** command to include the static default route in the OSPF updates that are sent from R2.

```
R2(config)# router ospf 1
R2(config-router)# default-information originate
```

Step 3: Verify OSPF static route propagation.

a. Issue the **show ip route static** command on R2.

```
R2# show ip route static
Codes: L - local, C - connected, S - static, R - RIP, M - mobile, B - BGP
       D - EIGRP, EX - EIGRP external, O - OSPF, IA - OSPF inter area
       N1 - OSPF NSSA external type 1, N2 - OSPF NSSA external type 2
       E1 - OSPF external type 1, E2 - OSPF external type 2
       i - IS-IS, su - IS-IS summary, L1 - IS-IS level-1, L2 - IS-IS level-2
       ia - IS-IS inter area, * - candidate default, U - per-user static route
       o - ODR, P - periodic downloaded static route, H - NHRP, l - LISP
       + - replicated route, % - next hop override


Gateway of last resort is 0.0.0.0 to network 0.0.0.0


S*      0.0.0.0/0 is directly connected, Loopback0
```

b. Issue the **show ip route** command on R1 to verify the propagation of the static route from R2.

```
R1# show ip route
Codes: L - local, C - connected, S - static, R - RIP, M - mobile, B - BGP
       D - EIGRP, EX - EIGRP external, O - OSPF, IA - OSPF inter area
       N1 - OSPF NSSA external type 1, N2 - OSPF NSSA external type 2
       E1 - OSPF external type 1, E2 - OSPF external type 2
       i - IS-IS, su - IS-IS summary, L1 - IS-IS level-1, L2 - IS-IS level-2
       ia - IS-IS inter area, * - candidate default, U - per-user static route
       o - ODR, P - periodic downloaded static route, H - NHRP, l - LISP
       + - replicated route, % - next hop override


Gateway of last resort is 192.168.12.2 to network 0.0.0.0
```

```
O*E2    0.0.0.0/0 [110/1] via 192.168.12.2, 00:02:57, Serial0/0/0
            192.168.1.0/24 is variably subnetted, 2 subnets, 2 masks
C           192.168.1.0/24 is directly connected, GigabitEthernet0/0
L           192.168.1.1/32 is directly connected, GigabitEthernet0/0
O       192.168.3.0/24 [110/15634] via 192.168.12.2, 00:03:35, Serial0/0/0
            192.168.12.0/24 is variably subnetted, 2 subnets, 2 masks
C           192.168.12.0/30 is directly connected, Serial0/0/0
L           192.168.12.1/32 is directly connected, Serial0/0/0
            192.168.13.0/24 is variably subnetted, 2 subnets, 2 masks
C           192.168.13.0/30 is directly connected, Serial0/0/1
L           192.168.13.1/32 is directly connected, Serial0/0/1
            192.168.23.0/30 is subnetted, 1 subnets
O           192.168.23.0 [110/15624] via 192.168.12.2, 00:05:18, Serial0/0/0
```

c.   Verify end-to-end connectivity by issuing a ping from PC-A to the ISP interface address 209.165.200.225.

Were the pings successful? _____

Part 5:   Configure OSPF Authentication

OSPF authentication can be set up at the link level or the area level. There are three authentication types available for OSPF authentication: Null, plain text, or MD5. In Part 5, you will set up OSPF MD5 authentication, which is the strongest available.

Step 1:   Set up MD5 OSPF authentication on a single link.

a.   Issue the **debug ip ospf adj** command on R2 to view OSPF adjacency messages.

```
R2# debug ip ospf adj
OSPF adjacency debugging is on
```

b.   Assign an MD5 key for OSPF Authentication on R1, interface S0/0/0.

```
R1(config)# interface s0/0/0
R1(config-if)# ip ospf message-digest-key 1 md5 MD5KEY
```

c.   Activate MD5 authentication on R1, interface S0/0/0.

```
R1(config-if)# ip ospf authentication message-digest
```

OSPF debug messages informing you of a Mismatched Authentication type displays on R2.

```
*Mar 19 00:03:18.187: OSPF-1 ADJ   Se0/0/0: Rcv pkt from 192.168.12.1 : Mismatched
Authentication type. Input packet specified type 2, we use type 0
```

d.   Issue the **u all** command, which is the shortest version of the **undebug all** command on R2 to disable debugging.

e.   Configure OSPF authentication on R2, interface S0/0/0. Use the same MD5 password you entered for R1.

f.   Issue a **show ip ospf interface s0/0/0** command on R2. This command displays the type of authentication at the bottom of the output.

```
R2# show ip ospf interface s0/0/0
Serial0/0/0 is up, line protocol is up
  Internet Address 192.168.12.2/30, Area 0, Attached via Network Statement
  Process ID 1, Router ID 2.2.2.2, Network Type POINT_TO_POINT, Cost: 7812
```

```
 Topology-MTID    Cost    Disabled    Shutdown      Topology Name
        0         7812       no          no             Base
   Transmit Delay is 1 sec, State POINT_TO_POINT
   Timer intervals configured, Hello 10, Dead 40, Wait 40, Retransmit 5
     oob-resync timeout 40
     Hello due in 00:00:03
   Supports Link-local Signaling (LLS)
   Cisco NSF helper support enabled
   IETF NSF helper support enabled
   Index 1/1, flood queue length 0
   Next 0x0(0)/0x0(0)
   Last flood scan length is 1, maximum is 1
   Last flood scan time is 0 msec, maximum is 0 msec
   Neighbor Count is 1, Adjacent neighbor count is 1
     Adjacent with neighbor 1.1.1.1
   Suppress hello for 0 neighbor(s)
   Message digest authentication enabled
     Youngest key id is 1
```

Step 2:   Set up OSPF authentication at the area level.

a. Issue the **area 0 authentication** command to set MD5 authentication for OSPF Area 0 on R1.

```
R1(config)# router ospf 1
R1(config-router)# area 0 authentication message-digest
```

b. This option still requires that you assign the MD5 password at the interface level.

```
R1(config)# interface s0/0/1
R1(config-if)# ip ospf message-digest-key 1 md5 MD5KEY
```

c. Issue the **show ip ospf neighbor** command on R3. R1 no longer has an adjacency with R3.

```
R3# show ip ospf neighbor
```

```
Neighbor ID     Pri   State         Dead Time   Address         Interface
2.2.2.2          0   FULL/ -        00:00:31    192.168.23.1    Serial0/0/1
```

d. Set up area authentication on R3 and assign the same MD5 password to interface S0/0/0.

```
R3(config)# router ospf 1
R3(config-router)# area 0 authentication message-digest
R3(config-router)# interface s0/0/0
R3(config-if)# ip ospf message-digest-key 1 md5 MD5KEY
```

e. Issue the **show ip ospf neighbor** command on R3. Notice that R1 is now showing as a neighbor, but R2 is missing.

```
R3# show ip ospf neighbor
```

```
Neighbor ID     Pri   State         Dead Time   Address         Interface
1.1.1.1          0   FULL/ -        00:00:38    192.168.13.1    Serial0/0/0
```

Why is R2 no longer showing as an OSPF neighbor?

_____

_____

f. Configure R2 to perform area-level MD5 authentication.

    R2(config)# **router ospf 1**

    R2(config-router)# **area 0 authentication message-digest**

g. Assign **MD5KEY** as the MD5 password for the link between R2 and R3.

h. Issue the **show ip ospf neighbor** command on all routers to verify that all adjacencies have been re-established.

    R1# **show ip ospf neighbor**

Neighbor ID	Pri	State	Dead Time	Address	Interface
3.3.3.3	0	FULL/ -	00:00:39	192.168.13.2	Serial0/0/1
2.2.2.2	0	FULL/ -	00:00:35	192.168.12.2	Serial0/0/0

    R2# **show ip ospf neighbor**

Neighbor ID	Pri	State	Dead Time	Address	Interface
3.3.3.3	0	FULL/ -	00:00:36	192.168.23.2	Serial0/0/1
1.1.1.1	0	FULL/ -	00:00:32	192.168.12.1	Serial0/0/0

    R3# **show ip ospf neighbor**

Neighbor ID	Pri	State	Dead Time	Address	Interface
2.2.2.2	0	FULL/ -	00:00:33	192.168.23.1	Serial0/0/1
1.1.1.1	0	FULL/ -	00:00:39	192.168.13.1	Serial0/0/0

Reflection

1. What is the easiest and preferred method of manipulating OSPF route costs?

   _____

   _____

2. What does the **default-information originate** command do for a network using the OSPF routing protocol?

   _____

3. Why is it a good idea to use OSPF authentication?

   _____

   _____

   _____

   _____

Router Interface Summary Table

Router Interface Summary				
Router Model	**Ethernet Interface #1**	**Ethernet Interface #2**	**Serial Interface #1**	**Serial Interface #2**
1800	Fast Ethernet 0/0 (F0/0)	Fast Ethernet 0/1 (F0/1)	Serial 0/0/0 (S0/0/0)	Serial 0/0/1 (S0/0/1)
1900	Gigabit Ethernet 0/0 (G0/0)	Gigabit Ethernet 0/1 (G0/1)	Serial 0/0/0 (S0/0/0)	Serial 0/0/1 (S0/0/1)
2801	Fast Ethernet 0/0 (F0/0)	Fast Ethernet 0/1 (F0/1)	Serial 0/1/0 (S0/1/0)	Serial 0/1/1 (S0/1/1)
2811	Fast Ethernet 0/0 (F0/0)	Fast Ethernet 0/1 (F0/1)	Serial 0/0/0 (S0/0/0)	Serial 0/0/1 (S0/0/1)
2900	Gigabit Ethernet 0/0 (G0/0)	Gigabit Ethernet 0/1 (G0/1)	Serial 0/0/0 (S0/0/0)	Serial 0/0/1 (S0/0/1)

Note: To find out how the router is configured, look at the interfaces to identify the type of router and how many interfaces the router has. There is no way to effectively list all the combinations of configurations for each router class. This table includes identifiers for the possible combinations of Ethernet and Serial interfaces in the device. The table does not include any other type of interface, even though a specific router may contain one. An example of this might be an ISDN BRI interface. The string in parenthesis is the legal abbreviation that can be used in Cisco IOS commands to represent the interface.

5.2.3.3 Lab – Troubleshooting Basic Single-Area OSPFv2 and OSPFv3

Topology

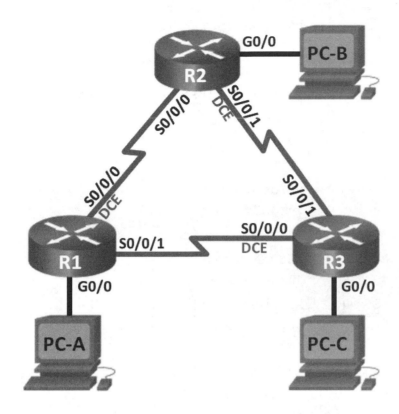

Addressing Table

Device	OSPF Router ID	Interface	IP Address	Default Gateway
R1	1.1.1.1	G0/0	192.168.1.1/24 2001:DB8:ACAD:A::1/64 FE80::1 link-local	N/A
		S0/0/0	192.168.12.1/30 2001:DB8:ACAD:12::1/64 FE80::1 link-local	N/A
		S0/0/1	192.18.13.1/30 2001:DB8:ACAD:13::1/64 FE80::1 link-local	N/A
R2	2.2.2.2	G0/0	192.168.2.1/24 2001:DB8:ACAD:B::2/64 FE80::2 link-local	N/A
		S0/0/0	192.168.12.2/30 2001:DB8:ACAD:12::2/64 FE80::2 link-local	N/A
		S0/0/1	192.168.23.1/30 2001:DB8:ACAD:23::2/64 FE80::2 link-local	N/A
R3	3.3.3.3	G0/0	192.168.3.1/24 2001:DB8:ACAD:C::3/64 FE80::3 link-local	N/A
		S0/0/0	192.168.13.2/30 2001:DB8:ACAD:13::3/64 FE80::3 link-local	N/A
		S0/0/1	192.168.23.2/30 2001:DB8:ACAD:23::3/64 FE80::3 link-local	N/A
PC-A		NIC	192.168.1.3/24 2001:DB8:ACAD:A::A/64	192.168.1.1 FE80::1
PC-B		NIC	192.168.2.3/24 2001:DB8:ACAD:B::B/64	192.168.2.1 FE80::2
PC-C		NIC	192.168.3.3/24 2001:DB8:ACAD:C::C/64	192.168.3.1 FE80::3

Objectives

Part 1: Build the Network and Load Device Configurations

Part 2: Troubleshoot Layer 3 Connectivity

Part 3: Troubleshoot OSPFv2

Part 4: Troubleshoot OSPFv3

Background / Scenario

Open Shortest Path First (OSPF) is a link-state routing protocol for IP networks. OSPFv2 is defined for IPv4 networks, and OSPFv3 is defined for IPv6 networks. OSPFv2 and OSPFv3 are completely isolated routing protocols, changes in OSPFv2 do not affect OSPFv3 routing, and vice versa.

In this lab, a single-area OSPF network running OSPFv2 and OSPFv3 is experiencing problems. You have been assigned to find the problems with the network and correct them.

Note: The routers used with CCNA hands-on labs are Cisco 1941 Integrated Services Routers (ISRs) with Cisco IOS Release 15.2(4)M3 (universalk9 image). Other routers and Cisco IOS versions can be used. Depending on the model and Cisco IOS version, the commands available and output produced might vary from what is shown in the labs. Refer to the Router Interface Summary Table at the end of this lab for the correct interface identifiers.

Note: Make sure that the routers have been erased and have no startup configurations. If you are unsure, contact your instructor.

Required Resources

- 3 Routers (Cisco 1941 with Cisco IOS Release 15.2(4)M3 universal image or comparable)
- 3 PCs (Windows 7, Vista, or XP with terminal emulation program, such as Tera Term)
- Console cables to configure the Cisco IOS devices via the console ports
- Ethernet and serial cables as shown in the topology

Part 1:   Build the Network and Load Device Configurations

In Part 1, you will set up the network topology and configure basic settings on the PC hosts and routers.

Step 1:   Cable the network as shown in the topology.

Step 2:   Configure PC hosts.

Step 3:   Load router configurations.

Load the following configurations into the appropriate router. All routers have the same passwords. The privileged EXEC password is **cisco**. The password for console and vty access is **class**.

Router R1 Configuration:

```
conf t
service password-encryption
no ip domain lookup
```

```
hostname R1
enable secret class
line con 0
 logging synchronous
 password cisco
 login
line vty 0
 password cisco
 login
banner motd @Unauthorized Access is Prohibited!@
ipv6 unicast-routing
ipv6 router ospf 1
 router-id 1.1.1.1
 passive-interface g0/0
interface g0/0
 ip address 192.168.1.1 255.255.255.0
 ipv6 address 2001:db8:acad:a::1/64
 ipv6 address fe80::1 link-local


interface s0/0/0
 clock rate 128000
 ip address 192.168.12.1 255.255.255.0

 ipv6 address 2001:db8:acad:12::1/64
 ipv6 address fe80::1 link-local
 ipv6 ospf 1 area 0
 no shutdown
interface s0/0/1
 ip address 192.168.13.1 255.255.255.0

 ipv6 address 2001:db8:acad:13::1/64
 ipv6 address fe80::1 link-local
 ipv6 ospf 1 area 0
 no shutdown
router ospf 1
 network 192.168.1.0 0.0.0.255 area 0
 network 129.168.12.0 0.0.0.3 area 0
```

```
    network 192.168.13.0 0.0.0.3 area 0
    passive-interface g0/0

  end
```

Router R2 Configuration:

```
conf t
service password-encryption
no ip domain lookup
hostname R2
enable secret class
line con 0
 logging synchronous
 password cisco
 login
line vty 0
 password cisco
 login
banner motd @Unauthorized Access is Prohibited!@
ipv6 unicast-routing
ipv6 router ospf 1
 router-id 2.2.2.2

interface g0/0
ip address 192.168.2.1 255.255.255.0
 ipv6 address 2001:db8:acad:B::2/64
 ipv6 address fe80::1 link-local



 no shutdown
interface s0/0/0
 ip address 192.168.12.2 255.255.255.252
 ipv6 address 2001:db8:acad:12::2/64
 ipv6 address fe80::2 link-local
 ipv6 ospf 1 area 0
 no shutdown
interface s0/0/1
 clock rate 128000
```

```
ipv6 address 2001:db8:acad:23::2/64
ipv6 address fe80::2 link-local

no shutdown
router ospf 1
 network 192.168.2.0 0.0.0.255 area 0
 network 192.168.12.0 0.0.0.3 area 0
 network 192.168.23.0 0.0.0.3 area 0

end
```

Router R3 Configuration:

```
conf t
service password-encryption
no ip domain lookup
enable secret class
hostname R3
line con 0
 logging synchronous
 password cisco
 login
line vty 0
 password cisco
 login
banner motd @Unauthorized Access is Prohibited!@
interface g0/0

 ipv6 address 2001:db8:acad:c::3/64
 ipv6 address fe80::3 link-local


interface s0/0/0
 clock rate 128000
 ip address 192.168.13.1 255.255.255.252

 ipv6 address 2001:db8:acad:13::3/64
 ipv6 address fe80::3 link-local
```

```
 no shutdown
interface s0/0/1
 ip address 192.168.23.2 255.255.255.252
 ipv6 address 2001:db8:acad:23::3/64
 ipv6 address fe80::3 link-local




router ospf 1
 network 192.168.3.0 0.0.0.255 area 0



 passive-interface g0/0
end
```

Part 2: Troubleshoot Layer 3 Connectivity

In Part 2, you will verify that Layer 3 connectivity is established on all interfaces. You will need to test both IPv4 and IPv6 connectivity for all device interfaces.

Step 1:   Verify that the interfaces listed in the Addressing Table are active and configured with the correct IP address information.

a. Issue the **show ip interface brief** command on all routers to verify that the interfaces are in an up/up state. Record your findings.

_____

_____

_____

_____

b. Issue the **show run interface** command to verify IP address assignments on all router interfaces. Compare the interface IP addresses against the Addressing Table and verify the subnet mask assignments. For IPv6, verify that the link-local address has been assigned. Record your findings.

_____

_____

_____

_____

c. Resolve all problems that are found. Record the commands used to correct the issues.

_____

_____

_____

_____

_____

_____

_____

_____

_____

d. Using the **ping** command, verify that each router has network connectivity with the serial interfaces on the neighbor routers. Verify that the PCs can ping their default gateways. If problems still exist, continue troubleshooting Layer 3 issues.

Part 3:   Troubleshoot OSPFv2

In Part 3, you will troubleshoot OSPFv2 problems and make the necessary changes needed to establish OS-PFv2 routes and end-to-end IPv4 connectivity.

Note: LAN (G0/0) interfaces should not advertise OSPF routing information, but routes to these networks should be in the routing tables.

Step 1:   Test IPv4 end-to-end connectivity.

From each PC host, ping the other PC hosts in the topology to verify end-to-end connectivity.

Note: It may be necessary to disable the PC firewall before testing, to ping between PCs.

a. Ping from PC-A to PC-B. Were the pings successful? _____

b. Ping from PC-A to PC-C. Were the pings successful? _____

c. Ping from PC-B to PC-C. Were the pings successful? _____

Step 2:   Verify that all interfaces are assigned to OSPFv2 area 0 on R1.

a. Issue the **show ip protocols** command to verify that OSPF is running and that all networks are advertised in area 0. Verify that the router ID is set correctly. Record your findings.

_____

_____

_____

b. Make the necessary changes to the configuration on R1 based on the output from the **show ip protocols** command. Record the commands used to correct the issues.

_____

_____

_____

c. Issue the **clear ip ospf process** command if necessary.

d. Re-issue the **show ip protocols** command to verify that your changes had the desired effect.

e. Issue the **show ip ospf interface brief** command to verify that all interfaces are listed as OSPF networks assigned to area 0.

f. Issue the **show ip ospf interface g0/0** command to verify that G0/0 is a passive interface.

   Note: This information is also in the **show ip protocols** command.

g. Resolve any problems discovered on R1. List any additional changes made to R1. If no problems were found on the device, then respond with "no problems were found".

_____

Step 3: Verify that all interfaces are assigned to OSPFv2 area 0 on R2.

a. Issue the **show ip protocols** command to verify that OSPF is running and that all networks are being advertised in area 0. Verify that the router ID is set correctly. Record your findings.

_____

_____

_____

b. Make the necessary changes to the configuration on R2 based on the output from the **show ip protocols** command. Record the commands used to correct the issues.

_____

_____

_____

c. Issue the **clear ip ospf process** command if necessary.

d. Re-issue the **show ip protocols** command to verify that your changes had the desired effect.

e. Issue the **show ip ospf interface brief** command to verify that all interfaces are listed as OSPF networks assigned to area 0.

f. Issue the **show ip ospf interface g0/0** command to verify that G0/0 is a passive interface.

   Note: This information is also available from the **show ip protocols** command.

g. Resolve any problems discovered on R2. List any additional changes made to R2. If no problems were found on the device, then respond with "no problems were found".

_____

Step 4: Verify that all interfaces are assigned to OSPFv2 area 0 on R3.

a. Issue the **show ip protocols** command to verify that OSPF is running and that all networks are being advertised in area 0. Verify that the router ID is set correctly as well. Record your findings.

_____

_____

_____

b. Make the necessary changes to the configuration on R3 based on the output from the **show ip protocols** command. Record the commands used to correct the issues.

_____

_____

_____

   c.   Issue the **clear ip ospf process** command if necessary.

   d.   Re-issue the **show ip protocols** command to verify that your changes had the desired effect.

   e.   Issue the **show ip ospf interface brief** command to verify that all interfaces are listed as OSPF networks assigned to area 0.

   f.   Issue the **show ip ospf interface g0/0** command to verify that G0/0 is a passive interface.

       Note: This information is also in the **show ip protocols** command.

   g.   Resolve any problems discovered on R3. List any additional changes made to R3. If no problems were found on the device, then respond with "no problems were found".

Step 5:   Verify OSPF neighbor information.

   a.   Issue the **show ip ospf neighbor** command on all routers to view the OSPF neighbor information.

Step 6:   Verify OSPFv2 Routing Information.

   a.   Issue the **show ip route ospf** command to verify that each router has OSPFv2 routes to all non-adjoining networks.

       Are all OSPFv2 routes available? _____

       If any OSPFv2 routes are missing, what is missing?

---

   b.   If any routing information is missing, resolve these issues.

Step 7:   Verify IPv4 end-to-end connectivity.

From each PC, verify that IPv4 end-to-end connectivity exists. PCs should be able to ping the other PC hosts in the topology. If IPv4 end-to-end connectivity does not exist, then continue troubleshooting to resolve any remaining issues.

Note: It may be necessary to disable the PC firewall to ping between PCs.

Part 4:   Troubleshoot OSPFv3

In Part 4, you will troubleshoot OSPFv3 problems and make the necessary changes needed to establish OSPFv3 routes and end-to-end IPv6 connectivity.

Note: LAN (G0/0) interfaces should not advertise OSPFv3 routing information, but routes to these networks should be contained in the routing tables.

Step 1:   Test IPv6 end-to-end connectivity.

From each PC host, ping the IPv6 addresses of the other PC hosts in the topology to verify IPv6 end-to-end connectivity.

Note: It may be necessary to disable the PC firewall to ping between PCs.

Step 2:   Verify that IPv6 unicast routing has been enabled on all routers.

a. An easy way to verify that IPv6 routing has been enabled on a router is to use the **show run | section ipv6 unicast** command. By adding this pipe (|) section to the **show run** command, the **ipv6 unicast-routing** command displays if IPv6 routing has been enabled.

Note: The **show run** command can also be issued without any pipe, and then a manual search for the **ipv6 unicast-routing** command can be done.

Issue the command on each router. Record your findings.

_____

_____

_____

b. If IPv6 unicast routing is not enabled on one or more routers, enable it now. Record the commands used to correct the issues.

_____

_____

Step 3:   Verify that all interfaces are assigned to OSPFv3 area 0 on R1.

a. Issue the **show ipv6 protocols** command and verify that the router ID is correct. Also verify that the expected interfaces are displayed under area 0.

Note: If no output is generated from this command, then the OSPFv3 process has not been configured.

Record your findings.

_____

_____

_____

b. Make the necessary configuration changes to R1. Record the commands used to correct the issues.

_____

_____

_____

c. Issue the **clear ipv6 ospf process** command if necessary.

d. Re-issue the **show ipv6 protocols** command to verify that your changes had the desired effect.

e. Issue the **show ipv6 ospf interface brief** command to verify that all interfaces are listed as OSPF networks assigned to area 0.

f. Issue the **show ipv6 ospf interface g0/0** command to verify that this interface is set not to advertise OSPFv3 routes.

g. Resolve any problems discovered on R1. List any additional changes made to R1. If no problems were found on the device, then respond with "no problems were found".

_____

Step 4:   Verify that all interfaces are assigned to OSPFv3 area 0 on R2.

    a.   Issue the **show ipv6 protocols** command and verify the router ID is correct. Also verify that the expected interfaces display under area 0.

        Note: If no output is generated from this command, then the OSPFv3 process has not been configured. Record your findings.

        _____

        _____

        _____

    b.   Make the necessary configuration changes to R2. Record the commands used to correct the issues.

        _____

        _____

        _____

    c.   Issue the **clear ipv6 ospf process** command if necessary.

    d.   Re-issue the **show ipv6 protocols** command to verify that your changes had the desired effect.

    e.   Issue the **show ipv6 ospf interface brief** command to verify that all interfaces are listed as OSPF networks assigned to area 0.

    f.   Issue the **show ipv6 ospf interface g0/0** command to verify that this interface is not set to advertise OSPFv3 routes.

    g.   List any additional changes made to R2. If no problems were found on the device, then respond with "no problems were found".

        _____

Step 5:   Verify that all interfaces are assigned to OSPFv3 area 0 on R3.

    a.   Issue the **show ipv6 protocols** command and verify that the router ID is correct. Also verify that the expected interfaces display under area 0.

        Note: If no output is generated from this command, then the OSPFv3 process has not been configured. Record your findings.

        _____

        _____

        _____

    b.   Make the necessary configuration changes to R3. Record the commands used to correct the issues.

        _____

        _____

        _____

    c.   Issue the **clear ipv6 ospf process** command if necessary.

    d.   Re-issue the **show ipv6 protocols** command to verify that your changes had the desired effect.

    e.   Issue the **show ipv6 ospf interface brief** command to verify that all interfaces are listed as OSPF networks assigned to area 0.

f. Issue the **show ipv6 ospf interface g0/0** command to verify that this interface is set not to advertise OSPFv3 routes.

g. Resolve any problems discovered on R3. List any additional changes made to R3. If no problems were found on the device, then respond with "no problems were found".

_____

Step 6: Verify that all routers have correct neighbor adjacency information.

a. Issue the **show ipv6 ospf neighbor** command to verify that adjacencies have formed between neighboring routers.

b. Resolve any OSPFv3 adjacency issues that still exist.

Step 7: Verify OSPFv3 routing information.

a. Issue the **show ipv6 route ospf** command, and verify that OSPFv3 routes exist to all non-adjoining networks.

Are all OSPFv3 routes available? _____

If any OSPFv3 routes are missing, what is missing?

_____

b. Resolve any routing issues that still exist.

Step 8: Verify IPv6 end-to-end connectivity.

From each PC, verify that IPv6 end-to-end connectivity exists. PCs should be able to ping each interface on the network. If IPv6 end-to-end connectivity does not exist, then continue troubleshooting to resolve remaining issues.

Note: It may be necessary to disable the PC firewall to ping between PCs.

Reflection

Why would you troubleshoot OSPFv2 and OSPFv3 separately?

_____

_____

Router Interface Summary Table

Router Interface Summary				
Router Model	**Ethernet Interface #1**	**Ethernet Interface #2**	**Serial Interface #1**	**Serial Interface #2**
1800	Fast Ethernet 0/0 (F0/0)	Fast Ethernet 0/1 (F0/1)	Serial 0/0/0 (S0/0/0)	Serial 0/0/1 (S0/0/1)
1900	Gigabit Ethernet 0/0 (G0/0)	Gigabit Ethernet 0/1 (G0/1)	Serial 0/0/0 (S0/0/0)	Serial 0/0/1 (S0/0/1)
2801	Fast Ethernet 0/0 (F0/0)	Fast Ethernet 0/1 (F0/1)	Serial 0/1/0 (S0/1/0)	Serial 0/1/1 (S0/1/1)
2811	Fast Ethernet 0/0 (F0/0)	Fast Ethernet 0/1 (F0/1)	Serial 0/0/0 (S0/0/0)	Serial 0/0/1 (S0/0/1)
2900	Gigabit Ethernet 0/0 (G0/0)	Gigabit Ethernet 0/1 (G0/1)	Serial 0/0/0 (S0/0/0)	Serial 0/0/1 (S0/0/1)

Note: To find out how the router is configured, look at the interfaces to identify the type of router and how many interfaces the router has. There is no way to effectively list all the combinations of configurations for each router class. This table includes identifiers for the possible combinations of Ethernet and Serial interfaces in the device. The table does not include any other type of interface, even though a specific router may contain one. An example of this might be an ISDN BRI interface. The string in parenthesis is the legal abbreviation that can be used in Cisco IOS commands to represent the interface.

5.2.3.4 Lab – Troubleshooting Advanced Single-Area OSPFv2

Topology

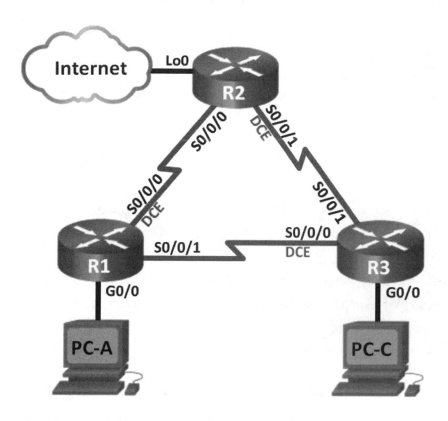

Addressing Table

Device	Interface	IP Address	Subnet Mask	Default Gateway
R1	G0/0	192.168.1.1	255.255.255.0	N/A
	S0/0/0 (DCE)	192.168.12.1	255.255.255.252	N/A
	S0/0/1	192.168.13.1	255.255.255.252	N/A
R2	Lo0	209.165.200.225	255.255.255.252	N/A
	S0/0/0	192.168.12.2	255.255.255.252	N/A
	S0/0/1 (DCE)	192.168.23.1	255.255.255.252	N/A
R3	G0/0	192.168.3.1	255.255.255.0	N/A
	S0/0/0 (DCE)	192.168.13.2	255.255.255.252	N/A
	S0/0/1	192.168.23.2	255.255.255.252	N/A
PC-A	NIC	192.168.1.3	255.255.255.0	192.168.1.1
PC-C	NIC	192.168.3.3	255.255.255.0	192.168.3.1

Objectives

Part 1: Build the Network and Load Device Configurations

Part 2: Troubleshoot OSPF

Background / Scenario

OSPF is a popular routing protocol used by businesses worldwide. A Network Administrator should be able to isolate OSPF issues and resolve those issues in a timely manner.

In this lab, you will troubleshoot a single-area OSPFv2 network and resolve all issues that exist.

Note: The routers used with CCNA hands-on labs are Cisco 1941 Integrated Services Routers (ISRs) with Cisco IOS Release 15.2(4)M3 (universalk9 image). Other routers and Cisco IOS versions can be used. Depending on the model and Cisco IOS version, the commands available and output produced might vary from what is shown in the labs. Refer to the Router Interface Summary Table at the end of this lab for the correct interface identifiers.

Note: Make sure that the routers have been erased and have no startup configurations. If you are unsure, contact your instructor.

Required Resources

- 3 Routers (Cisco 1941 with Cisco IOS Release 15.2(4)M3 universal image or comparable)
- 3 PCs (Windows 7, Vista, or XP with terminal emulation program, such as Tera Term)
- Console cables to configure the Cisco IOS devices via the console ports
- Ethernet and serial cables, as shown in the topology

Part 1:   Build the Network and Load Device Configurations

In Part 1, you will set up the network topology and configure basic settings on the PC hosts and routers.

Step 1:   Cable the network as shown in the topology.

Step 2:   Configure PC hosts.

Step 3:   Load router configurations.

Load the following configurations into the appropriate router. All routers have the same passwords. The privileged EXEC password is **class**. The password for console and vty lines is **cisco**.

Router R1 Configuration:

```
conf t
hostname R1
enable secret class
no ip domain lookup
interface GigabitEthernet0/0
 ip address 192.168.1.1 255.255.255.0
 duplex auto
 speed auto
 no shut
```

```
interface Serial0/0/0
 bandwidth 128
 ip address 192.168.12.1 255.255.255.252
 ip ospf message-digest-key 1 md5 MD5LINKS
 clock rate 128000
 no shut
interface Serial0/0/1
 bandwidth 64

 ip ospf message-digest-key 1 md5 MD5LINKS
 ip address 192.168.13.1 255.255.255.252
 no shut
router ospf 1
 auto-cost reference-bandwidth 1000

 area 0 authentication message-digest
 passive-interface g0/0
 network 192.168.1.0 0.0.0.255 area 0
 network 192.168.12.0 0.0.0.3 area 0
 network 192.168.13.0 0.0.0.3 area 0
banner motd ^
  Unauthorized Access is Prohibited!
^
line con 0
 password cisco
 logging synchronous
 login
line vty 0 4
 password cisco
 login
 transport input all
end
```

Router R2 Configuration:

```
conf t
hostname R2
enable secret class
no ip domain lookup
interface Loopback0
```

```
  ip address 209.165.200.225 255.255.255.252
interface Serial0/0/0
 bandwidth 182


 ip ospf message-digest-key 1 md5 MD5LINKS
 ip address 192.168.12.2 255.255.255.252
 no shut
interface Serial0/0/1
 bandwidth 128
 ip ospf message-digest-key 1 md5 MD5LINKS
 ip address 192.168.23.1 255.255.255.252
 clock rate 128000
 no shut
router ospf 1
 router-id 2.2.2.2
 auto-cost reference-bandwidth 1000
 area 0 authentication message-digest
 passive-interface g0/0
 network 192.168.12.0 0.0.0.3 area 0
 network 192.168.23.0 0.0.0.3 area 0


ip route 0.0.0.0 0.0.0.0 Loopback0
banner motd ^
  Unauthorized Access is Prohibited!
^
line con 0
 password cisco
 logging synchronous
 login
line vty 0 4
 password cisco
 login
 transport input all
end
```

Router R3 Configuration:

```
conf t
hostname R3
enable secret class
no ip domain lookup
```

```
interface GigabitEthernet0/0
 ip address 192.168.3.1 255.255.255.0
 duplex auto
 speed auto
 no shut
interface Serial0/0/0
 bandwidth 128
 ip ospf message-digest-key 1 md5 MD5LINKS
 ip address 192.168.13.2 255.255.255.252
 clock rate 128000
 no shut
interface Serial0/0/1
 bandwidth 128
 ip address 192.168.23.2 255.255.255.252

 no shut
router ospf 1
 router-id 3.3.3.3

 area 0 authentication message-digest
 passive-interface g0/0
 network 192.168.3.0 0.0.0.255 area 0
 network 192.168.13.0 0.0.0.3 area 0
 network 192.168.23.0 0.0.0.3 area 0
banner motd ^
  Unauthorized Access is Prohibited!
^
line con 0
 password cisco
 logging synchronous
 login
line vty 0 4
 password cisco
 login
 transport input all
end
```

Step 4:   Test end-to-end connectivity.

All interfaces should be up and the PCs should be able to ping the default gateway.

Part 2: Troubleshoot OSPF

In Part 2, verify that all routers have established neighbor adjacencies, and that all network routes are available.

Additional OSPF Requirements:

- Each router should have the following router ID assignments:
    - R1 Router ID: **1.1.1.1**
    - R2 Router ID: **2.2.2.2**
    - R3 Router ID: **3.3.3.3**
- All serial interface clocking rates should be set at 128 Kb/s and a matching bandwidth setting should be available to allow OSPF cost metrics to be calculated correctly.
- The 1941 routers have Gigabit interfaces, so the default OSPF reference bandwidth should be adjusted to allow cost metrics to reflect appropriate costs for all interfaces.
- OSPF should propagate a default route to the Internet. This is simulated by using Loopback interface 0 on R2.
- All interfaces advertising OSPF routing information should be configured with MD5 authentication, using **MD5LINKS** as the key.

List the commands used during your OSPF troubleshooting process:

_____

_____

_____

_____

List the changes made to resolve the OSPF issues. If no problems were found on the device, then respond with "no problems were found".

R1 Router:

_____

_____

_____

_____

R2 Router:

_____

_____

_____

_____

R3 Router:

_____

_____

_____

_____

Reflection

How would you change the network in this lab so all LAN traffic was routed through R2?

_____

_____

_____

_____

Router Interface Summary Table

Router Interface Summary				
Router Model	**Ethernet Interface #1**	**Ethernet Interface #2**	**Serial Interface #1**	**Serial Interface #2**
1800	Fast Ethernet 0/0 (F0/0)	Fast Ethernet 0/1 (F0/1)	Serial 0/0/0 (S0/0/0)	Serial 0/0/1 (S0/0/1)
1900	Gigabit Ethernet 0/0 (G0/0)	Gigabit Ethernet 0/1 (G0/1)	Serial 0/0/0 (S0/0/0)	Serial 0/0/1 (S0/0/1)
2801	Fast Ethernet 0/0 (F0/0)	Fast Ethernet 0/1 (F0/1)	Serial 0/1/0 (S0/1/0)	Serial 0/1/1 (S0/1/1)
2811	Fast Ethernet 0/0 (F0/0)	Fast Ethernet 0/1 (F0/1)	Serial 0/0/0 (S0/0/0)	Serial 0/0/1 (S0/0/1)
2900	Gigabit Ethernet 0/0 (G0/0)	Gigabit Ethernet 0/1 (G0/1)	Serial 0/0/0 (S0/0/0)	Serial 0/0/1 (S0/0/1)

Note: To find out how the router is configured, look at the interfaces to identify the type of router and how many interfaces the router has. There is no way to effectively list all the combinations of configurations for each router class. This table includes identifiers for the possible combinations of Ethernet and Serial interfaces in the device. The table does not include any other type of interface, even though a specific router may contain one. An example of this might be an ISDN BRI interface. The string in parenthesis is the legal abbreviation that can be used in Cisco IOS commands to represent the interface.

5.3.1.1 Class Activity – OSPF Troubleshooting Mastery

Objective

Explain the process and tools used to troubleshoot a single-area OSPF network.

Scenario

You have decided to change your routing protocol from RIPv2 to OSPFv2. Your small- to medium-sized business network topology will not change from its original physical settings. Use the diagram on the PDF for this activity as your company's small- to medium- business network design.

Your addressing design is complete and you then configure your routers with IPv4 and VLSM. OSPF has been applied as the routing protocol. However, some routers are sharing routing information with each other and some are not.

Open the PDF file that accompanies this modeling activity and follow the directions to complete the activity.

When the steps in the directions are complete, regroup as a class and compare recorded activity correction times. The group taking the shortest time to find and fix the configuration error will be declared the winner only after successfully explaining how they found the error, fixed it, and proved that the topology is now working.

Required Resources

- Topology diagram
- Packet Tracer software
- Timer

Topology Diagram

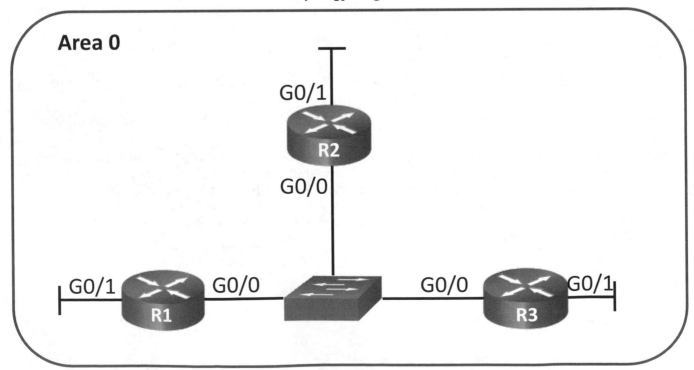

Directions

Choose a partner from the class with whom to work on this activity. Use Packet Tracer to create the topology diagram shown for this activity.

Step 1:   Build the topology based on the modeling activity page for this scenario.

Step 2:   Configure the routers.

a.   Use IPv4 for all interfaces.

b.   Incorporate VLSM into the addressing scheme.

c.   Make one intentional configuration error.

d.   Verify that the network does not work based upon the intentional error.

e.   Save your file to be used with Step 3.

Step 3:   Exchange your Packet Tracer file with another group.

a.   Find the configuration error on the Packet Tracer network file you received from another group.

b.   Fix the OSPF configuration error so that the network operates fully.

c.   Record the time it took to find and fix the OSPF network error.

d.   When complete, meet with your class to determine the Master Troubleshooter for the day.

Chapter 6 — Multiarea OSPF

6.0.1.2 Class Activity – Leaving on a Jet Plane

Objective

Explain the operation of multiarea OSPF to enable internetworking in a small- to medium-sized business network.

Scenario

You and a classmate are starting a new airline to serve your continent. In addition to your core area or headquarters airport, you will locate and map four intra-continental airport service areas and one trans-continental airport service area that can be used for additional source and destination travel.

Use the blank world map provided to design your airport locations. Additional instructions for completing this activity can be found in the accompanying PDF.

Required Resources

- Blank world map diagram
- Word processing software or alternative graphics software for marking airport locations and their connections

Blank World Map Diagram

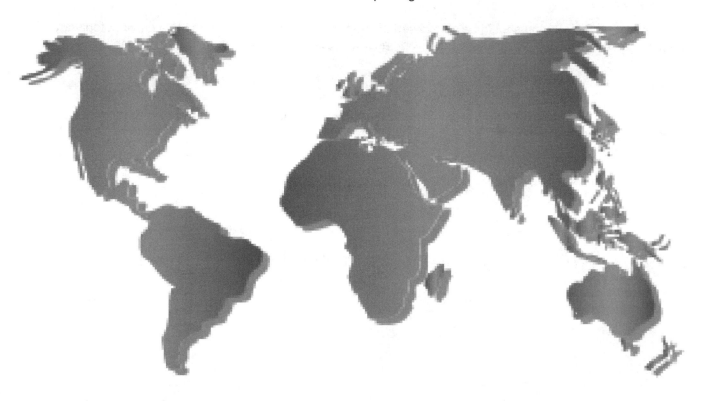

Directions

Step 1:   Design the airport locations.

a.   Use the blank world map diagram provided.

b.   On your map, place a star in the center of the continent in which you live. This is now the Airport Core Site and will serve as your core transit location. Label it as Airport Core Site. This is your first area of intra-continental service and all airports will be connected to the Airport Core Site.

Step 2:   Map airports within your continent to serve your passengers.

a.   Map four airport locations within your continent to connect to the Airport Core Site. Call them North, South, East, and West Airport Sites.

b.   Place four circles on your continent's map to represent the North, South, East, and West Airport Sites. Some circles may overlap due to the size of the continent and the sites placement on the map.

c.   Draw a straight line from each of these airports to the Airport Core Site. These intra-continent locations are your first level of service for your airlines. They are also known as area border airport sites.

Step 3:   Identify another continent your airline will serve.

a.   On the world map, locate another continent you would like to provide service to and from the Airlines Core Site.

b.   Place a circle in the center of the continent you chose for second-level service. This airport will be called Transcontinental Airport Site.

c.   Draw a line from your Airlines Core Site to the Transcontinental Airport Site. This airport will be known as an autonomous system border router (ASBR) airport site.

Summary

After completing Step 3, you should be able to see that the airport connections resemble a network topology. Complete the reflection questions, save your work, and be prepared to share your answers with the class.

Reflection

1.   While designing your airline travel routes, did you pay close attention to the headquarters location? Why would it be important to have a core site for airline travel?

2.   Would networks incorporate core, border, and ASBRs into area sites? Justify your answer.

3. What is the significance of mapping transcontinental areas?

4. What is the significance of mapping internal airline destination routes? Compare this to a routing topology.

5. Is it possible that the Airlines Core Site could serve several functions for your airlines (network)? Explain your answer.

6.2.3.8 Lab - Configuring Multiarea OSPFv2

Topology

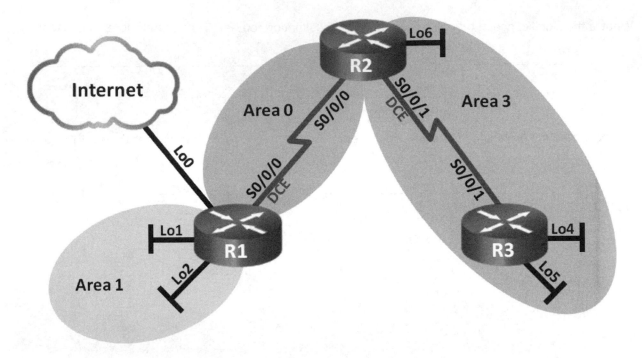

Addressing Table

Device	Interface	IP Address	Subnet Mask
R1	Lo0	209.165.200.225	255.255.255.252
	Lo1	192.168.1.1	255.255.255.0
	Lo2	192.168.2.1	255.255.255.0
	S0/0/0 (DCE)	192.168.12.1	255.255.255.252
R2	Lo6	192.168.6.1	255.255.255.0
	S0/0/0	192.168.12.2	255.255.255.252
	S0/0/1 (DCE)	192.168.23.1	255.255.255.252
R3	Lo4	192.168.4.1	255.255.255.0
	Lo5	192.168.5.1	255.255.255.0
	S0/0/1	192.168.23.2	255.255.255.252

Objectives

Part 1: Build the Network and Configure Basic Device Settings

Part 2: Configure a Multiarea OSPFv2 Network

Part 3: Configure Interarea Summary Routes

Background / Scenario

To make OSPF more efficient and scalable, OSPF supports hierarchical routing using the concept of areas. An OSPF area is a group of routers that share the same link-state information in their link-state databases (LSDBs). When a large OSPF area is divided into smaller areas, it is called multiarea OSPF. Multiarea OSPF is useful in larger network deployments to reduce processing and memory overhead.

In the lab, you will configure a multiarea OSPFv2 network with interarea summary routes.

Note: The routers used with CCNA hands-on labs are Cisco 1941 Integrated Services Routers (ISRs) with Cisco IOS Release 15.2(4)M3 (universalk9 image). Other routers and Cisco IOS versions can be used. Depending on the model and Cisco IOS version, the commands available and output produced might vary from what is shown in the labs. Refer to the Router Interface Summary Table at the end of this lab for the correct interface identifiers.

Note: Make sure that the routers have been erased and have no startup configurations. If you are unsure, contact your instructor.

Required Resources

- 3 Routers (Cisco 1941 with Cisco IOS Release 15.2(4)M3 universal image or comparable)
- Console cables to configure the Cisco IOS devices via the console ports
- Serial cables as shown in the topology

Part 1:   Build the Network and Configure Basic Device Settings

In Part 1, you will set up the network topology and configure basic settings on the routers.

Step 1:   Cable the network as shown in the topology.

Step 2:   Initialize and reload the routers as necessary.

Step 3:   Configure basic settings for each router.

a. Disable DNS lookup.

b. Configure device name, as shown in the topology.

c. Assign **class** as the privileged EXEC password.

d. Assign **cisco** as the console and vty passwords.

e. Configure **logging synchronous** for the console line.

f. Configure an MOTD banner to warn users that unauthorized access is prohibited.

g. Configure the IP addresses listed in the Addressing Table for all interfaces. DCE interfaces should be configured with a clock rate of 128000. Bandwidth should be set to 128 Kb/s on all serial interfaces.

h. Copy the running configuration to the startup configuration.

Step 4:   Verify Layer 3 connectivity.

Use the **show ip interface brief** command to verify that the IP addressing is correct and that the interfaces are active. Verify that each router can ping their neighbor's serial interface.

Part 2:   Configure a Multiarea OSPFv2 Network

In Part 2, you will configure a multiarea OSPFv2 network with process ID of 1. All LAN loopback interfaces should be passive, and all serial interfaces should be configured with MD5 authentication using **Cisco123** as the key.

Step 1:   Identify the OSPF router types in the topology.

Identify the Backbone router(s): _____

Identify the Autonomous System Boundary Router(s) (ASBR): _____

Identify the Area Border Router(s) (ABR): _____

Identify the Internal router(s): _____

Step 2:   Configure OSPF on R1.

a.   Configure a router ID of 1.1.1.1 with OSPF process ID of 1.

b.   Add the networks for R1 to OSPF.

```
R1(config-router)# network 192.168.1.0 0.0.0.255 area 1
R1(config-router)# network 192.168.2.0 0.0.0.255 area 1
R1(config-router)# network 192.168.12.0 0.0.0.3 area 0
```

c.   Set all LAN loopback interfaces, Lo1 and Lo2, as passive.

d.   Create a default route to the Internet using exit interface Lo0.

Note: You may see the "%Default route without gateway, if not a point-to-point interface, may impact performance" message. This is normal behavior if using a Loopback interface to simulate a default route.

e.   Configure OSPF to propagate the routes throughout the OSPF areas.

Step 3:   Configure OSPF on R2.

a.   Configure a router ID of 2.2.2.2 with OSPF process ID of 1.

b. Add the networks for R2 to OSPF. Add the networks to the correct area. Write the commands used in the space below.

_____

_____

_____

c. Set all LAN loopback interfaces as passive.

Step 4:   Configure OSPF on R3.

a. Configure a router ID of 3.3.3.3 with OSPF process ID of 1.

b. Add the networks for R3 to OSPF. Write the commands used in the space below.

_____

_____

_____

c. Set all LAN loopback interfaces as passive.

Step 5:   Verify that OSPF settings are correct and adjacencies have been established between routers.

a. Issue the **show ip protocols** command to verify OSPF settings on each router. Use this command to identify the OSPF router types and to determine the networks assigned to each area.

```
R1# show ip protocols
*** IP Routing is NSF aware ***


Routing Protocol is "ospf 1"
  Outgoing update filter list for all interfaces is not set
  Incoming update filter list for all interfaces is not set
  Router ID 1.1.1.1
  It is an area border and autonomous system boundary router
 Redistributing External Routes from,
  Number of areas in this router is 2. 2 normal 0 stub 0 nssa
```

```
    Maximum path: 4
    Routing for Networks:
        192.168.1.0 0.0.0.255 area 1
        192.168.2.0 0.0.0.255 area 1
        192.168.12.0 0.0.0.3 area 0
    Passive Interface(s):
        Loopback1
        Loopback2
    Routing Information Sources:
        Gateway          Distance      Last Update
        2.2.2.2               110      00:01:45
    Distance: (default is 110)
```

R2# **show ip protocols**

```
*** IP Routing is NSF aware ***


Routing Protocol is "ospf 1"
    Outgoing update filter list for all interfaces is not set
    Incoming update filter list for all interfaces is not set
    Router ID 2.2.2.2
    It is an area border router
    Number of areas in this router is 2. 2 normal 0 stub 0 nssa
    Maximum path: 4
    Routing for Networks:
        192.168.6.0 0.0.0.255 area 3
        192.168.12.0 0.0.0.3 area 0
        192.168.23.0 0.0.0.3 area 3
    Passive Interface(s):
        Loopback6
    Routing Information Sources:
        Gateway          Distance      Last Update
        3.3.3.3               110      00:01:20
        1.1.1.1               110      00:10:12
    Distance: (default is 110)
```

R3# **show ip protocols**

```
*** IP Routing is NSF aware ***


Routing Protocol is "ospf 1"
    Outgoing update filter list for all interfaces is not set
    Incoming update filter list for all interfaces is not set
    Router ID 3.3.3.3
    Number of areas in this router is 1. 1 normal 0 stub 0 nssa
```

```
      Maximum path: 4
      Routing for Networks:
         192.168.4.0 0.0.0.255 area 3
         192.168.5.0 0.0.0.255 area 3
         192.168.23.0 0.0.0.3 area 3
      Passive Interface(s):
         Loopback4
         Loopback5
      Routing Information Sources:
         Gateway          Distance       Last Update
         1.1.1.1              110        00:07:46
         2.2.2.2              110        00:07:46
      Distance: (default is 110)
```

What is the OSPF router type for each router?

R1: _____

R2: _____

R3: _____

b. Issue the **show ip ospf neighbor** command to verify that OSPF adjacencies have been established between routers.

```
R1# show ip ospf neighbor


Neighbor ID      Pri   State          Dead Time    Address         Interface
2.2.2.2            0   FULL/  -       00:00:34     192.168.12.2    Serial0/0/0


R2# show ip ospf neighbor


Neighbor ID      Pri   State          Dead Time    Address         Interface
1.1.1.1            0   FULL/  -       00:00:36     192.168.12.1    Serial0/0/0
3.3.3.3            0   FULL/  -       00:00:36     192.168.23.2    Serial0/0/1


R3# show ip ospf neighbor


Neighbor ID      Pri   State          Dead Time    Address         Interface
2.2.2.2            0   FULL/  -       00:00:38     192.168.23.1    Serial0/0/1
```

c. Issue the **show ip ospf interface brief** command to display a summary of interface route costs.

```
R1# show ip ospf interface brief
Interface    PID   Area       IP Address/Mask       Cost  State Nbrs F/C
Se0/0/0       1     0         192.168.12.1/30       781   P2P   1/1
```

```
Lo1          1     1                192.168.1.1/24    1    LOOP  0/0
Lo2          1     1                192.168.2.1/24    1    LOOP  0/0


R2# show ip ospf interface brief
Interface    PID   Area             IP Address/Mask   Cost State Nbrs F/C
Se0/0/0      1     0                192.168.12.2/30   781  P2P   1/1
Lo6          1     3                192.168.6.1/24    1    LOOP  0/0
Se0/0/1      1     3                192.168.23.1/30   781  P2P   1/1


R3# show ip ospf interface brief
Interface    PID   Area             IP Address/Mask   Cost State Nbrs F/C
Lo4          1     3                192.168.4.1/24    1    LOOP  0/0
Lo5          1     3                192.168.5.1/24    1    LOOP  0/0
Se0/0/1      1     3                192.168.23.2/30   781  P2P   1/1
```

Step 6:   Configure MD5 authentication on all serial interfaces.

Configure OSPF MD5 authentication at the interface level with an authentication key of **Cisco123**.

Why is it a good idea to verify that OSPF is functioning correctly before configuring OSPF authentication?

_____

_____

Step 7:   Verify OSPF adjacencies have been re-established.

Issue the **show ip ospf neighbor** command again to verify that adjacencies have been re-established after MD5 authentication was implemented. Troubleshoot any issues found before moving on to Part 3.

Part 3:   Configure Interarea Summary Routes

OSPF does not perform automatic summarization. Interarea summarization must be manually configured on ABRs. In Part 3, you will apply interarea summary routes on the ABRs. Using **show** commands, you will be able to observe how summarization affects the routing table and LSDBs.

Step 1:   Display the OSPF routing tables on all routers.

a.   Issue the **show ip route ospf** command on R1. OSPF routes that originate from a different area have a descriptor (O IA) indicating that these are interarea routes.

```
R1# show ip route ospf
Codes: L - local, C - connected, S - static, R - RIP, M - mobile, B - BGP
       D - EIGRP, EX - EIGRP external, O - OSPF, IA - OSPF inter area
       N1 - OSPF NSSA external type 1, N2 - OSPF NSSA external type 2
       E1 - OSPF external type 1, E2 - OSPF external type 2
```

```
        i - IS-IS, su - IS-IS summary, L1 - IS-IS level-1, L2 - IS-IS level-2
        ia - IS-IS inter area, * - candidate default, U - per-user static route
        o - ODR, P - periodic downloaded static route, H - NHRP, l - LISP
        + - replicated route, % - next hop override

Gateway of last resort is 0.0.0.0 to network 0.0.0.0


      192.168.4.0/32 is subnetted, 1 subnets
O IA     192.168.4.1 [110/1563] via 192.168.12.2, 00:23:49, Serial0/0/0
      192.168.5.0/32 is subnetted, 1 subnets
O IA     192.168.5.1 [110/1563] via 192.168.12.2, 00:23:49, Serial0/0/0
      192.168.23.0/30 is subnetted, 1 subnets
O IA     192.168.6.1 [110/782] via 192.168.12.2, 00:02:01, Serial0/0/0
      192.168.23.0/30 is subnetted, 1 subnets
O IA     192.168.23.0 [110/1562] via 192.168.12.2, 00:23:49, Serial0/0/0
```

b. Repeat the **show ip route ospf** command for R2 and R3. Record the OSPF interarea routes for each router.

R2:

_____

_____

_____

R3:

_____

_____

_____

Step 2: Display the LSDB on all routers.

a. Issue the **show ip ospf database** command on R1. A router maintains a separate LSDB for every area that it is a member.

```
R1# show ip ospf database


            OSPF Router with ID (1.1.1.1) (Process ID 1)


                Router Link States (Area 0)


Link ID          ADV Router       Age        Seq#        Checksum Link count
1.1.1.1          1.1.1.1          1295       0x80000003 0x0039CD 2
2.2.2.2          2.2.2.2          1282       0x80000002 0x00D430 2
```

Summary Net Link States (Area 0)

Link ID	ADV Router	Age	Seq#	Checksum
192.168.1.1	1.1.1.1	1387	0x80000002	0x00AC1F
192.168.2.1	1.1.1.1	1387	0x80000002	0x00A129
192.168.4.1	2.2.2.2	761	0x80000001	0x000DA8
192.168.5.1	2.2.2.2	751	0x80000001	0x0002B2
192.168.6.1	2.2.2.2	1263	0x80000001	0x00596A
192.168.23.0	2.2.2.2	1273	0x80000001	0x00297E

Router Link States (Area 1)

Link ID	ADV Router	Age	Seq#	Checksum	Link count
1.1.1.1	1.1.1.1	1342	0x80000006	0x0094A4	2

Summary Net Link States (Area 1)

Link ID	ADV Router	Age	Seq#	Checksum
192.168.4.1	1.1.1.1	760	0x80000001	0x00C8E0
192.168.5.1	1.1.1.1	750	0x80000001	0x00BDEA
192.168.6.1	1.1.1.1	1262	0x80000001	0x0015A2
192.168.12.0	1.1.1.1	1387	0x80000001	0x00C0F5
192.168.23.0	1.1.1.1	1272	0x80000001	0x00E4B6

Type-5 AS External Link States

Link ID	ADV Router	Age	Seq#	Checksum	Tag
0.0.0.0	1.1.1.1	1343	0x80000001	0x001D91	1

b. Repeat the **show ip ospf database** command for R2 and R3. Record the Link IDs for the Summary Net Link States for each area.

R2:

_____

_____

R3:

_____

_____

Step 3: Configure the interarea summary routes.

a. Calculate the summary route for the networks in area 1.

b. Configure the summary route for area 1 on R1.

```
R1(config)# router ospf 1
R1(config-router)# area 1 range 192.168.0.0 255.255.252.0
```

c. Calculate the summary route for the networks in area 3. Record your results.

_____

d. Configure the summary route for area 3 on R2. Write the commands you used in the space below.

_____

_____

Step 4:   Re-display the OSPF routing tables on all routers.

Issue the **show ip route ospf** command on each router. Record the results for the summary and interarea routes.

R1:

_____

_____

R2:

_____

_____

R3:

_____

_____

Step 5:   Display the LSDB on all routers.

Issue the **show ip ospf database** command again on each router. Record the Link IDs for the Summary Net Link States for each area.

R1:

_____

_____

R2:

_____

_____

R3:

_____

_____

What type of LSA is injected into the backbone by the ABR when interarea summarization is enabled?

_____

Step 6:   Verify end-to-end connectivity.

Verify that all networks can be reached from each router. If any issues exist, troubleshoot until they have been resolved.

Reflection

What are three advantages for designing a network with multiarea OSPF?

_____

_____

_____

Router Interface Summary Table

Router Interface Summary				
Router Model	**Ethernet Interface #1**	**Ethernet Interface #2**	**Serial Interface #1**	**Serial Interface #2**
1800	Fast Ethernet 0/0 (F0/0)	Fast Ethernet 0/1 (F0/1)	Serial 0/0/0 (S0/0/0)	Serial 0/0/1 (S0/0/1)
1900	Gigabit Ethernet 0/0 (G0/0)	Gigabit Ethernet 0/1 (G0/1)	Serial 0/0/0 (S0/0/0)	Serial 0/0/1 (S0/0/1)
2801	Fast Ethernet 0/0 (F0/0)	Fast Ethernet 0/1 (F0/1)	Serial 0/1/0 (S0/1/0)	Serial 0/1/1 (S0/1/1)
2811	Fast Ethernet 0/0 (F0/0)	Fast Ethernet 0/1 (F0/1)	Serial 0/0/0 (S0/0/0)	Serial 0/0/1 (S0/0/1)
2900	Gigabit Ethernet 0/0 (G0/0)	Gigabit Ethernet 0/1 (G0/1)	Serial 0/0/0 (S0/0/0)	Serial 0/0/1 (S0/0/1)
Note: To find out how the router is configured, look at the interfaces to identify the type of router and how many interfaces the router has. There is no way to effectively list all the combinations of configurations for each router class. This table includes identifiers for the possible combinations of Ethernet and Serial interfaces in the device. The table does not include any other type of interface, even though a specific router may contain one. An example of this might be an ISDN BRI interface. The string in parenthesis is the legal abbreviation that can be used in Cisco IOS commands to represent the interface.				

6.2.3.9 Lab - Configuring Multiarea OSPFv3

Topology

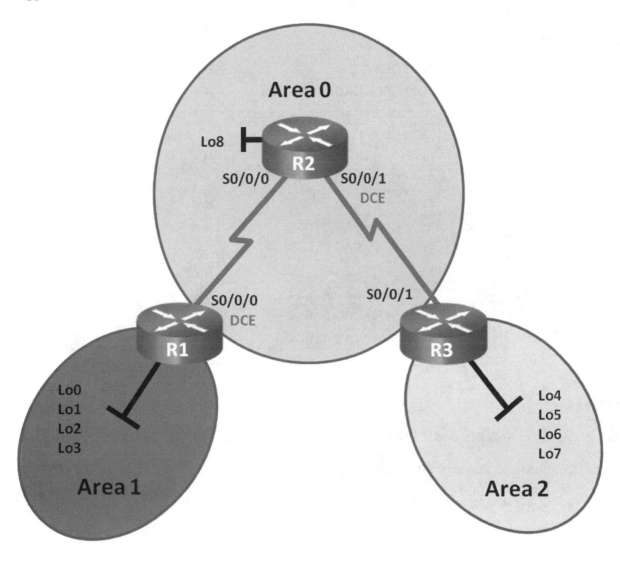

Addressing Table

Device	Interface	IPv6 Address	Default Gateway
R1	S0/0/0 (DCE)	2001:DB8:ACAD:12::1/64	
		FE80::1 link-local	N/A
	Lo0	2001:DB8:ACAD::1/64	N/A
	Lo1	2001:DB8:ACAD:1::1/64	N/A
	Lo2	2001:DB8:ACAD:2::1/64	N/A
	Lo3	2001:DB8:ACAD:3::1/64	N/A
R2	S0/0/0	2001:DB8:ACAD:12::2/64	
		FE80::2 link-local	N/A
	S0/0/1 (DCE)	2001:DB8:ACAD:23::2/64	
		FE80::2 link-local	N/A
	Lo8	2001:DB8:ACAD:8::1/64	N/A
R3	S0/0/1	2001:DB8:ACAD:23::3/64	
		FE80::3 link-local	N/A
	Lo4	2001:DB8:ACAD:4::1/64	N/A
	Lo5	2001:DB8:ACAD:5::1/64	N/A
	Lo6	2001:DB8:ACAD:6::1/64	N/A
	Lo7	2001:DB8:ACAD:7::1/64	N/A

Objectives

Part 1: Build the Network and Configure Basic Device Settings

Part 2: Configure Multiarea OSPFv3 Routing

Part 3: Configure Interarea Route Summarization

Background / Scenario

Using multiarea OSPFv3 in large IPv6 network deployments can reduce router processing by creating smaller routing tables and requiring less memory overhead. In multiarea OSPFv3, all areas are connected to the backbone area (area 0) through area border routers (ABRs).

In this lab, you will implement OSPFv3 routing for multiple areas and configure interarea route summarizations on the Area Border Routers (ABRs). You will also use a number of **show** commands to display and verify OSPFv3 routing information. This lab uses loopback addresses to simulate networks in multiple OSPFv3 areas.

Note: The routers used with CCNA hands-on labs are Cisco 1941 Integrated Services Routers (ISRs) with Cisco IOS Release 15.2(4)M3 (universalk9 image). Other routers and Cisco IOS versions can be used. Depending on the model and Cisco IOS version, the commands available and output produced might vary from what is shown in the labs. Refer to the Router Interface Summary Table at this end of this lab for the correct interface identifiers.

Note: Make sure that the routers have been erased and have no startup configurations. If you are unsure, contact your instructor.

Required Resources

- 3 Routers (Cisco 1941 with Cisco IOS Release 15.2(4)M3 universal image or comparable)
- 3 PCs (Windows 7, Vista, or XP with terminal emulation program, such as Tera Term)
- Console cables to configure the Cisco IOS devices via the console ports
- Serial cables as shown in the topology

Part 1: Build the Network and Configure Basic Device Settings

In Part 1, you will set up the network topology and configure basic settings on the routers.

Step 1: Cable the network as shown in the topology.

Step 2: Initialize and reload the routers as necessary.

Step 3: Configure basic settings for each router.

a. Disable DNS lookup.

b. Configure device name as shown in the topology.

c. Assign **class** as the privileged EXEC password.

d. Assign **cisco** as the vty password.

e. Configure a MOTD banner to warn users that unauthorized access is prohibited.

f. Configure **logging synchronous** for the console line.

g. Encrypt plain text passwords.

h. Configure the IPv6 unicast and link-local addresses listed in the Addressing Table for all interfaces.

i. Enable IPv6 unicast routing on each router.

j. Copy the running configuration to the startup configuration.

Step 4: Test connectivity.

The routers should be able to ping one another. The routers are unable to ping distant loopbacks until OS-PFv3 routing is configured. Verify and troubleshoot if necessary.

Part 2: Configure Multiarea OSPFv3 Routing

In Part 2, you will configure OSPFv3 routing on all routers to separate the network domain into three distinct areas, and then verify that routing tables are updated correctly.

Step 1: Assign router IDs.

a. On R1, issue the **ipv6 router ospf** command to start an OSPFv3 process on the router.

```
R1(config)# ipv6 router ospf 1
```

Note: The OSPF process ID is kept locally and has no meaning to other routers on the network.

b. Assign the OSPFv3 router ID **1.1.1.1** to R1.

```
R1(config-rtr)# router-id 1.1.1.1
```

c. Assign a router ID of **2.2.2.2** to R2 and a router ID of **3.3.3.3** to R3.

   d.   Issue the **show ipv6 ospf** command to verify the router IDs on all routers.

```
R2# show ipv6 ospf
Routing Process "ospfv3 1" with ID 2.2.2.2
Event-log enabled, Maximum number of events: 1000, Mode: cyclic
Router is not originating router-LSAs with maximum metric
<output omitted>
```

Step 2:   Configure multiarea OSPFv3.

   a.   Issue the **ipv6 ospf 1 area** *area-id* command for each interface on R1 that is to participate in OSPFv3 routing. The loopback interfaces are assigned to area 1 and the serial interface is assigned to area 0. You will change the network type on the loopback interfaces to ensure that the correct subnet is advertised.

```
R1(config)# interface lo0
R1(config-if)# ipv6 ospf 1 area 1
R1(config-if)# ipv6 ospf network point-to-point
R1(config-if)# interface lo1
R1(config-if)# ipv6 ospf 1 area 1
R1(config-if)# ipv6 ospf network point-to-point
R1(config-if)# interface lo2
R1(config-if)# ipv6 ospf 1 area 1
R1(config-if)# ipv6 ospf network point-to-point
R1(config-if)# interface lo3
R1(config-if)# ipv6 ospf 1 area 1
R1(config-if)# ipv6 ospf network point-to-point
R1(config-if)# interface s0/0/0
R1(config-if)# ipv6 ospf 1 area 0
```

   b.   Use the **show ipv6 protocols** command to verify multiarea OSPFv3 status.

```
R1# show ipv6 protocols
IPv6 Routing Protocol is "connected"
IPv6 Routing Protocol is "ND"
IPv6 Routing Protocol is "ospf 1"
  Router ID 1.1.1.1
  Area border router
  Number of areas: 2 normal, 0 stub, 0 nssa
  Interfaces (Area 0):
    Serial0/0/0
  Interfaces (Area 1):
    Loopback0
    Loopback1
    Loopback2
    Loopback3
  Redistribution:
    None
```

c. Assign all interfaces on R2 to participate in OSPFv3 area 0. For the loopback interface, change the network type to point-to point. Write the commands used in the space below.

_____

_____

_____

_____

_____

_____

d. Use the **show ipv6 ospf interface brief** command to view OSPFv3 enabled interfaces.

```
R2# show ipv6 ospf interface brief
Interface     PID   Area            Intf ID    Cost   State  Nbrs F/C
Lo8           1     0               13         1      P2P    0/0
Se0/0/1       1     0               7          64     P2P    1/1
Se0/0/0       1     0               6          64     P2P    1/1
```

e. Assign the loopback interfaces on R3 to participate in OSPFv3 area 2 and change the network type to point-to-point. Assign the serial interface to participate in OSPFv3 area 0. Write the commands used in the space below.

_____

_____

_____

_____

_____

_____

_____

_____

_____

f. Use the **show ipv6 ospf** command to verify configurations.

```
R3# show ipv6 ospf
Routing Process "ospfv3 1" with ID 3.3.3.3
Event-log enabled, Maximum number of events: 1000, Mode: cyclic
It is an area border router
Router is not originating router-LSAs with maximum metric
Initial SPF schedule delay 5000 msecs
Minimum hold time between two consecutive SPFs 10000 msecs
Maximum wait time between two consecutive SPFs 10000 msecs
```

```
       Minimum LSA interval 5 secs

       Minimum LSA arrival 1000 msecs

       LSA group pacing timer 240 secs

       Interface flood pacing timer 33 msecs

       Retransmission pacing timer 66 msecs

       Number of external LSA 0. Checksum Sum 0x000000

       Number of areas in this router is 2. 2 normal 0 stub 0 nssa

       Graceful restart helper support enabled

       Reference bandwidth unit is 100 mbps

       RFC1583 compatibility enabled

           Area BACKBONE(0)

               Number of interfaces in this area is 1

               SPF algorithm executed 2 times

               Number of LSA 16. Checksum Sum 0x0929F8

               Number of DCbitless LSA 0

               Number of indication LSA 0

               Number of DoNotAge LSA 0

               Flood list length 0

           Area 2

               Number of interfaces in this area is 4

               SPF algorithm executed 2 times

               Number of LSA 13. Checksum Sum 0x048E3C

               Number of DCbitless LSA 0

               Number of indication LSA 0

               Number of DoNotAge LSA 0

               Flood list length 0
```

Step 3: Verify OSPFv3 neighbors and routing information.

   a. Issue the **show ipv6 ospf neighbor** command on all routers to verify that each router is listing the correct routers as neighbors.

```
R1# show ipv6 ospf neighbor


            OSPFv3 Router with ID (1.1.1.1) (Process ID 1)



Neighbor ID     Pri    State          Dead Time    Interface ID    Interface
2.2.2.2           0    FULL/  -       00:00:39     6               Serial0/0/0
```

   b. Issue the **show ipv6 route ospf** command on all routers to verify that each router has learned routes to all networks in the Addressing Table.

```
R1# show ipv6 route ospf
IPv6 Routing Table - default - 16 entries
Codes: C - Connected, L - Local, S - Static, U - Per-user Static route
       B - BGP, R - RIP, H - NHRP, I1 - ISIS L1
```

```
          I2 - ISIS L2, IA - ISIS interarea, IS - ISIS summary, D - EIGRP
          EX - EIGRP external, ND - ND Default, NDp - ND Prefix, DCE - Destination
          NDr - Redirect, O - OSPF Intra, OI - OSPF Inter, OE1 - OSPF ext 1
          OE2 - OSPF ext 2, ON1 - OSPF NSSA ext 1, ON2 - OSPF NSSA ext 2
OI  2001:DB8:ACAD:4::/64 [110/129]
      via FE80::2, Serial0/0/0
OI  2001:DB8:ACAD:5::/64 [110/129]
      via FE80::2, Serial0/0/0
OI  2001:DB8:ACAD:6::/64 [110/129]
      via FE80::2, Serial0/0/0
OI  2001:DB8:ACAD:7::/64 [110/129]
      via FE80::2, Serial0/0/0
O   2001:DB8:ACAD:8::/64 [110/65]
      via FE80::2, Serial0/0/0
O   2001:DB8:ACAD:23::/64 [110/128]
      via FE80::2, Serial0/0/0
```

What is the significance of an OI route?

_____

c. Issue the **show ipv6 ospf database** command on all routers.

R1# **show ipv6 ospf database**

```
          OSPFv3 Router with ID (1.1.1.1) (Process ID 1)


          Router Link States (Area 0)


ADV Router      Age        Seq#        Fragment ID  Link count  Bits
  1.1.1.1       908        0x80000001  0            1           B
  2.2.2.2       898        0x80000003  0            2           None
  3.3.3.3       899        0x80000001  0            1           B


          Inter Area Prefix Link States (Area 0)


ADV Router      Age        Seq#        Prefix
  1.1.1.1       907        0x80000001  2001:DB8:ACAD::/62
  3.3.3.3       898        0x80000001  2001:DB8:ACAD:4::/62


          Link (Type-8) Link States (Area 0)
```

ADV Router	Age	Seq#	Link ID	Interface
1.1.1.1	908	0x80000001	6	Se0/0/0
2.2.2.2	909	0x80000002	6	Se0/0/0

Intra Area Prefix Link States (Area 0)

ADV Router	Age	Seq#	Link ID	Ref-lstype	Ref-LSID
1.1.1.1	908	0x80000001	0	0x2001	0
2.2.2.2	898	0x80000003	0	0x2001	0
3.3.3.3	899	0x80000001	0	0x2001	0

Router Link States (Area 1)

ADV Router	Age	Seq#	Fragment ID	Link count	Bits
1.1.1.1	908	0x80000001	0	0	B

Inter Area Prefix Link States (Area 1)

ADV Router	Age	Seq#	Prefix
1.1.1.1	907	0x80000001	2001:DB8:ACAD:12::/64
1.1.1.1	907	0x80000001	2001:DB8:ACAD:8::/64
1.1.1.1	888	0x80000001	2001:DB8:ACAD:23::/64
1.1.1.1	888	0x80000001	2001:DB8:ACAD:4::/62

Link (Type-8) Link States (Area 1)

ADV Router	Age	Seq#	Link ID	Interface
1.1.1.1	908	0x80000001	13	Lo0
1.1.1.1	908	0x80000001	14	Lo1
1.1.1.1	908	0x80000001	15	Lo2
1.1.1.1	908	0x80000001	16	Lo3

Intra Area Prefix Link States (Area 1)

ADV Router	Age	Seq#	Link ID	Ref-lstype	Ref-LSID
1.1.1.1	908	0x80000001	0	0x2001	0

How many link state databases are found on R1? _____

How many link state databases are found on R2? _____

How many link state databases are found on R3? _____

Part 3: Configure Interarea Route Summarization

In Part 3, you will manually configure interarea route summarization on the ABRs.

Step 1: Summarize networks on R1.

a. List the network addresses for the loopback interfaces and identify the hextet section where the addresses differ.

2001:DB8:ACAD:0000::1/64

2001:DB8:ACAD:0001::1/64

2001:DB8:ACAD:0002::1/64

2001:DB8:ACAD:0003::1/64

b. Convert the differing section from hex to binary.

2001:DB8:ACAD: 0000 0000 0000 0000::1/64

2001:DB8:ACAD: 0000 0000 0000 0001::1/64

2001:DB8:ACAD: 0000 0000 0000 0010::1/64

2001:DB8:ACAD: 0000 0000 0000 0011::1/64

c. Count the number of leftmost matching bits to determine the prefix for the summary route.

2001:DB8:ACAD: 0000 0000 0000 0000::1/64

2001:DB8:ACAD: 0000 0000 0000 0001::1/64

2001:DB8:ACAD: 0000 0000 0000 0010::1/64

2001:DB8:ACAD: 0000 0000 0000 0011::1/64

How many bits match? _____

d. Copy the matching bits and then add zero bits to determine the summarized network address.

2001:DB8:ACAD: 0000 0000 0000 0000::0

e. Convert the binary section back to hex.

2001:DB8:ACAD::

f. Append the prefix of the summary route (result of Step 1c).

2001:DB8:ACAD::/62

Step 2: Configure interarea route summarization on R1.

a. To manually configure interarea route summarization on R1, use the **area** *area-id* **range** *address mask* command.

```
R1(config)# ipv6 router ospf 1
R1(config-rtr)# area 1 range 2001:DB8:ACAD::/62
```

b. View the OSPFv3 routes on R3.

```
R3# show ipv6 route ospf
IPv6 Routing Table - default - 14 entries
Codes: C - Connected, L - Local, S - Static, U - Per-user Static route
```

```
        B - BGP, R - RIP, H - NHRP, I1 - ISIS L1

        I2 - ISIS L2, IA - ISIS interarea, IS - ISIS summary, D - EIGRP

        EX - EIGRP external, ND - ND Default, NDp - ND Prefix, DCE - Destination

        NDr - Redirect, O - OSPF Intra, OI - OSPF Inter, OE1 - OSPF ext 1

        OE2 - OSPF ext 2, ON1 - OSPF NSSA ext 1, ON2 - OSPF NSSA ext 2

OI  2001:DB8:ACAD::/62 [110/129]

     via FE80::2, Serial0/0/1

O   2001:DB8:ACAD:8::/64 [110/65]

     via FE80::2, Serial0/0/1

O   2001:DB8:ACAD:12::/64 [110/128]

     via FE80::2, Serial0/0/1
```

Compare this output to the output from Part 2, Step 3b. How are the networks in area 1 now expressed in the routing table on R3?

_____

c. View the OSPFv3 routes on R1.

R1# **show ipv6 route ospf**

```
IPv6 Routing Table - default - 18 entries

Codes: C - Connected, L - Local, S - Static, U - Per-user Static route

        B - BGP, R - RIP, H - NHRP, I1 - ISIS L1

        I2 - ISIS L2, IA - ISIS interarea, IS - ISIS summary, D - EIGRP

        EX - EIGRP external, ND - ND Default, NDp - ND Prefix, DCE - Destination

        NDr - Redirect, O - OSPF Intra, OI - OSPF Inter, OE1 - OSPF ext 1

        OE2 - OSPF ext 2, ON1 - OSPF NSSA ext 1, ON2 - OSPF NSSA ext 2

O   2001:DB8:ACAD::/62 [110/1]

     via Null0, directly connected

OI  2001:DB8:ACAD:4::/64 [110/129]

     via FE80::2, Serial0/0/0

OI  2001:DB8:ACAD:5::/64 [110/129]

     via FE80::2, Serial0/0/0

OI  2001:DB8:ACAD:6::/64 [110/129]

     via FE80::2, Serial0/0/0

OI  2001:DB8:ACAD:7::/64 [110/129]

     via FE80::2, Serial0/0/0

O   2001:DB8:ACAD:8::/64 [110/65]

     via FE80::2, Serial0/0/0

O   2001:DB8:ACAD:23::/64 [110/128]

     via FE80::2, Serial0/0/0
```

Compare this output to the output from Part 2, Step 3b. How are the summarized networks expressed in the routing table on R1?

_____

Step 3: Summarize networks and configure interarea route summarization on R3.

a. Summarize the loopback interfaces on R3.

   1) List the network addresses and identify the hextet section where the addresses differ.

   2) Convert the differing section from hex to binary.

   3) Count the number of left-most matching bits to determine the prefix for the summary route.

   4) Copy the matching bits and then add zero bits to determine the summarized network address.

   5) Convert the binary section back to hex.

   6) Append the prefix of the summary route.

   Write the summary address in the space provided.

   _____

b. Manually configure interarea route summarization on R3. Write the commands in the space provided.

   _____

c. Verify that area 2 routes are summarized on R1. What command was used?

   _____

d. Record the routing table entry on R1 for the summarized route advertised from R3.

   _____

Reflection

1. Why would multiarea OSPFv3 be used?

   _____

   _____

2. What is the benefit of configuring interarea route summarization?

   _____

   _____

Router Interface Summary Table

Router Interface Summary				
Router Model	Ethernet Interface #1	Ethernet Interface #2	Serial Interface #1	Serial Interface #2
1800	Fast Ethernet 0/0 (F0/0)	Fast Ethernet 0/1 (F0/1)	Serial 0/0/0 (S0/0/0)	Serial 0/0/1 (S0/0/1)
1900	Gigabit Ethernet 0/0 (G0/0)	Gigabit Ethernet 0/1 (G0/1)	Serial 0/0/0 (S0/0/0)	Serial 0/0/1 (S0/0/1)
2801	Fast Ethernet 0/0 (F0/0)	Fast Ethernet 0/1 (F0/1)	Serial 0/1/0 (S0/1/0)	Serial 0/1/1 (S0/1/1)
2811	Fast Ethernet 0/0 (F0/0)	Fast Ethernet 0/1 (F0/1)	Serial 0/0/0 (S0/0/0)	Serial 0/0/1 (S0/0/1)
2900	Gigabit Ethernet 0/0 (G0/0)	Gigabit Ethernet 0/1 (G0/1)	Serial 0/0/0 (S0/0/0)	Serial 0/0/1 (S0/0/1)
Note: To find out how the router is configured, look at the interfaces to identify the type of router and how many interfaces the router has. There is no way to effectively list all the combinations of configurations for each router class. This table includes identifiers for the possible combinations of Ethernet and Serial interfaces in the device. The table does not include any other type of interface, even though a specific router may contain one. An example of this might be an ISDN BRI interface. The string in parenthesis is the legal abbreviation that can be used in Cisco IOS commands to represent the interface.				

6.2.3.10 Lab – Troubleshooting Multiarea OSPFv2 and OSPFv3

Topology

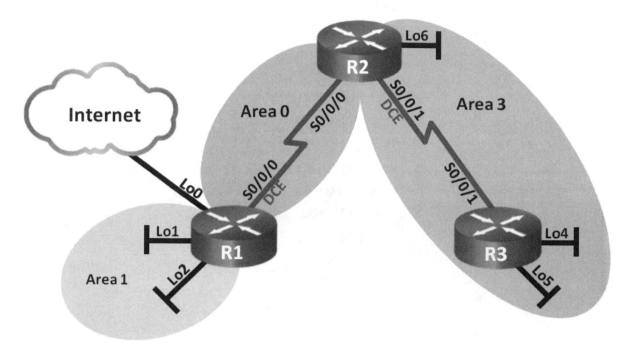

Addressing Table

Device	Interface	IP Address
R1	Lo0	209.165.200.225/30
	Lo1	192.168.1.1/24
		2001:DB8:ACAD:1::1/64
		FE80::1 link-local
	Lo2	192.168.2.1/24
		2001:DB8:ACAD:2::1/64
		FE80::1 link-local
	S0/0/0 (DCE)	192.168.12.1/30
		2001:DB8:ACAD:12::1/64
		FE80::1 link-local
R2	S0/0/0	192.168.12.2/30
		2001:DB8:ACAD:12::2/64
		FE80::2 link-local
	S0/0/1 (DCE)	192.168.23.2/30
		2001:DB8:ACAD:23::2/64
		FE80::2 link-local
	Lo6	192.168.6.1/24
		2001:DB8:ACAD:6::1/64
		FE80::2 link-local
R3	Lo4	192.168.4.1/24
		2001:DB8:ACAD:4::1/64
		FE80::3 link-local
	Lo5	192.168.5.1/24
		2001:DB8:ACAD:5::1/64
		FE80::3 link-local
	S0/0/1	192.168.23.1/30
		2001:DB8:ACAD:23::1/64
		FE80::3 link-local

Objectives

Part 1: Build the Network and Load Device Configurations

Part 2: Troubleshoot Layer 3 Connectivity

Part 3: Troubleshoot OSPFv2

Part 4: Troubleshoot OSPFv3

Background / Scenario

Open Shortest Path First (OSPF) is an open-standard link-state routing protocol for IP networks. OSPFv2 is defined for IPv4 networks, while OSPFv3 is defined for IPv6 networks. OSPFv2 and OSPFv3 are completely isolated routing protocols, meaning changes in OSPFv2 do not affect OSPFv3 routing, and vice versa.

In this lab, a multiarea OSPF network running OSPFv2 and OSPFv3 is experiencing problems. You have been assigned to find the problems with the network and correct them.

Note: The routers used with CCNA hands-on labs are Cisco 1941 Integrated Services Routers (ISRs) with Cisco IOS Release 15.2(4)M3 (universalk9 image). Other routers and Cisco IOS versions can be used. Depending on the model and Cisco IOS version, the commands available and output produced might vary from what is shown in the labs. Refer to the Router Interface Summary Table at the end of this lab for the correct interface identifiers.

Note: Make sure that the routers have been erased and have no startup configurations. If you are unsure, contact your instructor.

Required Resources

- 3 Routers (Cisco 1941 with Cisco IOS Release 15.2(4)M3 universal image or comparable)
- Console cables to configure the Cisco IOS devices via the console ports
- Serial cables as shown in the topology

Part 1: Build the Network and Load Device Configurations

Step 1: Cable the network as shown in the topology.

Step 2: Load router configuration files.

Load the following configurations into the appropriate router. All routers have the same passwords. The enable password is **class**, and the line password is **cisco**.

Router R1 Configuration:

```
enable
conf t
hostname R1
enable secret class
ipv6 unicast-routing
no ip domain lookup
interface Loopback0
 ip address 209.165.200.225 255.255.255.252
interface Loopback1
 ip address 192.168.1.1 255.255.255.0
 ipv6 address 2001:DB80:ACAD:1::1/64



 ipv6 ospf network point-to-point
```

```
interface Loopback2
 ip address 192.168.2.1 255.255.255.0
 ipv6 address 2001:DB8:ACAD:2::1/64
 ipv6 ospf 1 area 1
 ipv6 ospf network point-to-point
interface Serial0/0/0
 ip address 192.168.21.1 255.255.255.252

 ipv6 address FE80::1 link-local
 ipv6 address 2001:DB8:ACAD:12::1/64
 ipv6 ospf 1 area 0
 clock rate 128000
 shutdown

router ospf 1
 router-id 1.1.1.1
 passive-interface Loopback1
 passive-interface Loopback2

 network 192.168.2.0 0.0.0.255 area 1
 network 192.168.12.0 0.0.0.3 area 0
 default-information originate
ipv6 router ospf 1

 area 1 range 2001:DB8:ACAD::/61

ip route 0.0.0.0 0.0.0.0 Loopback0
banner motd @
  Unauthorized Access is Prohibited! @
line con 0
 password cisco
 logging synchronous
 login
line vty 0 4
 password cisco
 logging synchronous
 login
 transport input all
end
```

Router R2 Configuration:

```
enable
conf t
hostname R2
ipv6 unicast-routing
no ip domain lookup
enable secret class
interface Loopback6
  ip address 192.168.6.1 255.255.255.0
  ipv6 address 2001:DB8:CAD:6::1/64


interface Serial0/0/0
  ip address 192.168.12.2 255.255.255.252
  ipv6 address FE80::2 link-local
  ipv6 address 2001:DB8:ACAD:12::2/64
  ipv6 ospf 1 area 0
  no shutdown
interface Serial0/0/1
  ip address 192.168.23.2 255.255.255.252
  ipv6 address FE80::2 link-local
  ipv6 address 2001:DB8:ACAD:23::2/64
  ipv6 ospf 1 area 3
  clock rate 128000
  no shutdown
router ospf 1
  router-id 2.2.2.2
  passive-interface Loopback6
  network 192.168.6.0 0.0.0.255 area 3
  network 192.168.12.0 0.0.0.3 area 0
  network 192.168.23.0 0.0.0.3 area 3
ipv6 router ospf 1
  router-id 2.2.2.2
banner motd @
  Unauthorized Access is Prohibited! @
line con 0
  password cisco
  logging synchronous
  login
```

```
line vty 0 4
 password cisco
 logging synchronous
 login
 transport input all
end
```

Router R3 Configuration:

```
enable
conf t
hostname R3
no ip domain lookup
ipv6 unicast-routing
enable secret class
interface Loopback4
 ip address 192.168.4.1 255.255.255.0
 ipv6 address 2001:DB8:ACAD:4::1/64
 ipv6 ospf 1 area 3
interface Loopback5
 ip address 192.168.5.1 255.255.255.0
 ipv6 address 2001:DB8:ACAD:5::1/64
 ipv6 ospf 1 area 3
interface Serial0/0/1
 ip address 192.168.23.1 255.255.255.252
 ipv6 address FE80::3 link-local
 ipv6 address 2001:DB8:ACAD:23::1/64
 ipv6 ospf 1 area 3
 no shutdown
router ospf 1
 router-id 3.3.3.3
 passive-interface Loopback4
 passive-interface Loopback5
 network 192.168.4.0 0.0.0.255 area 3
 network 192.168.5.0 0.0.0.255 area 3

 ipv6 router ospf 1
 router-id 3.3.3.3
banner motd @
  Unauthorized Access is Prohibited! @
line con 0
```

```
  password cisco
  logging synchronous
  login
 line vty 0 4
  password cisco
  logging synchronous
  login
  transport input all
 end
```

Step 3:   Save your configuration.

Part 2:   Troubleshoot Layer 3 Connectivity

In Part 2, you will verify that Layer 3 connectivity is established on all interfaces. You will need to test both IPv4 and IPv6 connectivity for all device interfaces.

Step 1:   Verify the interfaces listed in the Addressing Table are active and configured with correct IP address information.

a. Issue the **show ip interface brief** command on all three routers to verify that the interfaces are in an up/up state.

b. Issue the **show run | section interface** command to view all the commands related to interfaces.

c. Resolve all problems found. Record the commands used to correct the configuration.

_____

_____

_____

_____

_____

_____

_____

_____

d. Using the **ping** command, verify that IPv4 and IPv6 connectivity has been established on all directly connected router interfaces. If problems still exist, continue troubleshooting Layer 3 issues.

Part 3:   Troubleshoot OSPFv2

Note: LAN (loopback) interfaces should not advertise OSPF routing information, but routes to these networks should be contained in the routing tables.

Step 1:   Test IPv4 end-to-end connectivity.

From each router, ping all interfaces on the other routers. Record your results below as IPv4 OSPFv2 connectivity problems do exist.

_____

_____

_____

_____

Step 2:   Verify that all interfaces are assigned to the proper OSPFv2 areas on R1.

a.   Issue the **show ip protocols** command to verify that OSPF is running and that all networks are being advertised in the correct areas. Verify that the router ID is set correctly, as well for OSPF.

b.   If required, make the necessary changes needed to the configuration on R1 based on the output from the **show ip protocols** command. Record the commands used to correct the configuration.

_____

_____

_____

c.   If required, re-issue the **show ip protocols** command to verify that your changes had the desired effect.

d.   Issue the **show ip ospf interface brief** command to verify that the serial interface and loopback interfaces 1 and 2 are listed as OSPF networks assigned to their respective areas.

e.   Resolve any problems discovered on R1 for OSPFv2.

Step 3:   Verify that all interfaces are assigned to the proper OSPFv2 areas on R2.

a.   Issue the **show ip protocols** command to verify that OSPF is running and that all networks are being advertised in their proper respective areas. Verify that the router ID is also set correctly.

b.   If required, make any necessary changes to the configuration on R2 based on the output from the **show ip protocols** command. Record the commands used to correct the configuration.

_____

_____

_____

c. If required, re-issue the **show ip protocols** command to verify that your changes had the desired effect.

d. Issue the **show ip ospf interface brief** command to verify that all interfaces are listed as OSPF networks assigned to their proper respective areas.

e. Resolve any problems discovered on R2 for OSPFv2.

Step 4: Verify that all interfaces are assigned to the proper OSPFv2 areas on R3.

a. Issue the **show ip protocols** command to verify that OSPF is running and that all networks are being advertised in their respective areas. Verify that the router ID is also set correctly.

b. If required, make the necessary changes to the configuration on R3 based on the output from the **show ip protocols** command. Record the commands used to correct the configuration.

_____

_____

_____

c. If required, re-issue the **show ip protocols** command to verify that your changes had the desired effect.

d. Issue the **show ip ospf interface brief** command to verify that all interfaces are listed as OSPF networks assigned to their proper areas.

e. Resolve any problems discovered on R3 for OSPFv2.

Step 5: Verify OSPFv2 neighbor information.

Issue the **show ip ospf neighbor** command to verify that each router has all OSPFv2 neighbors listed.

Step 6: Verify OSPFv2 routing information.

a. Issue the **show ip route ospf** command to verify that each router has all OSPFv2 routes in their respective routing tables.

b. If any OSPFv2 routes are missing, troubleshoot and resolve the problems.

Step 7: Verify IPv4 end-to-end connectivity.

From each router, ping all interfaces on other routers. If IPv4 end-to-end connectivity does not exist, then continue troubleshooting to resolve any remaining issues.

Part 4: Troubleshoot OSPFv3

Note: LAN (loopback) interfaces should not advertise OSPFv3 routing information, but routes to these networks should be contained in the routing tables.

Step 1: Test IPv6 end-to-end connectivity.

From each router, ping all interfaces on the other routers. Record your results as IPv6 connectivity problems do exist.

_____

_____

_____

_____

Step 2: Verify that IPv6 unicast routing has been enabled on all routers.

a. An easy way to verify that IPv6 routing has been enabled on a router is to use the **show run | section ipv6 unicast** command. By adding the pipe section to the **show run** command, the **ipv6 unicast-routing** command is displayed if IPv6 routing has been enabled.

b. If IPv6 unicast routing is not enabled on one or more routers, enable it now. If required, record the commands used to correct the configuration.

_____

_____

Step 3: Verify that all interfaces are assigned to the proper OSPFv3 areas on R1.

a. Issue the **show ipv6 protocols** command to verify that the router ID is correct and the expected interfaces display in their proper areas.

b. If required, make any necessary changes to the configuration on R1 based on the output from the **show ipv6 protocols** command. Record the commands used to correct the configuration. It may be necessary to reset OSPF process by issuing the **clear ipv6 ospf process** command.

_____

_____

_____

c. Re-issue the **show ipv6 protocols** command on R1 to make sure changes took effect.

d. Enter the **show ipv6 route ospf** command on R1 to verify that the interarea route summarization is configured correctly.

```
R1# show ipv6 route ospf
IPv6 Routing Table - default - 12 entries
Codes: C - Connected, L - Local, S - Static, U - Per-user Static route
       B - BGP, R - RIP, I1 - ISIS L1, I2 - ISIS L2
       IA - ISIS interarea, IS - ISIS summary, D - EIGRP, EX - EIGRP external
       ND - ND Default, NDp - ND Prefix, DCE - Destination, NDr - Redirect
       O - OSPF Intra, OI - OSPF Inter, OE1 - OSPF ext 1, OE2 - OSPF ext 2
       ON1 - OSPF NSSA ext 1, ON2 - OSPF NSSA ext 2
O   2001:DB8:ACAD::/61 [110/1]
     via Null0, directly connected
OI  2001:DB8:ACAD:4::/64 [110/129]
     via FE80::2, Serial0/0/0
OI  2001:DB8:ACAD:5::/64 [110/129]
     via FE80::2, Serial0/0/0
OI  2001:DB8:ACAD:23::/64 [110/128]
     via FE80::2, Serial0/0/0
```

e. Which IPv6 networks are included in the interarea route summarization shown in the routing table?

_____

_____

f. If required, make the necessary configuration changes on R1. Record the commands used to correct the configuration.

_____

_____

g. If required, re-issue the **show ipv6 route ospf** command on R1 to verify the changes.

```
R1# show ipv6 route ospf
IPv6 Routing Table - default - 11 entries
Codes: C - Connected, L - Local, S - Static, U - Per-user Static route
       B - BGP, R - RIP, I1 - ISIS L1, I2 - ISIS L2
       IA - ISIS interarea, IS - ISIS summary, D - EIGRP, EX - EIGRP external
       ND - ND Default, NDp - ND Prefix, DCE - Destination, NDr - Redirect
       O - OSPF Intra, OI - OSPF Inter, OE1 - OSPF ext 1, OE2 - OSPF ext 2
       ON1 - OSPF NSSA ext 1, ON2 - OSPF NSSA ext 2
O   2001:DB8:ACAD::/62 [110/1]
     via Null0, directly connected
OI  2001:DB8:ACAD:4::1/128 [110/128]
```

```
          via FE80::2, Serial0/0/0
   OI  2001:DB8:ACAD:5::1/128 [110/128]
          via FE80::2, Serial0/0/0
   OI  2001:DB8:ACAD:23::/64 [110/128]
          via FE80::2, Serial0/0/0
```

Step 4:   Verify that all interfaces are assigned to the proper OSPFv3 areas on R2.

  a.   Issue the **show ipv6 protocols** command and verify that the router ID is correct and that the expected interfaces are showing up under their proper areas.

  b.   If required, make any necessary changes to the configuration on R2 based on the output from the **show ipv6 protocols** command. Record the commands used to correct the configuration. It may be necessary to reset OSPF process by issuing the **clear ipv6 ospf process** command.

_____

_____

_____

  c.   Verify that the configuration change has the desired effect.

Step 5:   Verify that all interfaces are assigned to the proper OSPFv3 areas on R3.

  a.   Issue the **show ipv6 protocols** command to verify that the router ID is correct and the expected interfaces display under their respective areas.

  b.   If required, make any necessary changes to the configuration on R3 based on the output from the **show ipv6 protocols** command. Record the commands used to correct the configuration. It may be necessary to reset OSPF process by issuing the **clear ipv6 ospf process** command.

_____

_____

_____

  c.   Verify that the configuration changes have the desired effect.

Step 6:   Verify that all routers have correct neighbor adjacency information.

  a.   Issue the **show ipv6 ospf neighbor** command to verify that adjacencies have formed between neighboring routers.

Step 7:   Verify OSPFv3 routing information.

  a.   Issue the **show ipv6 route ospf** command, and verify that OSPFv3 routes exist to all networks.

  b.   Resolve any routing issues that still exist.

Step 8: Verify IPv6 end-to-end connectivity.

From each router, ping all of the IPv6 interfaces on the other routers. If IPv6 end-to-end issues still exist, continue troubleshooting to resolve any remaining issues.

Reflection

Why not just use the **show running-config** command to resolve all issues?

_____

Router Interface Summary Table

Router Interface Summary				
Router Model	**Ethernet Interface #1**	**Ethernet Interface #2**	**Serial Interface #1**	**Serial Interface #2**
1800	Fast Ethernet 0/0 (F0/0)	Fast Ethernet 0/1 (F0/1)	Serial 0/0/0 (S0/0/0)	Serial 0/0/1 (S0/0/1)
1900	Gigabit Ethernet 0/0 (G0/0)	Gigabit Ethernet 0/1 (G0/1)	Serial 0/0/0 (S0/0/0)	Serial 0/0/1 (S0/0/1)
2801	Fast Ethernet 0/0 (F0/0)	Fast Ethernet 0/1 (F0/1)	Serial 0/1/0 (S0/1/0)	Serial 0/1/1 (S0/1/1)
2811	Fast Ethernet 0/0 (F0/0)	Fast Ethernet 0/1 (F0/1)	Serial 0/0/0 (S0/0/0)	Serial 0/0/1 (S0/0/1)
2900	Gigabit Ethernet 0/0 (G0/0)	Gigabit Ethernet 0/1 (G0/1)	Serial 0/0/0 (S0/0/0)	Serial 0/0/1 (S0/0/1)
Note: To find out how the router is configured, look at the interfaces to identify the type of router and how many interfaces the router has. There is no way to effectively list all the combinations of configurations for each router class. This table includes identifiers for the possible combinations of Ethernet and Serial interfaces in the device. The table does not include any other type of interface, even though a specific router may contain one. An example of this might be an ISDN BRI interface. The string in parenthesis is the legal abbreviation that can be used in Cisco IOS commands to represent the interface.				

6.3.1.1 Class Activity – Digital Trolleys

Objective

Use CLI commands to verify operational status of a multiarea OSPF network.

Scenario

Your city has an aging digital trolley system based on a one-area design. All communications within this one area are taking longer to process as trolleys are being added to routes serving the population of your growing city. Trolley departures and arrivals are also taking a little longer, because each trolley must check large routing tables to determine where to pick up and deliver residents from their source and destination streets.

A concerned citizen has come up with the idea of dividing the city into different areas for a more efficient way to determine trolley routing information. It is thought that if the trolley maps are smaller, the system might be improved because of faster and smaller updates to the routing tables.

Your city board approves and implements the new area-based, digital trolley system. But to ensure the new area routes are more efficient, the city board needs data to show the results at the next open board meeting.

Complete the activity directions as stated below.

Save your work and explain the differences between the old, single area and new, multiarea system to another group or the entire class.

Required Resources

- Packet Tracer software
- Word processing software

Directions

Step 1:   Map the single-area city trolley routing topology.

a. Use Packet Tracer to map the old routing topology for the city. Cisco 1941 Integrated Services Routers (ISRs) are preferred.

b. Create a core area and place one of the routers in the core area.

c. Connect at least two routers to the core area router.

d. Choose to connect two more routers to the routers from Step 1c or create loopback addresses for the LAN interfaces on the routers from Step 1c.

e. Address the connected links or interfaces using IPv4 and VLSM.

f. Configure OSPF on each router for area 0 only.

g. Ping all routers to ensure full connectivity within the entire area.

Step 2:   Map the multiarea city trolley routing topology.

a. Use your cursor to highlight all devices from Step 1, and copy and paste them to another area of the Packet Tracer desktop.

b. Assign at least three areas to your topology. One must be the backbone (or core area) and the other two areas will be joined to the backbone area using current routers, which will now become area border routers.

c. Configure the appropriate routers to their new area assignments. Remove old area configuration commands and assign new area commands to the appropriate interfaces.

d. Save each router's changes as you make changes.

e. When complete, you should have three areas represented on the topology and all routers should be able to ping each other throughout the network.

f. Use the drawing tool and identify your areas by drawing circles or rectangles around the three areas.

g. Save your work.

Step 3: Verify the network for city council members.

a. Use at least three commands learned (or used in this chapter) to help the city council prove that the new area, digital trolley routing topology works.

b. Save a copy of topology graphics and verification commands comparisons in table format to a word processing file.

c. Share your work with another group or the class. You may also want to add this activity and its files to a portfolio for this course.

Chapter 7 — EIGRP

7.0.1.2 Class Activity – Classless EIGRP

Objectives

Describe the basic features of EIGRP.

Scenario

EIGRP was introduced as a distance vector routing protocol in 1992. It was originally designed to work as a proprietary protocol on Cisco devices only. In 2013, EIGRP became a multi-vendor routing protocol, meaning that it can be used by other device vendors in addition to Cisco devices.

View the *Fundamental Configuration and Verification of EIGRP* video located at http://www.cisco.com/E-Learning/bulk/subscribed/tac/netbits/iprouting/eigrp/01_fundamental_eigrp/start.htm. In order to view the video you must have a cisco.com account. If you do not have a cisco.com account, please register to create one.

While viewing the video, pay close attention to the following concepts and terms:

- Subnet mask reporting to routing tables for classful and classless networks
- Auto-summarization of networks in routing tables
- Autonomous system numbers
- Wildcard masks
- Passive interfaces
- EIGRP configuration commands
- EIGRP verification commands

Complete the reflection questions which accompany the PDF file for this activity. Save your work and be prepared to share your answers with the class.

Resources

Internet access

Reflection

1. Explain classful routing protocols.

2. Explain classless routing protocols.

3. What is network auto-summarization?

    _____

4. What is an autonomous system number?

    _____

5. What are wildcard masks?

    _____

6. What is a passive interface?

    _____

7. Is EIGRP considered a distance-vector or a link-state routing protocol?

    _____

7.2.2.5 Lab – Configuring Basic EIGRP for IPv4

Topology

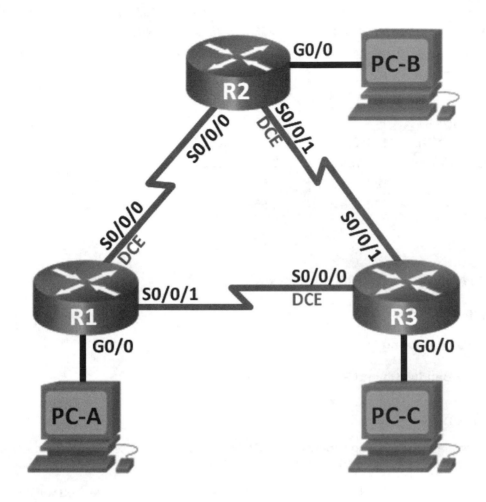

Addressing Table

Device	Interface	IP Address	Subnet Mask	Default Gateway
R1	G0/0	192.168.1.1	255.255.255.0	N/A
	S0/0/0 (DCE)	10.1.1.1	255.255.255.252	N/A
	S0/0/1	10.3.3.1	255.255.255.252	N/A
R2	G0/0	192.168.2.1	255.255.255.0	N/A
	S0/0/0	10.1.1.2	255.255.255.252	N/A
	S0/0/1 (DCE)	10.2.2.2	255.255.255.252	N/A
R3	G0/0	192.168.3.1	255.255.255.0	N/A
	S0/0/0 (DCE)	10.3.3.2	255.255.255.252	N/A
	S0/0/1	10.2.2.1	255.255.255.252	N/A
PC-A	NIC	192.168.1.3	255.255.255.0	192.168.1.1
PC-B	NIC	192.168.2.3	255.255.255.0	192.168.2.1
PC-C	NIC	192.168.3.3	255.255.255.0	192.168.3.1

Objectives

Part 1: Build the Network and Verify Connectivity

Part 2: Configure EIGRP Routing

Part 3: Verify EIGRP Routing

Part 4: Configure Bandwidth and Passive Interfaces

Background / Scenario

Enhanced Interior Gateway Routing Protocol (EIGRP) is a powerful distance vector routing protocol and is relatively easy to configure for basic networks.

In this lab, you will configure EIGRP for the topology and networks shown above. You will modify bandwidth and configure passive interfaces to allow EIGRP to function more efficiently.

Note: The routers used with CCNA hands-on labs are Cisco 1941 Integrated Services Routers (ISRs) with Cisco IOS Release 15.2(4)M3 (universalk9 image). Other routers and Cisco IOS versions can be used. Depending on the model and Cisco IOS version, the commands available and output produced might vary from what is shown in the labs. Refer to the Router Interface Summary Table at the end of this lab for the correct interface identifiers.

Note: Make sure that the routers have been erased and have no startup configurations. If you are unsure, contact your instructor.

Required Resources

- 3 Routers (Cisco 1941 with Cisco IOS Release 15.2(4)M3 universal image or comparable)
- 3 PCs (Windows 7, Vista, or XP with terminal emulation program, such as Tera Term)
- Console cables to configure the Cisco IOS devices via the console ports
- Ethernet and serial cables as shown in the topology

Part 1:   Build the Network and Verify Connectivity

In Part 1, you will set up the network topology and configure basic settings, such as the interface IP addresses, device access, and passwords.

Step 1:   Cable the network as shown in the topology.

Step 2:   Configure PC hosts.

Step 3:   Initialize and reload the routers as necessary.

Step 4:   Configure basic settings for each router.

a.   Disable DNS lookup.

b.   Configure IP addresses for the routers, as listed in the Addressing Table.

c.   Configure device name as shown in the topology.

d.   Assign **cisco** as the console and vty passwords.

e.   Assign **class** as the privileged EXEC password.

f.   Configure **logging synchronous** to prevent console and vty messages from interrupting command entry.

g.   Configure a message of the day.

h.   Copy the running configuration to the startup configuration.

Step 5:   Verify connectivity.

The routers should be able to ping one another, and each PC should be able to ping its default gateway. The PCs will not be able to ping other PCs until EIGRP routing is configured. Verify and troubleshoot if necessary.

Part 2:   Configure EIGRP Routing

Step 1:   Enable EIGRP routing on R1. Use AS number 10.

```
R1(config)# router eigrp 10
```

Step 2:   Advertise the directly connected networks on R1 using the wildcard mask.

```
R1(config-router)# network 10.1.1.0 0.0.0.3
R1(config-router)# network 192.168.1.0 0.0.0.255
R1(config-router)# network 10.3.3.0 0.0.0.3
```

Why is it a good practice to use wildcard masks when advertising networks? Could the mask have been omitted from any of the network statements above? If so, which one(s)?

_____

_____

_____

Step 3:   Enable EIGRP routing and advertise the directly connected networks on R2 and R3.

You will see neighbor adjacency messages as interfaces are added to the EIGRP routing process. The messages on R2 are displayed as an example.

```
*Apr 14 15:24:59.543: %DUAL-5-NBRCHANGE: EIGRP-IPv4 10: Neighbor 10.1.1.1 (Serial0/0/0) is up: new adjacency
```

Step 4:   Verify end-to-end connectivity.

All devices should be able to ping each other if EIGRP is configured correctly.

Note: Depending on the operating system, it may be necessary to disable the firewall for the pings to the host PCs to be successful.

Part 3:   Verify EIGRP Routing

Step 1:   Examine the EIGRP neighbor table.

On R1, issue the **show ip eigrp neighbors** command to verify that the adjacency has been established with its neighboring routers.

```
R1# show ip eigrp neighbors

EIGRP-IPv4 Neighbors for AS(10)

H   Address              Interface        Hold Uptime    SRTT   RTO  Q   Seq
                                          (sec)          (ms)        Cnt Num
1   10.3.3.2             Se0/0/1          13 00:24:58     8    100  0   17
0   10.1.1.2             Se0/0/0          13 00:29:23     7    100  0   23
```

Step 2:   Examine the IP EIGRP routing table.

```
R1# show ip route eigrp

Codes: L - local, C - connected, S - static, R - RIP, M - mobile, B - BGP
       D - EIGRP, EX - EIGRP external, O - OSPF, IA - OSPF inter area
       N1 - OSPF NSSA external type 1, N2 - OSPF NSSA external type 2
       E1 - OSPF external type 1, E2 - OSPF external type 2
       i - IS-IS, su - IS-IS summary, L1 - IS-IS level-1, L2 - IS-IS level-2
       ia - IS-IS inter area, * - candidate default, U - per-user static route
       o - ODR, P - periodic downloaded static route, H - NHRP, l - LISP
       + - replicated route, % - next hop override


Gateway of last resort is not set

      10.0.0.0/8 is variably subnetted, 5 subnets, 2 masks
D        10.2.2.0/30 [90/2681856] via 10.3.3.2, 00:29:01, Serial0/0/1
                     [90/2681856] via 10.1.1.2, 00:29:01, Serial0/0/0
D        192.168.2.0/24 [90/2172416] via 10.1.1.2, 00:29:01, Serial0/0/0
D        192.168.3.0/24 [90/2172416] via 10.3.3.2, 00:27:56, Serial0/0/1
```

Why does R1 have two paths to the 10.2.2.0/30 network?

_____

_____

Step 3: Examine the EIGRP topology table.

```
R1# show ip eigrp topology
EIGRP-IPv4 Topology Table for AS(10)/ID(192.168.1.1)
Codes: P - Passive, A - Active, U - Update, Q - Query, R - Reply,
       r - reply Status, s - sia Status

P 192.168.3.0/24, 1 successors, FD is 2172416
        via 10.3.3.2 (2172416/28160), Serial0/0/1
P 192.168.2.0/24, 1 successors, FD is 2172416
        via 10.1.1.2 (2172416/28160), Serial0/0/0
P 10.2.2.0/30, 2 successors, FD is 2681856
        via 10.1.1.2 (2681856/2169856), Serial0/0/0
        via 10.3.3.2 (2681856/2169856), Serial0/0/1
P 10.3.3.0/30, 1 successors, FD is 2169856
        via Connected, Serial0/0/1
P 192.168.1.0/24, 1 successors, FD is 2816
        via Connected, GigabitEthernet0/0
P 10.1.1.0/30, 1 successors, FD is 2169856
        via Connected, Serial0/0/0
```

Why are there no feasible successors listed in the R1 topology table?

_____

_____

Step 4: Verify the EIGRP routing parameters and networks advertised.

Issue the **show ip protocols** command to verify the EIGRP routing parameters used.

```
R1# show ip protocols
*** IP Routing is NSF aware ***

Routing Protocol is "eigrp 10"
  Outgoing update filter list for all interfaces is not set
  Incoming update filter list for all interfaces is not set
  Default networks flagged in outgoing updates
  Default networks accepted from incoming updates
  EIGRP-IPv4 Protocol for AS(10)
    Metric weight K1=1, K2=0, K3=1, K4=0, K5=0
```

```
    NSF-aware route hold timer is 240

    Router-ID: 192.168.1.1

    Topology : 0 (base)

        Active Timer: 3 min

        Distance: internal 90 external 170

        Maximum path: 4

        Maximum hopcount 100

        Maximum metric variance 1


    Automatic Summarization: disabled

    Maximum path: 4

    Routing for Networks:

        10.1.1.0/30

        10.3.3.0/30

        192.168.1.0

    Routing Information Sources:

        Gateway          Distance      Last Update

        10.3.3.2               90      02:38:34

        10.1.1.2               90      02:38:34

    Distance: internal 90 external 170
```

Based on the output of issuing the **show ip protocols** command, answer the following questions.

What AS number is used? _____

What networks are advertised?

_____

What is the administrative distance for EIGRP? _____

How many equal cost paths does EIGRP use by default? _____

Part 4: Configure Bandwidth and Passive Interfaces

EIGRP uses a default bandwidth based on the type of interface in the router. In Part 4, you will modify the bandwidth so that the link between R1 and R3 has a lower bandwidth than the link between R1/R2 and R2/R3. In addition, you will set passive interfaces on each router.

Step 1:   Observe the current routing settings.

a.   Issue the **show interface s0/0/0** command on R1.

```
R1# show interface s0/0/0

Serial0/0/0 is up, line protocol is up

    Hardware is WIC MBRD Serial

    Internet address is 10.1.1.1/30
```

```
MTU 1500 bytes, BW 1544 Kbit/sec, DLY 20000 usec,
    reliability 255/255, txload 1/255, rxload 1/255
Encapsulation HDLC, loopback not set
Keepalive set (10 sec)
Last input 00:00:01, output 00:00:02, output hang never
Last clearing of "show interface" counters 03:43:45
Input queue: 0/75/0/0 (size/max/drops/flushes); Total output drops: 0
Queueing strategy: fifo
Output queue: 0/40 (size/max)
5 minute input rate 0 bits/sec, 0 packets/sec
5 minute output rate 0 bits/sec, 0 packets/sec
    4050 packets input, 270294 bytes, 0 no buffer
    Received 1554 broadcasts (0 IP multicasts)
    0 runts, 0 giants, 0 throttles
    1 input errors, 0 CRC, 0 frame, 0 overrun, 0 ignored, 1 abort
    4044 packets output, 271278 bytes, 0 underruns
    0 output errors, 0 collisions, 5 interface resets
    4 unknown protocol drops
    0 output buffer failures, 0 output buffers swapped out
    12 carrier transitions
    DCD=up  DSR=up  DTR=up  RTS=up  CTS=up
```

What is the default bandwidth for this serial interface?

_____

b. How many routes are listed in the routing table to reach the 10.2.2.0/30 network? _____

Step 2:   Modify the bandwidth on the routers.

a. Modify the bandwidth on R1 for the serial interfaces.

```
R1(config)# interface s0/0/0
R1(config-if)# bandwidth 2000
R1(config-if)# interface s0/0/1
R1(config-if)# bandwidth 64
```

Issue **show ip route** command on R1. Is there a difference in the routing table? If so, what is it?

```
Codes: L - local, C - connected, S - static, R - RIP, M - mobile, B - BGP
       D - EIGRP, EX - EIGRP external, O - OSPF, IA - OSPF inter area
       N1 - OSPF NSSA external type 1, N2 - OSPF NSSA external type 2
       E1 - OSPF external type 1, E2 - OSPF external type 2
       i - IS-IS, su - IS-IS summary, L1 - IS-IS level-1, L2 - IS-IS level-2
       ia - IS-IS inter area, * - candidate default, U - per-user static route
       o - ODR, P - periodic downloaded static route, H - NHRP, l - LISP
       + - replicated route, % - next hop override


Gateway of last resort is not set


      10.0.0.0/8 is variably subnetted, 5 subnets, 2 masks
C        10.1.1.0/30 is directly connected, Serial0/0/0
L        10.1.1.1/32 is directly connected, Serial0/0/0
D        10.2.2.0/30 [90/2681856] via 10.1.1.2, 00:03:09, Serial0/0/0
C        10.3.3.0/30 is directly connected, Serial0/0/1
L        10.3.3.1/32 is directly connected, Serial0/0/1
      192.168.1.0/24 is variably subnetted, 2 subnets, 2 masks
C        192.168.1.0/24 is directly connected, GigabitEthernet0/0
L        192.168.1.1/32 is directly connected, GigabitEthernet0/0
D     192.168.2.0/24 [90/1794560] via 10.1.1.2, 00:03:09, Serial0/0/0
D     192.168.3.0/24 [90/2684416] via 10.1.1.2, 00:03:08, Serial0/0/0
```

---

b. Modify the bandwidth on the R2 and R3 serial interfaces.

```
R2(config)# interface s0/0/0
R2(config-if)# bandwidth 2000
R2(config-if)# interface s0/0/1
R2(config-if)# bandwidth 2000
```

```
R3(config)# interface s0/0/0
R3(config-if)# bandwidth 64
R3(config-if)# interface s0/0/1
R3(config-if)# bandwidth 2000
```

Step 3:   Verify the bandwidth modifications.

a. Verify bandwidth modifications. Issue a **show interface serial 0/0/x** command, with x being the appropriate serial interface on all three routers to verify that bandwidth is set correctly. R1 is shown as an example.

```
R1# show interface s0/0/0
Serial0/0/0 is up, line protocol is up
  Hardware is WIC MBRD Serial
  Internet address is 10.1.1.1/30
  MTU 1500 bytes, BW 2000 Kbit/sec, DLY 20000 usec,
     reliability 255/255, txload 1/255, rxload 1/255
  Encapsulation HDLC, loopback not set
  Keepalive set (10 sec)
  Last input 00:00:01, output 00:00:02, output hang never
  Last clearing of "show interface" counters 04:06:06
  Input queue: 0/75/0/0 (size/max/drops/flushes); Total output drops: 0
  Queueing strategy: fifo
  Output queue: 0/40 (size/max)
  5 minute input rate 0 bits/sec, 0 packets/sec
  5 minute output rate 0 bits/sec, 0 packets/sec
     4767 packets input, 317155 bytes, 0 no buffer
     Received 1713 broadcasts (0 IP multicasts)
     0 runts, 0 giants, 0 throttles
     1 input errors, 0 CRC, 0 frame, 0 overrun, 0 ignored, 1 abort
     4825 packets output, 316451 bytes, 0 underruns
     0 output errors, 0 collisions, 5 interface resets
     4 unknown protocol drops
     0 output buffer failures, 0 output buffers swapped out
     12 carrier transitions
     DCD=up  DSR=up  DTR=up  RTS=up  CTS=up
```

Based on your bandwidth configuration, try and determine what the R2 and R3 routing tables will look like before you issue a **show ip route** command. Are their routing tables the same or different?

_____

_____

_____

Step 4: Configure G0/0 interface as passive on R1, R2, and R3.

A passive interface does not allow outgoing and incoming routing updates over the configured interface. The **passive-interface** *interface* command causes the router to stop sending and receiving Hello packets over an interface; however, the network associated with the interface is still advertised to other routers through the non-passive interfaces. Router interfaces connected to LANs are typically configured as passive.

```
R1(config)# router eigrp 10
R1(config-router)# passive-interface g0/0

R2(config)# router eigrp 10
R2(config-router)# passive-interface g0/0

R3(config)# router eigrp 10
R3(config-router)# passive-interface g0/0
```

Step 5: Verify the passive interface configuration.

Issue a **show ip protocols** command on R1, R2, and R3 and verify that G0/0 has been configured as passive.

```
R1# show ip protocols
*** IP Routing is NSF aware ***

Routing Protocol is "eigrp 10"
  Outgoing update filter list for all interfaces is not set
  Incoming update filter list for all interfaces is not set
  Default networks flagged in outgoing updates
  Default networks accepted from incoming updates
  EIGRP-IPv4 Protocol for AS(10)
    Metric weight K1=1, K2=0, K3=1, K4=0, K5=0
    NSF-aware route hold timer is 240
    Router-ID: 192.168.1.1
    Topology : 0 (base)
      Active Timer: 3 min
      Distance: internal 90 external 170
      Maximum path: 4
      Maximum hopcount 100
      Maximum metric variance 1

  Automatic Summarization: disabled
  Maximum path: 4
  Routing for Networks:
    10.1.1.0/30
    10.3.3.0/30
```

```
   192.168.1.0
Passive Interface(s):
   GigabitEthernet0/0
Routing Information Sources:
   Gateway          Distance       Last Update
   10.3.3.2               90        00:48:09
   10.1.1.2               90        00:48:26
Distance: internal 90 external 170
```

Reflection

You could have used only static routing for this lab. What is an advantage of using EIGRP?

_____

_____

_____

Router Interface Summary Table

Router Interface Summary				
Router Model	Ethernet Interface #1	Ethernet Interface #2	Serial Interface #1	Serial Interface #2
1800	Fast Ethernet 0/0 (F0/0)	Fast Ethernet 0/1 (F0/1)	Serial 0/0/0 (S0/0/0)	Serial 0/0/1 (S0/0/1)
1900	Gigabit Ethernet 0/0 (G0/0)	Gigabit Ethernet 0/1 (G0/1)	Serial 0/0/0 (S0/0/0)	Serial 0/0/1 (S0/0/1)
2801	Fast Ethernet 0/0 (F0/0)	Fast Ethernet 0/1 (F0/1)	Serial 0/1/0 (S0/1/0)	Serial 0/1/1 (S0/1/1)
2811	Fast Ethernet 0/0 (F0/0)	Fast Ethernet 0/1 (F0/1)	Serial 0/0/0 (S0/0/0)	Serial 0/0/1 (S0/0/1)
2900	Gigabit Ethernet 0/0 (G0/0)	Gigabit Ethernet 0/1 (G0/1)	Serial 0/0/0 (S0/0/0)	Serial 0/0/1 (S0/0/1)
Note: To find out how the router is configured, look at the interfaces to identify the type of router and how many interfaces the router has. There is no way to effectively list all the combinations of configurations for each router class. This table includes identifiers for the possible combinations of Ethernet and Serial interfaces in the device. The table does not include any other type of interface, even though a specific router may contain one. An example of this might be an ISDN BRI interface. The string in parenthesis is the legal abbreviation that can be used in Cisco IOS commands to represent the interface.				

7.4.3.5 Lab – Configuring Basic EIGRP for IPv6

Topology

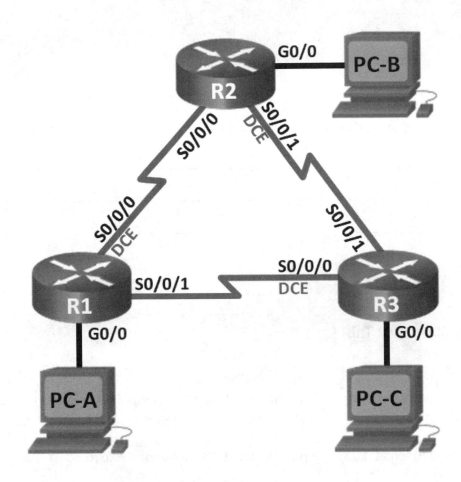

Addressing Table

Device	Interface	IP Address	Default Gateway
R1	G0/0	2001:DB8:ACAD:A::1/64 FE80::1 link-local	N/A
	S0/0/0 (DCE)	2001:DB8:ACAD:12::1/64 FE80::1 link-local	N/A
	S0/0/1	2001:DB8:ACAD:13::1/64 FE80::1 link-local	N/A
R2	G0/0	2001:DB8:ACAD:B::1/64 FE80::2 link-local	N/A
	S0/0/0	2001:DB8:ACAD:12::2/64 FE80::2 link-local	N/A
	S0/0/1 (DCE)	2001:DB8:ACAD:23::2/64 FE80::2 link-local	N/A
R3	G0/0	2001:DB8:ACAD:C::1/64 FE80::3 link-local	N/A
	S0/0/0 (DCE)	2001:DB8:ACAD:13::3/64 FE80::3 link-local	N/A
	S0/0/1	2001:DB8:ACAD:23::3/64 FE80::3 link-local	N/A
PC-A	NIC	2001:DB8:ACAD:A::3/64	FE80::1
PC-B	NIC	2001:DB8:ACAD:B::3/64	FE80::2
PC-C	NIC	2001:DB8:ACAD:C::3/64	FE80::3

Objectives

Part 1: Build the Network and Verify Connectivity

Part 2: Configure EIGRP for IPv6 Routing

Part 3: Verify EIGRP for IPv6 Routing

Part 4: Configure and Verify Passive Interfaces

Background / Scenario

EIGRP for IPv6 has the same overall operation and features as EIGRP for IPv4. However, there are a few major differences between them:

- EIGRP for IPv6 is configured directly on the router interfaces.
- With EIGRP for IPv6, a router ID is required on each router or the routing process does not start.
- The EIGRP for IPv6 routing process uses a shutdown feature.

In this lab, you will configure the network with EIGRP routing for IPv6. You will also assign router IDs, configure passive interfaces, verify the network is fully converged, and display routing information using CLI **show** commands.

Note: The routers used with CCNA hands-on labs are Cisco 1941 Integrated Services Routers (ISRs) with Cisco IOS Release 15.2(4)M3 (universalk9 image). Other routers and Cisco IOS versions can be used. Depending on the model and Cisco IOS version, the commands available and output produced might vary from what is shown in the labs. Refer to the Router Interface Summary Table at the end of this lab for the correct interface identifiers.

Note: Make sure that the routers have been erased and have no startup configurations. If you are unsure, contact your instructor.

Required Resources

- 3 Routers (Cisco 1941 with Cisco IOS Release 15.2(4)M3 universal image or comparable)
- 3 PCs (Windows 7, Vista, or XP with terminal emulation program, such as Tera Term)
- Console cables to configure the Cisco IOS devices via the console ports
- Ethernet and serial cables as shown in the topology

Part 1: Build the Network and Verify Connectivity

In Part 1, you will set up the network topology and configure basic settings, such as the interface IP addresses, device access, and passwords.

Step 1: Cable the network as shown in the topology.

Step 2: Configure PC hosts.

Step 3: Initialize and reload the routers as necessary.

Step 4: Configure basic settings for each router.

a. Disable DNS lookup.

b. Configure IP addresses for the routers as listed in Addressing Table.

   Note: Configure the FE80::x link-local address and the unicast address for each router interface.

c. Configure the device name as shown in the topology.

d. Assign **cisco** as the console and vty passwords.

e. Assign **class** as the privileged EXEC password.

f. Configure **logging synchronous** to prevent console and vty messages from interrupting command entry.

g. Configure a message of the day.

h. Copy the running configuration to the startup configuration.

Step 5: Verify connectivity.

The routers should be able to ping one another, and each PC should be able to ping its default gateway. The PCs will not be able to ping other PCs until EIGRP routing is configured. Verify and troubleshoot if necessary.

Part 2:   Configure EIGRP for IPv6 Routing

Step 1:   Enable IPv6 routing on the routers.

```
R1(config)# ipv6 unicast-routing
```

Step 2:   Assign a router ID to each router.

a. To begin the EIGRP for IPv6 routing configuration process, issue the **ipv6 router eigrp 1** command, where **1** is the AS number.

```
R1(config)# ipv6 router eigrp 1
```

b. EIGRP for IPv6 requires a 32-bit address for the router ID. Use the **router-id** command to configure the router ID in the router configuration mode.

```
R1(config)# ipv6 router eigrp 1
R1(config-rtr)# router-id 1.1.1.1


R2(config)# ipv6 router eigrp 1
R2(config-rtr)# router-id 2.2.2.2


R3(config)# ipv6 router eigrp 1
R3(config-rtr)# router-id 3.3.3.3
```

Step 3:   Enable EIGRP for IPv6 routing on each router.

The IPv6 routing process is shut down by default. Issue the **no shutdown** command to enable EIGRP for IPv6 routing on all routers.

```
R1(config)# ipv6 router eigrp 1
R1(config-rtr)# no shutdown


R2(config)# ipv6 router eigrp 1
R2(config-rtr)# no shutdown


R3(config)# ipv6 router eigrp 1
R3(config-rtr)# no shutdown
```

Step 4:   Configure EIGRP for IPv6 using AS 1 on the Serial and Gigabit Ethernet interfaces on the routers.

a. Issue the **ipv6 eigrp 1** command on the interfaces that participate in the EIGRP routing process. The AS number is 1 as assigned in Step 2. The configuration for R1 is displayed below as an example.

```
R1(config)# interface g0/0
R1(config-if)# ipv6 eigrp 1
R1(config-if)# interface s0/0/0
R1(config-if)# ipv6 eigrp 1
R1(config-if)# interface s0/0/1
```

```
R1(config-if)# ipv6 eigrp 1
```

b. Assign EIGRP participating interfaces on R2 and R3. You will see neighbor adjacency messages as interfaces are added to the EIGRP routing process. The messages on R1 are displayed below as an example.

```
R1(config-if)#
*Apr 12 00:25:49.183: %DUAL-5-NBRCHANGE: EIGRP-IPv6 1: Neighbor FE80::2 (Serial0/0/0)
is up: new adjacency
*Apr 12 00:26:15.583: %DUAL-5-NBRCHANGE: EIGRP-IPv6 1: Neighbor FE80::3 (Serial0/0/1)
is up: new adjacency
```

What address is used to indicate the neighbor in the adjacency messages? _____

Step 5:   Verify end-to-end connectivity.

Part 3:   Verify EIGRP for IPv6 Routing

Step 1:   Examine the neighbor adjacencies.

On R1, issue the **show ipv6 eigrp neighbors** command to verify that the adjacency has been established
with its neighboring routers. The link-local addresses of the neighboring routers are displayed in the adjacency table.

```
R1# show ipv6 eigrp neighbors
EIGRP-IPv6 Neighbors for AS(1)
H   Address                   Interface        Hold Uptime   SRTT   RTO  Q   Seq
                                               (sec)         (ms)        Cnt Num
1   Link-local address:       Se0/0/1          13 00:02:42    1     100  0   7
    FE80::3
0   Link-local address:       Se0/0/0          13 00:03:09    12    100  0   9
    FE80::2
```

Step 2:   Examine the IPv6 EIGRP routing table.

Use the **show ipv6 route eigrp** command to display IPv6 specific EIGRP routes on all the routers.

```
R1# show ipv6 route eigrp
IPv6 Routing Table - default - 10 entries
Codes: C - Connected, L - Local, S - Static, U - Per-user Static route
       B - BGP, R - RIP, I1 - ISIS L1, I2 - ISIS L2
       IA - ISIS interarea, IS - ISIS summary, D - EIGRP, EX - EIGRP external
       ND - ND Default, NDp - ND Prefix, DCE - Destination, NDr - Redirect
       O - OSPF Intra, OI - OSPF Inter, OE1 - OSPF ext 1, OE2 - OSPF ext 2
       ON1 - OSPF NSSA ext 1, ON2 - OSPF NSSA ext 2
D   2001:DB8:ACAD:B::/64 [90/2172416]
     via FE80::2, Serial0/0/0
D   2001:DB8:ACAD:C::/64 [90/2172416]
     via FE80::3, Serial0/0/1
```

```
D   2001:DB8:ACAD:23::/64 [90/2681856]

    via FE80::2, Serial0/0/0

    via FE80::3, Serial0/0/1
```

Step 3:   Examine the EIGRP topology.

```
R1# show ipv6 eigrp topology

EIGRP-IPv6 Topology Table for AS(1)/ID(1.1.1.1)

Codes: P - Passive, A - Active, U - Update, Q - Query, R - Reply,

       r - reply Status, s - sia Status


P 2001:DB8:ACAD:A::/64, 1 successors, FD is 28160

        via Connected, GigabitEthernet0/0

P 2001:DB8:ACAD:C::/64, 1 successors, FD is 2172416

        via FE80::3 (2172416/28160), Serial0/0/1

P 2001:DB8:ACAD:12::/64, 1 successors, FD is 2169856

        via Connected, Serial0/0/0

P 2001:DB8:ACAD:B::/64, 1 successors, FD is 2172416

        via FE80::2 (2172416/28160), Serial0/0/0

P 2001:DB8:ACAD:23::/64, 2 successors, FD is 2681856

        via FE80::2 (2681856/2169856), Serial0/0/0

        via FE80::3 (2681856/2169856), Serial0/0/1

P 2001:DB8:ACAD:13::/64, 1 successors, FD is 2169856

        via Connected, Serial0/0/1
```

Compare the highlighted entries to the routing table. What can you conclude from the comparison?

_____

_____

_____

Step 4:   Verify the parameters and current state of the active IPv6 routing protocol processes.

Issue the **show ipv6 protocols** command to verify the configured parameter. From the output, EIGRP is the configured IPv6 routing protocol with 1.1.1.1 as the router ID for R1. This routing protocol is associated with autonomous system 1 with three active interfaces: G0/0, S0/0/0, and S0/0/1.

```
R1# show ipv6 protocols

IPv6 Routing Protocol is "connected"

IPv6 Routing Protocol is "ND"

IPv6 Routing Protocol is "eigrp 1"

EIGRP-IPv6 Protocol for AS(1)

  Metric weight K1=1, K2=0, K3=1, K4=0, K5=0
```

```
        NSF-aware route hold timer is 240
        Router-ID: 1.1.1.1
        Topology : 0 (base)
          Active Timer: 3 min
          Distance: internal 90 external 170
          Maximum path: 16
          Maximum hopcount 100
          Maximum metric variance 1

        Interfaces:
          GigabitEthernet0/0
          Serial0/0/0
          Serial0/0/1
        Redistribution:
          None
```

Part 4:   Configure and Verify Passive Interfaces

A passive interface does not allow outgoing and incoming routing updates over the configured interface. The **passive-interface** *interface* command causes the router to stop sending and receiving Hello packets over an interface.

Step 1:   Configure interface G0/0 as passive on R1 and R2.

```
R1(config)# ipv6 router eigrp 1
R1(config-rtr)# passive-interface g0/0


R2(config)# ipv6 router eigrp 1
R2(config-rtr)# passive-interface g0/0
```

Step 2:   Verify the passive interface configuration.

Issue the **show ipv6 protocols** command on R1 and verify that G0/0 has been configured as passive.

```
R1# show ipv6 protocols
IPv6 Routing Protocol is "connected"
IPv6 Routing Protocol is "ND"
IPv6 Routing Protocol is "eigrp 1"
EIGRP-IPv6 Protocol for AS(1)
  Metric weight K1=1, K2=0, K3=1, K4=0, K5=0
  NSF-aware route hold timer is 240
  Router-ID: 1.1.1.1
  Topology : 0 (base)
    Active Timer: 3 min
    Distance: internal 90 external 170
```

```
       Maximum path: 16
       Maximum hopcount 100
       Maximum metric variance 1

     Interfaces:
       Serial0/0/0
       Serial0/0/1
       GigabitEthernet0/0 (passive)
     Redistribution:
       None
```

Step 3:   Configure the G0/0 passive interface on R3.

If a few interfaces are configured as passive, use the **passive-interface default** command to configure all the interfaces on the router as passive. Use the **no passive-interface** *interface* command to allow EIGRP Hello messages in and out of the router interface.

a. Configure all interfaces as passive on R3.

```
R3(config)# ipv6 router eigrp 1

R3(config-rtr)# passive-interface default

R3(config-rtr)#

*Apr 13 00:07:03.267: %DUAL-5-NBRCHANGE: EIGRP-IPv6 1: Neighbor FE80::1 (Serial0/0/0)
is down: interface passive

*Apr 13 00:07:03.267: %DUAL-5-NBRCHANGE: EIGRP-IPv6 1: Neighbor FE80::2 (Serial0/0/1)
is down: interface passive
```

b. After you have issued the **passive-interface default** command, R3 no longer participates in the routing process. What command can you use to verify it?

_____

c. What command can you use to display the passive interfaces on R3?

_____

d. Configure the serial interfaces to participate in the routing process.

```
R3(config)# ipv6 router eigrp 1

R3(config-rtr)# no passive-interface s0/0/0

R3(config-rtr)# no passive-interface s0/0/1

R3(config-rtr)#

*Apr 13 00:21:23.807: %DUAL-5-NBRCHANGE: EIGRP-IPv6 1: Neighbor FE80::1 (Serial0/0/0)
is up: new adjacency

*Apr 13 00:21:25.567: %DUAL-5-NBRCHANGE: EIGRP-IPv6 1: Neighbor FE80::2 (Serial0/0/1)
is up: new adjacency
```

e. The neighbor relationships have been established again with R1 and R2. Verify that only G0/0 has been configured as passive. What command do you use to verify the passive interface?

Reflection

1. Where would you configure passive interfaces? Why?

_____

_____

_____

2. What are some advantages with using EIGRP as the routing protocol in your network?

_____

_____

_____

Router Interface Summary Table

Router Interface Summary				
Router Model	**Ethernet Interface #1**	**Ethernet Interface #2**	**Serial Interface #1**	**Serial Interface #2**
1800	Fast Ethernet 0/0 (F0/0)	Fast Ethernet 0/1 (F0/1)	Serial 0/0/0 (S0/0/0)	Serial 0/0/1 (S0/0/1)
1900	Gigabit Ethernet 0/0 (G0/0)	Gigabit Ethernet 0/1 (G0/1)	Serial 0/0/0 (S0/0/0)	Serial 0/0/1 (S0/0/1)
2801	Fast Ethernet 0/0 (F0/0)	Fast Ethernet 0/1 (F0/1)	Serial 0/1/0 (S0/1/0)	Serial 0/1/1 (S0/1/1)
2811	Fast Ethernet 0/0 (F0/0)	Fast Ethernet 0/1 (F0/1)	Serial 0/0/0 (S0/0/0)	Serial 0/0/1 (S0/0/1)
2900	Gigabit Ethernet 0/0 (G0/0)	Gigabit Ethernet 0/1 (G0/1)	Serial 0/0/0 (S0/0/0)	Serial 0/0/1 (S0/0/1)

Note: To find out how the router is configured, look at the interfaces to identify the type of router and how many interfaces the router has. There is no way to effectively list all the combinations of configurations for each router class. This table includes identifiers for the possible combinations of Ethernet and Serial interfaces in the device. The table does not include any other type of interface, even though a specific router may contain one. An example of this might be an ISDN BRI interface. The string in parenthesis is the legal abbreviation that can be used in Cisco IOS commands to represent the interface.

7.5.1.1 Class Activity – Portfolio RIP and EIGRP

Objectives

Configure EIGRP for IPv4 in a small routed network (review).

Scenario

You are preparing a portfolio file for comparison of RIP and EIGRP routing protocols.

Think of a network with three interconnected routers with each router providing a LAN for PCs, printers, and other end devices. The graphic on this page depicts one example of a topology like this.

In this modeling activity scenario, you will be creating, addressing and configuring a topology, using verification commands, and comparing/contrasting RIP and EIGRP routing protocol outputs.

Complete the PDF reflection questions. Save your work and be prepared to share your answers with the class. Also save a copy of this activity for later use within this course or for portfolio reference.

Resources

Packet Tracer and word processing software programs

Directions

Step 1: WAN and LAN topology design

a. Use Packet Tracer to design a network with three routers (1941 model, suggested). If necessary, add NIC cards to the routers to provide connectivity to the routers to provide for at least one LAN to each router. Add at least one PC to each LAN.

b. Address the networks. You may use a flat addressing scheme or VLSM. Use only IPv4 networks for this entire activity.

Step 2: Copy the topology

a. Highlight the entire topology by using your cursor.

b. Use Ctrl+C to make a copy of the highlighted topology.

c. Use Ctrl+V to insert a full copy of the topology to the desktop of Packet Tracer. You will now have displayed two exact, IPv4-addressed topologies with which to work for routing protocols configurations.

d. While highlighted, move the copied topology to a different location on the Packet Tracer desktop to create room between the two for configuration purposes.

Step 3: Configure RIP and EIGRP on the separate topologies.

a. Configure the RIP routing protocol on the first topology and EIGRP on the second routing topology.

b. Once you have successfully configured RIP on one topology and EIGRP on the other, check to make sure your PCs can ping each other.

c. Save your work so no configuration information is lost.

Step 4:   Use verification commands to check output for the routing protocols.

   a. To compare/contrast routing protocol information from the two topologies, issue the **show ip route** command on R1 for topology 1 and 2.

   b. Copy the output into a table in your word processing program file. Label each column with RIP or EIGRP and place the output you received from the **show ip route** command.

   c. Issue the **show ip protocols** command on R1 for topology table 1 and 2. Create another table in your word processing software file and place the output information below RIP or EIGRP.

   d. Issue the **show cdp neighbors** command on R1's topology 1. Copy the output to a third table with RIP as the heading and issue the **show ip eigrp neighbors** command on R1's topology 2. Copy the output from this command in column 2 of table 3 under the heading EIGRP.

Reflection

1. Compare and contrast the output for the **show ip route** verification command.

   _____

2. Compare and contrast the output for the **show ip protocol** verification command.

   _____

3. Compare and contrast the **show cdp neighbors** command for the RIP topology and the **show ip eigrp neighbors** command for the EIGRP topology.

   _____

4. After comparing and contrasting the RIP and EIGRP output, which do you find most informative? Support your answer.

   _____

Chapter 8 — EIGRP Advanced Configurations and Troubleshooting

8.0.1.2 Class Activity – EIGRP – Back to the Future

Objectives

Implement advanced EIGRP features to enhance operation in a small- to medium-sized business network.

Scenario

Many of these bulleted concepts were mentioned in the previous chapter's curriculum content and will be the focus of this chapter:

- Auto-summarization
- Load balancing
- Default routes
- Hold-down timers
- Authentication

With a partner, write 10 EIGRP review questions based on the previous chapter's curriculum content. Three of the questions must focus on the bulleted items above. Ideally, Multiple Choice, True/False, or Fill in the Blank question types will be designed. As you design your questions, make sure you record the curriculum section and page numbers of the supporting content in case you need to refer back for answer verification.

Save your work and then meet with another group, or the entire class, and quiz them using the questions you developed.

Resources

- Word processing software program
- Curriculum content from the previous chapter

8.1.5.5 Lab – Configuring Advanced EIGRP for IPv4 Features

Topology

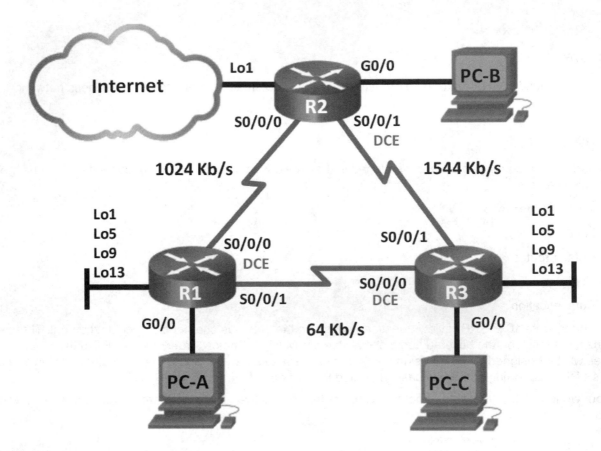

Addressing Table

Device	Interface	IP Address	Subnet Mask	Default Gateway
R1	G0/0	192.168.1.1	255.255.255.0	N/A
	S0/0/0 (DCE)	192.168.12.1	255.255.255.252	N/A
	S0/0/1	192.168.13.1	255.255.255.252	N/A
	Lo1	192.168.11.1	255.255.255.252	N/A
	Lo5	192.168.11.5	255.255.255.252	N/A
	Lo9	192.168.11.9	255.255.255.252	N/A
	Lo13	192.168.11.13	255.255.255.252	N/A
R2	G0/0	192.168.2.1	255.255.255.0	N/A
	S0/0/0	192.168.12.2	255.255.255.252	N/A
	S0/0/1 (DCE)	192.168.23.1	255.255.255.252	N/A
	Lo1	192.168.22.1	255.255.255.252	N/A
R3	G0/0	192.168.3.1	255.255.255.0	N/A
	S0/0/0 (DCE)	192.168.13.2	255.255.255.252	N/A
	S0/0/1	192.168.23.2	255.255.255.252	N/A
	Lo1	192.168.33.1	255.255.255.252	N/A
	Lo5	192.168.33.5	255.255.255.252	N/A
	Lo9	192.168.33.9	255.255.255.252	N/A
	Lo13	192.168.33.13	255.255.255.252	N/A
PC-A	NIC	192.168.1.3	255.255.255.0	192.168.1.1
PC-B	NIC	192.168.2.3	255.255.255.0	192.168.2.1
PC-C	NIC	192.168.3.3	255.255.255.0	192.168.3.1

Objectives

Part 1: Build the Network and Configure Basic Device Settings

Part 2: Configure EIGRP and Verify Connectivity

Part 3: Configure Summarization for EIGRP

- Configure EIGRP for automatic summarization.

- Configure manual summarization for EIGRP.

Part 4: Configure and Propagate a Default Static Route

Part 5: Fine-Tune EIGRP

- Configure bandwidth utilization for EIGRP.

- Configure the hello interval and hold timer for EIGRP.

Part 6: Configure EIGRP Authentication

Background / Scenario

EIGRP has advanced features to allow changes related to summarization, default route propagation, bandwidth utilization, metrics, and security.

In this lab, you will configure automatic and manual summarization for EIGRP, configure EIGRP route propagation, fine-tune EIGRP metrics, and use MD5 authentication to secure EIGRP routing information.

Note: The routers used with CCNA hands-on labs are Cisco 1941 Integrated Services Routers (ISRs) with Cisco IOS Release 15.2(4)M3 (universalk9 image). Other routers and Cisco IOS versions can be used. Depending on the model and Cisco IOS version, the commands available and output produced might vary from what is shown in the labs. Refer to the Router Interface Summary Table at this end of the lab for the correct interface identifiers.

Note: Ensure that the routers have been erased and have no startup configurations. If you are unsure, contact your instructor.

Required Resources

- 3 Routers (Cisco 1941 with Cisco IOS Release 15.2(4)M3 universal image or comparable)
- 3 PCs (Windows 7, Vista, or XP with terminal emulation program, such as Tera Term)
- Console cables to configure the Cisco IOS devices via the console ports
- Ethernet and serial cables as shown in the topology

Part 1: Build the Network and Configure Basic Device Settings

In Part 1, you will set up the network topology and configure basic settings on the PC hosts and routers.

Step 1: Cable the network as shown in the topology.

Step 2: Configure PC hosts.

Step 3: Initialize and reload the routers as necessary.

Step 4: Configure basic settings for each router.

a. Disable DNS lookup.

b. Configure device name as shown in the topology.

c. Assign **cisco** as the console and vty passwords.

d. Assign **class** as the privileged EXEC password.

e. Configure **logging synchronous** to prevent console messages from interrupting command entry.

f. Configure the IP address listed in the Addressing Table for all interfaces.

   Note: Do **NOT** configure the loopback interfaces at this time.

g. Copy the running configuration to the startup configuration.

Part 2: Configure EIGRP and Verify Connectivity

In Part 2, you will configure basic EIGRP for the topology and set bandwidths for the serial interfaces.

Note: This lab provides minimal assistance with the actual commands necessary to configure EIGRP. However, the required commands are provided in Appendix A. Test your knowledge by trying to configure the devices without referring to the appendix.

Step 1: Configure EIGRP.

a. On R1, configure EIGRP routing with an autonomous system (AS) ID of 1 for all directly connected networks. Write the commands used in the space below.

_____

_____

_____

_____

b. For the LAN interface on R1, disable the transmission of EIGRP hello packets. Write the command used in the space below.

_____

c. On R1, configure the bandwidth for S0/0/0 to 1024 Kb/s and the bandwidth for S0/0/1 to 64 Kb/s. Write the commands used in the space below. **Note**: The **bandwidth** command only affects the EIGRP metric calculation, not the actual bandwidth of the serial link.

_____

_____

d. On R2, configure EIGRP routing with an AS ID of 1 for all networks, disable the transmission of EIGRP hello packets for the LAN interface, and configure the bandwidth for S0/0/0 to 1024 Kb/s.

e. On R3, configure EIGRP routing with an AS ID of 1 for all networks, disable the transmission of EIGRP hello packets for the LAN interface, and configure the bandwidth for S0/0/0 to 64 Kb/s.

Step 2: Test connectivity.

All PCs should be able to ping one another. Verify and troubleshoot if necessary.

Note: It may be necessary to disable the PC firewall to ping between PCs.

Part 3: Configure Summarization for EIGRP

In Part 3, you will add loopback interfaces to R1, enable EIGRP automatic summarization on R1, and observe the effects on the routing table for R2. You will also add loopback interfaces on R3.

Step 1: Configure EIGRP for automatic summarization.

a. Issue the **show ip protocols** command on R1. What is the default status of automatic summarization in EIGRP?

_____

b. Configure the loopback addresses on R1.

c. Add the appropriate network statements to the EIGRP process on R1. Record the commands used in the space below.

_____

_____

_____

_____

_____

d. On R2, issue the **show ip route eigrp** command. How are the loopback networks represented in the output?

_____

e. On R1, issue the **auto-summary** command inside the EIGRP process.

```
R1(config)# router eigrp 1
R1(config-router)# auto-summary
R1(config-router)#
*Apr 14 01:14:55.463: %DUAL-5-NBRCHANGE: EIGRP-IPv4 1: Neighbor 192.168.13.2
(Serial0/0/1) is resync: summary configured
*Apr 14 01:14:55.463: %DUAL-5-NBRCHANGE: EIGRP-IPv4 1: Neighbor 192.168.12.2
(Serial0/0/0) is resync: summary configured
*Apr 14 01:14:55.463: %DUAL-5-NBRCHANGE: EIGRP-IPv4 1: Neighbor 192.168.13.2
(Serial0/0/1) is resync: summary up, remove components
R1(config-router)#67: %DUAL-5-NBRCHANGE: EIGRP-IPv4 1: Neighbor 192.168.12.2
(Serial0/0/0) is resync: summary up, remove components
*Apr 14 01:14:55.467: %DUAL-5-NBRCHANGE: EIGRP-IPv4 1: Neighbor 192.168.12.2
(Serial0/0/0) is resync: summary up, remove components
*Apr 14 01:14:55.467: %DUAL-5-NBRCHANGE: EIGRP-IPv4 1: Neighbor 192.168.13.2
(Serial0/0/1) is resync: summary up, remove components
```

How does the routing table on R2 change?

_____

Step 2: Configure manual summarization for EIGRP.

a. Configure the loopback addresses on R3.

b. Add the appropriate network statements to the EIGRP process on R3.

c. On R2, issue the **show ip route eigrp** command. How are the loopback networks from R3 represented in the output?

_____

_____

d. Determine the summary EIGRP route for the loopback addresses on R3. Write the summary route in the space below.

_____

_____

e. For the serial interfaces on R3, issue the **ip summary-address eigrp 1** *network address subnet mask* command to manually summarize the networks.

```
R3(config)# interface s0/0/0

R3(config-if)# ip summary-address eigrp 1 192.168.33.0 255.255.255.240

R3(config-if)# exit

R3(config)# interface s0/0/1

R3(config-if)# ip summary-address eigrp 1 192.168.33.0 255.255.255.240

*Apr 14 01:33:46.433: %DUAL-5-NBRCHANGE: EIGRP-IPv4 1: Neighbor 192.168.13.1
(Serial0/0/0) is resync: summary configured

*Apr 14 01:33:46.433: %DUAL-5-NBRCHANGE: EIGRP-IPv4 1: Neighbor 192.168.23.1
(Serial0/0/1) is resync: summary configured
```

How does the routing table on R2 change?

_____

_____

Part 4: Configure and Propagate a Default Static Route

In Part 4, you will configure a default static route on R2 and propagate the route to all other routers.

a. Configure the loopback address on R2.

b. Configure a default static route with an exit interface of Lo1.

```
R2(config)# ip route 0.0.0.0 0.0.0.0 Lo1
```

c. Use the **redistribute static** command within the EIGRP process to propagate the default static route to other participating routers.

```
R2(config)# router eigrp 1

R2(config-router)# redistribute static
```

d. Use the **show ip protocols** command on R2 to verify the static route is being distributed.

```
R2# show ip protocols
*** IP Routing is NSF aware ***


Routing Protocol is "eigrp 1"
    Outgoing update filter list for all interfaces is not set
```

```
Incoming update filter list for all interfaces is not set
Default networks flagged in outgoing updates
Default networks accepted from incoming updates
Redistributing: static
EIGRP-IPv4 Protocol for AS(1)
  Metric weight K1=1, K2=0, K3=1, K4=0, K5=0
  NSF-aware route hold timer is 240
  Router-ID: 192.168.23.1
  Topology : 0 (base)
    Active Timer: 3 min
    Distance: internal 90 external 170
    Maximum path: 4
    Maximum hopcount 100
    Maximum metric variance 1

Automatic Summarization: disabled
Maximum path: 4
Routing for Networks:
  192.168.2.0
  192.168.12.0/30
  192.168.23.0/30
Passive Interface(s):
  GigabitEthernet0/0
Routing Information Sources:
  Gateway         Distance      Last Update
  192.168.12.1         90       00:13:20
  192.168.23.2         90       00:13:20
Distance: internal 90 external 170
```

e. On R1, issue the **show ip route eigrp | include 0.0.0.0** command to view statements specific to the default route. How is the static default route represented in the output? What is the administrative distance (AD) for the propagated route?

_____

_____

Part 5: Fine-Tune EIGRP

In Part 5, you will configure the percentage of bandwidth that can be used by an EIGRP interface and change the hello interval and hold timers for EIGRP interfaces.

Step 1:   Configure bandwidth utilization for EIGRP.

a. Configure the serial link between R1 and R2 to allow only 75 percent of the link bandwidth for EIGRP traffic.

```
R1(config)# interface s0/0/0
R1(config-if)# ip bandwidth-percent eigrp 1 75
R2(config)# interface s0/0/0
R2(config-if)# ip bandwidth-percent eigrp 1 75
```

b. Configure the serial link between R1 and R3 to allow 40 percent of the links bandwidth for EIGRP traffic.

Step 2:   Configure the hello interval and hold timer for EIGRP.

a.   On R2, use the **show ip eigrp interfaces detail** command to view the hello interval and hold timer for EIGRP.

```
R2# show ip eigrp interfaces detail
EIGRP-IPv4 Interfaces for AS(1)
                         Xmit Queue    PeerQ       Mean   Pacing Time   Multicast    Pending
Interface        Peers   Un/Reliable   Un/Reliable SRTT   Un/Reliable   Flow Timer   Routes
Se0/0/0            1        0/0          0/0          1       0/15          50           0
   Hello-interval is 5, Hold-time is 15
   Split-horizon is enabled
   Next xmit serial <none>
   Packetized sent/expedited: 29/1
   Hello's sent/expedited: 390/2
   Un/reliable mcasts: 0/0  Un/reliable ucasts: 35/39
   Mcast exceptions: 0  CR packets: 0  ACKs suppressed: 0
   Retransmissions sent: 0  Out-of-sequence rcvd: 0
   Topology-ids on interface - 0
   Interface BW percentage is 75
   Authentication mode is not set
Se0/0/1            1        0/0          0/0          1       0/16          50           0
   Hello-interval is 5, Hold-time is 15
   Split-horizon is enabled
   Next xmit serial <none>
   Packetized sent/expedited: 34/5
   Hello's sent/expedited: 382/2
   Un/reliable mcasts: 0/0  Un/reliable ucasts: 31/42
   Mcast exceptions: 0  CR packets: 0  ACKs suppressed: 2
   Retransmissions sent: 0  Out-of-sequence rcvd: 0
   Topology-ids on interface - 0
   Authentication mode is not set
```

What is the default value for hello time? _____

What is the default value for hold time? _____

b.   Configure S0/0/0 and S0/0/1 interfaces on R1 to use a hello interval of 60 seconds and a hold time of 180 seconds in that specific order.

```
R1(config)# interface s0/0/0
R1(config-if)# ip hello-interval eigrp 1 60
R1(config-if)# ip hold-time eigrp 1 180
R1(config)# interface s0/0/1
R1(config-if)# ip hello-interval eigrp 1 60
R1(config-if)# ip hold-time eigrp 1 180
```

c.   Configure the serial interfaces on R2 and R3 to use a hello interval of 60 seconds and a hold time of 180 seconds.

d.   Use the **show ip eigrp interfaces detail** command on R2 to verify configuration.

Part 6: Configure EIGRP Authentication

In Part 6, you will create an authentication key on all routers and configure router interfaces to use MD5 authentication for EIGRP message authentication.

Step 1: Configure authentication keys.

a. On R1, use the **key chain** *name* command in global configuration mode to create a key chain with the label EIGRP-KEYS.

```
R1(config)# key chain EIGRP-KEYS
R1(config-keychain)# key 1
R1(config-keychain-key)# key-string cisco
```

b. Complete the configuration on R2 and R3.

c. Issue the **show key chain** command. You should have the same output on every router.

Step 2: Configure EIGRP link authentication.

a. Apply the following commands to active EIGRP authentication on the serial interfaces on R1.

```
R1# conf t
R1(config)# interface s0/0/0
R1(config-if)# ip authentication key-chain eigrp 1 EIGRP-KEYS
R1(config-if)# ip authentication mode eigrp 1 md5
R1(config-if)# interface s0/0/1
R1(config-if)# ip authentication key-chain eigrp 1 EIGRP-KEYS
R1(config-if)# ip authentication mode eigrp 1 md5
```

b. Activate EIGRP authentication on the serial interfaces on R2 and R3.

c. On R2, use the **show ip eigrp interfaces detail** command to verify authentication.

```
R2# show ip eigrp interfaces detail
EIGRP-IPv4 Interfaces for AS(1)
                          Xmit Queue   PeerQ        Mean   Pacing Time   Multicast    Pending
Interface        Peers   Un/Reliable  Un/Reliable  SRTT   Un/Reliable   Flow Timer   Routes
Se0/0/0            1        0/0          0/0          1       0/23           50          0
  Hello-interval is 60, Hold-time is 180
  Split-horizon is enabled
  Next xmit serial <none>
  Packetized sent/expedited: 30/5
  Hello's sent/expedited: 1163/5
  Un/reliable mcasts: 0/0  Un/reliable ucasts: 25/34
  Mcast exceptions: 0  CR packets: 0  ACKs suppressed: 0
  Retransmissions sent: 0  Out-of-sequence rcvd: 0
  Topology-ids on interface - 0
  Authentication mode is md5,  key-chain is "EIGRP-KEYS"
Se0/0/1            1        0/0          0/0          2       0/15           50          0
  Hello-interval is 60, Hold-time is 180
  Split-horizon is enabled
```

```
Next xmit serial <none>

Packetized sent/expedited: 31/1

Hello's sent/expedited: 1354/3

Un/reliable mcasts: 0/0  Un/reliable ucasts: 28/34

Mcast exceptions: 0  CR packets: 0  ACKs suppressed: 4

Retransmissions sent: 0  Out-of-sequence rcvd: 0

Topology-ids on interface - 0

Authentication mode is md5,  key-chain is "EIGRP-KEYS"
```

Reflection

1. What are the benefits of summarizing routes?

2. When setting EIGRP timers, why is it important to make the hold time value equal to or greater than the hello interval?

3. Why is it important to configure authentication for EIGRP?

Router Interface Summary Table

Router Interface Summary				
Router Model	**Ethernet Interface #1**	**Ethernet Interface #2**	**Serial Interface #1**	**Serial Interface #2**
1800	Fast Ethernet 0/0 (F0/0)	Fast Ethernet 0/1 (F0/1)	Serial 0/0/0 (S0/0/0)	Serial 0/0/1 (S0/0/1)
1900	Gigabit Ethernet 0/0 (G0/0)	Gigabit Ethernet 0/1 (G0/1)	Serial 0/0/0 (S0/0/0)	Serial 0/0/1 (S0/0/1)
2801	Fast Ethernet 0/0 (F0/0)	Fast Ethernet 0/1 (F0/1)	Serial 0/1/0 (S0/1/0)	Serial 0/1/1 (S0/1/1)
2811	Fast Ethernet 0/0 (F0/0)	Fast Ethernet 0/1 (F0/1)	Serial 0/0/0 (S0/0/0)	Serial 0/0/1 (S0/0/1)
2900	Gigabit Ethernet 0/0 (G0/0)	Gigabit Ethernet 0/1 (G0/1)	Serial 0/0/0 (S0/0/0)	Serial 0/0/1 (S0/0/1)
Note: To find out how the router is configured, look at the interfaces to identify the type of router and how many interfaces the router has. There is no way to effectively list all the combinations of configurations for each router class. This table includes identifiers for the possible combinations of Ethernet and Serial interfaces in the device. The table does not include any other type of interface, even though a specific router may contain one. An example of this might be an ISDN BRI interface. The string in parenthesis is the legal abbreviation that can be used in Cisco IOS commands to represent the interface.				

Appendix A: Configuration Commands

Router R1

```
R1(config)# router eigrp 1
R1(config-router)# network 192.168.1.0
R1(config-router)# network 192.168.12.0 0.0.0.3
R1(config-router)# network 192.168.13.0 0.0.0.3
R1(config-router)# network 192.168.11.0 0.0.0.3
R1(config-router)# network 192.168.11.4 0.0.0.3
R1(config-router)# network 192.168.11.8 0.0.0.3
R1(config-router)# network 192.168.11.12 0.0.0.3
R1(config-router)# passive-interface g0/0
R1(config)# int s0/0/0
R1(config-if)# bandwidth 1024
R1(config-if)# int s0/0/1
R1(config-if)# bandwidth 64
```

Router R2

```
R2(config)# router eigrp 1
R2(config-router)# network 192.168.2.0
R2(config-router)# network 192.168.12.0 0.0.0.3
R2(config-router)# network 192.168.23.0 0.0.0.3
R2(config-router)# passive-interface g0/0
R2(config)# int s0/0/0
R2(config-if)# bandwidth 1024
```

Router R3

```
R3(config)# router eigrp 1
R3(config-router)# network 192.168.3.0
R3(config-router)# network 192.168.13.0 0.0.0.3
R3(config-router)# network 192.168.23.0 0.0.0.3
R3(config-router)# network 192.168.33.0 0.0.0.3
R3(config-router)# network 192.168.33.4 0.0.0.3
R3(config-router)# network 192.168.33.8 0.0.0.3
R3(config-router)# network 192.168.33.12 0.0.0.3
R3(config-router)# passive-interface g0/0
R3(config)# int s0/0/0
R3(config-if)# bandwidth 64
```

8.2.3.6 Lab – Troubleshooting Basic EIGRP for IPv4 and IPv6

Topology

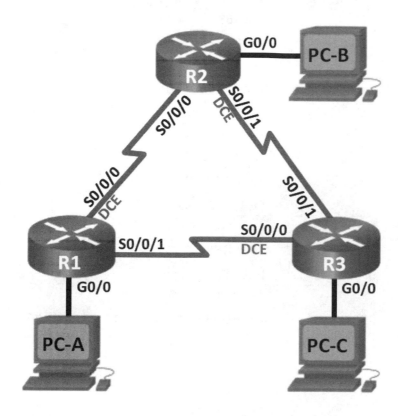

Addressing Table

Device	EIGRP Router ID	Interface	IP Address	Default Gateway
R1	1.1.1.1	G0/0	192.168.1.1/24 2001:DB8:ACAD:A::1/64 FE80::1 link-local	N/A
		S0/0/0 (DCE)	192.168.12.1/30 2001:DB8:ACAD:12::1/64 FE80::1 link-local	N/A
		S0/0/1	192.18.13.1/30 2001:DB8:ACAD:13::1/64 FE80::1 link-local	N/A
R2	2.2.2.2	G0/0	192.168.2.1/24 2001:DB8:ACAD:B::2/64 FE80::2 link-local	N/A
		S0/0/0	192.168.12.2/30 2001:DB8:ACAD:12::2/64 FE80::2 link-local	N/A
		S0/0/1 (DCE)	192.168.23.1/30 2001:DB8:ACAD:23::2/64 FE80::2 link-local	N/A
R3	3.3.3.3	G0/0	192.168.3.1/24 2001:DB8:ACAD:C::3/64 FE80::3 link-local	N/A
		S0/0/0 (DCE)	192.168.13.2/30 2001:DB8:ACAD:13::3/64 FE80::3 link-local	N/A
		S0/0/1	192.168.23.2/30 2001:DB8:ACAD:23::3/64 FE80::3 link-local	N/A
PC-A		NIC	192.168.1.3/24 2001:DB8:ACAD:A::A/64	192.168.1.1 FE80::1
PC-B		NIC	192.168.2.3/24 2001:DB8:ACAD:B::B/64	192.168.2.1 FE80::2
PC-C		NIC	192.168.3.3/24 2001:DB8:ACAD:C::C/64	192.168.3.1 FE80::3

Objectives

Part 1: Build the Network and Load Device Configurations

Part 2: Troubleshoot Layer 3 Connectivity

Part 3: Troubleshoot EIGRP for IPv4

Part 4: Troubleshoot EIGRP for IPv6

Background / Scenario

The Enhanced Interior Gateway Routing Protocol (EIGRP) is an advanced distance vector routing protocol developed by Cisco Systems. EIGRP routers discover neighbors and establish and maintain adjacencies with neighbor routers using Hello packets. An EIGRP router assumes that as long as it is receiving Hello packets from a neighboring router, that neighbor is up and its routes remain viable.

EIGRP for IPv4 runs over the IPv4 network layer, communicating with other EIGRP IPv4 peers, and advertising only IPv4 routes. EIGRP for IPv6 has the same functionality as EIGRP for IPv4 but uses IPv6 as the network layer protocol, communicating with EIGRP for IPv6 peers and advertising IPv6 routes.

In this lab, you will troubleshoot a network that runs EIGRP for IPv4 and EIGRP for IPv6 routing protocols. This network is experiencing problems and you are tasked with finding the problems and correcting them.

Note: The routers used with CCNA hands-on labs are Cisco 1941 Integrated Services Routers (ISRs) with Cisco IOS Release 15.2(4)M3 (universalk9 image). Other routers and Cisco IOS versions can be used. Depending on the model and Cisco IOS version, the commands available and output produced might vary from what is shown in the labs. Refer to the Router Interface Summary Table at the end of this lab for the correct interface identifiers.

Note: Make sure that the routers have been erased and have no startup configurations. If you are unsure, contact your instructor.

Required Resources

- 3 Router (Cisco 1941 with Cisco IOS Release 15.2(4)M3 universal image or comparable)
- 3 PCs (Windows 7, Vista, or XP with terminal emulation program, such as Tera Term)
- Console cables to configure the Cisco IOS devices via the console ports
- Ethernet and serial cables as shown in the topology

Part 1:   Build the Network and Load Device Configurations

In Part 1, you will set up the network topology and configure basic settings on the PC hosts and routers.

Step 1:   Cable the network as shown in the topology.

Step 2:   Configure PC hosts.

Step 3:   Load router configurations.

Load the following configurations into the appropriate router. All routers have the same passwords. The privileged EXEC password is **class**, and the console and vty password is **cisco**.

Router R1 Configuration:

```
conf t
service password-encryption
hostname R1
enable secret class
no ip domain lookup
ipv6 unicast-routing
interface GigabitEthernet0/0
 ip address 192.168.1.1 255.255.255.0
 duplex auto
 speed auto
 ipv6 address FE80::1 link-local
 ipv6 address 2001:DB8:ACAD:A::1/64
 ipv6 eigrp 1
 no shutdown
interface Serial0/0/0
 bandwidth 128
 ip address 192.168.21.1 255.255.255.252

 ipv6 address FE80::1 link-local
 ipv6 address 2001:DB8:ACAD:12::1/64
 ipv6 eigrp 1
 clock rate 128000
 no shutdown
interface Serial0/0/1

 ip address 192.168.13.1 255.255.255.252
 ipv6 address FE80::1 link-local
 ipv6 address 2001:DB8:ACAD:31::1/64

 ipv6 eigrp 1
 no shutdown
router eigrp 1
 network 192.168.1.0
 network 192.168.12.0 0.0.0.3
 network 192.168.13.0 0.0.0.3
 passive-interface GigabitEthernet0/0
 eigrp router-id 1.1.1.1
ipv6 router eigrp 1
```

```
 no shutdown
banner motd @
  Unauthorized Access is Prohibited! @
line con 0
 password cisco
 logging synchronous
line vty 0 4
 password cisco
login
 transport input all
end
```

Router R2 Configuration:

```
conf t
service password-encryption
hostname R2
enable secret class
no ip domain lookup
ipv6 unicast-routing
interface GigabitEthernet0/0
 ip address 192.168.2.1 255.255.255.0
 duplex auto
 speed auto
 ipv6 address FE80::2 link-local
 ipv6 address 2001:DB8:ACAD:B::2/64
 ipv6 eigrp 1

interface Serial0/0/0

 ip address 192.168.12.2 255.255.255.252
 ipv6 address FE80::2 link-local
 ipv6 address 2001:DB8:ACAD:12::2/64
 ipv6 eigrp 1
 no shutdown
interface Serial0/0/1
 bandwidth 128
 ip address 192.168.23.1 255.255.255.0

 ipv6 address FE80::2 link-local
```

```
   ipv6 address 2001:DB8:ACAD:23::2/64
   ipv6 eigrp 1
   clock rate 128000
   no shutdown
router eigrp 1

  network 192.168.12.0 0.0.0.3
  network 192.168.23.0 0.0.0.3
  passive-interface GigabitEthernet0/0
  eigrp router-id 2.2.2.2
ipv6 router eigrp 1

  no shutdown
  passive-interface GigabitEthernet0/0
banner motd @
  Unauthorized Access is Prohibited! @
line con 0
  password cisco
  login
  logging synchronous
line vty 0 4
  password cisco
  login
  transport input all
end
```

Router R3 Configuration:

```
conf t
service password-encryption
hostname R3
enable secret class
no ip domain lookup

interface GigabitEthernet0/0
  ip address 192.168.3.1 255.255.255.0
  duplex auto
  speed auto
  ipv6 address FE80::3 link-local
  ipv6 address 2001:DB8:ACAD:C::3/64
```

```
  ipv6 eigrp 1


interface Serial0/0/0


  ip address 192.168.13.2 255.255.255.252
  ipv6 address FE80::3 link-local
  ipv6 address 2001:DB8:ACAD:13::3/64
  ipv6 eigrp 1
  no shutdown


interface Serial0/0/1
  bandwidth 128
  ip address 192.168.23.2 255.255.255.252
  ipv6 address FE80::3 link-local
  ipv6 address 2001:DB8:ACAD:23::3/64
  ipv6 eigrp 1
  no shutdown
router eigrp 1
  network 192.168.3.0
  network 192.168.13.0 0.0.0.3


  passive-interface GigabitEthernet0/0
  eigrp router-id 3.3.3.3




banner motd @
  Unauthorized Access is Prohibited! @
line con 0
  password cisco
  login
  logging synchronous
line vty 0 4
  password cisco
  login
  transport input all
end
```

Step 4:   Save the running configuration for all routers.

Part 2:   Troubleshoot Layer 3 Connectivity

In Part 2, you will verify that Layer 3 connectivity is established on all interfaces. You will need to test both IPv4 and IPv6 connectivity for all device interfaces.

Note: All serial interfaces should be set with a bandwidth of 128 Kb/s. The clock rate on the DCE interface should be set to 128000.

Step 1:   Verify that the interfaces listed in the Addressing Table are active and configured with correct IP address information.

a.   Issue the **show ip interface brief** command on all routers to verify that the interfaces are in an up/up state. Record your findings.

_____

_____

_____

_____

b.   Issue the **show run interface** command to verify IP address assignments on all router interfaces. Compare the interface IP addresses against the Addressing Table and verify the subnet mask assignments. For IPv6, verify that the link-local address has been assigned. Record your findings.

_____

_____

_____

_____

c.   Issue the **show interfaces** *interface-id* command to verify bandwidth setting on the serial interfaces. Record your findings.

_____

_____

_____

d.   Issue the **show controllers** *interface-id* command to verify that clock rates have been set to 128 Kb/s on all DCE serial interfaces. Issue the **show interfaces** *interface-id* command to verify bandwidth setting on the serial interfaces. Record your findings.

_____

_____

_____

e.   Resolve all problems found. Record the commands used to correct the issues.

_____

_____

_____

_____

_____

_____

_____

_____

_____

_____

Step 2:   Verify Layer 3 connectivity.

Use the **ping** command and verify that each router has network connectivity with the serial interfaces on the neighbor routers. Verify that the PCs can ping their default gateways. If problems still exist, continue trouble-shooting Layer 3 issues.

Part 3:   Troubleshoot EIGRP for IPv4

In Part 3, you will troubleshoot EIGRP for IPv4 problems and make the necessary changes needed to establish EIGRP for IPv4 routes and end-to-end IPv4 connectivity.

Note: LAN (G0/0) interfaces should not advertise EIGRP routing information, but routes to these networks should be contained in the routing tables.

Step 1:   Test IPv4 end-to-end connectivity.

From each PC host, ping the other PC hosts in the topology to verify end-to-end connectivity.

Note: It may be necessary to disable the PC firewall before testing, to ping between PCs.

a.   Ping from PC-A to PC-B. Were the pings successful? _____

b.   Ping from PC-A to PC-C. Were the pings successful? _____

c.   Ping from PC-B to PC-C. Were the pings successful? _____

Step 2:   Verify that all interfaces are assigned to EIGRP for IPv4.

a.   Issue the **show ip protocols** command to verify that EIGRP is running and that all networks are advertised. This command also allows you to verify that the router ID is set correctly, and that the LAN interfaces are set as passive interfaces. Record your findings.

_____

_____

_____

b.   Make the necessary changes based on the output from the **show ip protocols** command. Record the commands that were used to correct the issues.

_____

_____

_____

c.   Re-issue the **show ip protocols** command to verify that your changes had the desired effect.

Step 3: Verify EIGRP neighbor information.

a. Issue the **show ip eigrp neighbor** command to verify that EIGRP adjacencies have been established between the neighboring routers.

b. Resolve any outstanding problems that were discovered.

Step 4: Verify EIGRP for IPv4 routing information.

a. Issue the **show ip route eigrp** command to verify that each router has EIGRP for IPv4 routes to all non-adjoining networks.

Are all EIGRP routes available? _____

If any EIGRP for IPv4 routes are missing, what is missing?

_____

b. If any routing information is missing, resolve these issues.

Step 5: Verify IPv4 end-to-end connectivity.

From each PC, verify that IPv4 end-to-end connectivity exists. PCs should be able to ping the other PC hosts in the topology. If IPv4 end-to-end connectivity does not exist, then continue troubleshooting to resolve remaining issues.

Note: It may be necessary to disable the PCs firewall.

Part 4: Troubleshoot EIGRP for IPv6

In Part 3, you will troubleshoot EIGRP for IPv6 problems and make the necessary changes needed to establish EIGRP for IPv6 routes and end-to-end IPv6 connectivity.

Note: LAN (G0/0) interfaces should not advertise EIGRP routing information, but routes to these networks should be contained in the routing tables.

Step 1: Test IPv6 end-to-end connectivity.

From each PC host, ping the IPv6 addresses of the other PC hosts in the topology to verify end-to-end connectivity.

Step 2: Verify that IPv6 unicast routing has been enabled on all routers.

a. An easy way to verify that IPv6 routing has been enabled on a router is to use the **show run | section ipv6 unicast** command. By adding this pipe to the **show run** command, the **ipv6 unicast-routing** command is displayed if IPv6 routing has been enabled.

Note: The **show run** command can also be issued without any pipe, and then a manual search for the **ipv6 unicast-routing** command can be done.

Issue the command on each router. Record your findings.

_____

_____

_____

b. If IPv6 unicast routing is not enabled on one or more routers, enable it now. Record the commands that were used to correct the issues.

_____

_____

Step 3: Verify that all interfaces are assigned to EIGRP for IPv6.

a. Issue the **show ipv6 protocols** command and verify that the router ID is correct. This command also allows you to verify that the LAN interfaces are set as passive interfaces.

Note: If no output is generated from this command, then the EIGRP for IPv6 process has not been configured.

Record your findings.

_____

_____

_____

b. Make the necessary configuration changes. Record the commands used to correct the issues.

_____

_____

_____

_____

_____

_____

_____

_____

_____

c. Re-issue the **show ipv6 protocols** command to verify that your changes are correct.

Step 4: Verify that all routers have correct neighbor adjacency information.

a. Issue the **show ipv6 eigrp neighbor** command to verify that adjacencies have formed between neighboring routers.

b. Resolve any EIGRP adjacency issues that still exist.

Step 5: Verify EIGRP for IPv6 routing information.

a. Issue the **show ipv6 route eigrp** command, and verify that EIGRP for IPv6 routes exist to all non-adjoining networks.

Are all EIGRP routes available? _____

If any EIGRP for IPv6 routes are missing, what is missing?

_____

b. Resolve any routing issues that still exist.

Step 6: Test IPv6 end-to-end connectivity.

From each PC, verify that IPv6 end-to-end connectivity exists. PCs should be able to ping the other PC hosts in the topology. If IPv6 end-to-end connectivity does not exist, then continue troubleshooting to resolve remaining issues.

Note: It may be necessary to disable the PCs firewall.

Reflection

Why would you troubleshoot EIGRP for IPv4 and EIGRP for IPv6 separately?

_____

Router Interface Summary Table

Router Interface Summary				
Router Model	**Ethernet Interface #1**	**Ethernet Interface #2**	**Serial Interface #1**	**Serial Interface #2**
1800	Fast Ethernet 0/0 (F0/0)	Fast Ethernet 0/1 (F0/1)	Serial 0/0/0 (S0/0/0)	Serial 0/0/1 (S0/0/1)
1900	Gigabit Ethernet 0/0 (G0/0)	Gigabit Ethernet 0/1 (G0/1)	Serial 0/0/0 (S0/0/0)	Serial 0/0/1 (S0/0/1)
2801	Fast Ethernet 0/0 (F0/0)	Fast Ethernet 0/1 (F0/1)	Serial 0/1/0 (S0/1/0)	Serial 0/1/1 (S0/1/1)
2811	Fast Ethernet 0/0 (F0/0)	Fast Ethernet 0/1 (F0/1)	Serial 0/0/0 (S0/0/0)	Serial 0/0/1 (S0/0/1)
2900	Gigabit Ethernet 0/0 (G0/0)	Gigabit Ethernet 0/1 (G0/1)	Serial 0/0/0 (S0/0/0)	Serial 0/0/1 (S0/0/1)

Note: To find out how the router is configured, look at the interfaces to identify the type of router and how many interfaces the router has. There is no way to effectively list all the combinations of configurations for each router class. This table includes identifiers for the possible combinations of Ethernet and Serial interfaces in the device. The table does not include any other type of interface, even though a specific router may contain one. An example of this might be an ISDN BRI interface. The string in parenthesis is the legal abbreviation that can be used in Cisco IOS commands to represent the interface.

8.2.3.7 Lab – Troubleshooting Advanced EIGRP

Topology

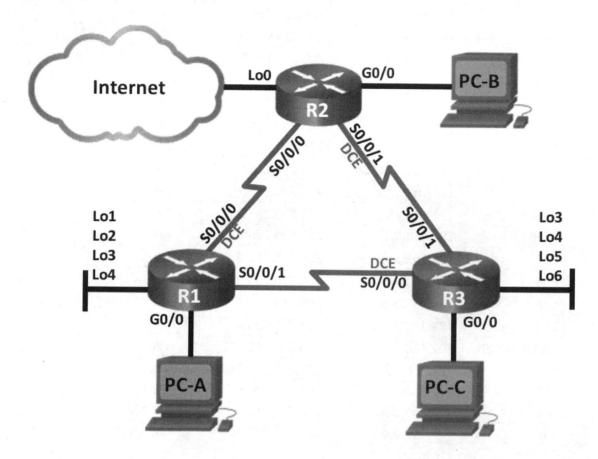

Addressing Table

Device	Interface	IP Address	Subnet Mask	Default Gateway
R1	G0/0	192.168.1.1	255.255.255.0	N/A
	Lo1	172.16.11.1	255.255.255.0	N/A
	Lo2	172.16.12.1	255.255.255.0	N/A
	Lo3	172.16.13.1	255.255.255.0	N/A
	Lo4	172.16.14.1	255.255.255.0	N/A
	S0/0/0 (DCE)	192.168.12.1	255.255.255.252	N/A
	S0/0/1	192.168.13.1	255.255.255.252	N/A
R2	G0/0	192.168.2.1	255.255.255.0	N/A
	Lo0	209.165.200.225	255.255.255.252	N/A
	S0/0/0	192.168.12.2	255.255.255.252	N/A
	S0/0/1 (DCE)	192.168.23.1	255.255.255.252	N/A
R3	G0/0	192.168.3.1	255.255.255.0	N/A
	Lo3	172.16.33.1	255.255.255.0	N/A
	Lo4	172.16.34.1	255.255.255.0	N/A
	Lo5	172.16.35.1	255.255.255.0	N/A
	Lo6	172.16.36.1	255.255.255.0	N/A
	S0/0/0 (DCE)	192.168.13.2	255.255.255.252	N/A
	S0/0/1	192.168.23.2	255.255.255.252	N/A
PC-A	NIC	192.168.1.3	255.255.255.0	192.168.1.1
PC-B	NIC	192.168.2.3	255.255.255.0	192.168.2.1
PC-C	NIC	192.168.3.3	255.255.255.0	192.168.3.1

Objectives

Part 1: Build the Network and Load Device Configurations

Part 2: Troubleshoot EIGRP

Background / Scenario

The Enhanced Interior Gateway Routing Protocol (EIGRP) has advanced features to allow changes related to summarization, default route propagation, bandwidth utilization, metrics, and security.

In this lab, you will troubleshoot a network that is running EIGRP. Advanced EIGRP features have been implemented, but the network is now experiencing problems. You are tasked with finding and correcting the network issues.

Note: The routers used with CCNA hands-on labs are Cisco 1941 Integrated Services Routers (ISRs) with Cisco IOS, Release 15.2(4)M3 (universalk9 image). Other routers and Cisco IOS versions can be used. Depending on the model and Cisco IOS version, the commands available and output produced might vary from what is shown in the labs. Refer to the Router Interface Summary Table at the end of this lab for the correct interface identifiers.

Note: Ensure that the routers have been erased and have no startup configurations. If you are unsure, contact your instructor.

Required Resources

- 3 Routers (Cisco 1941 with Cisco IOS Release 15.2(4)M3 universal image or comparable)
- 3 PCs (Windows 7, Vista, or XP with terminal emulation program, such as Tera Term)
- Console cables to configure the Cisco IOS devices via the console ports
- Ethernet cables as shown in the topology

Part 1:   Build the Network and Load Device Configurations

Step 1:   Cable the network as shown in the topology.

Step 2:   Configure PC hosts.

Step 3:   Load router configurations.

Load the following configurations into the appropriate router. All routers have the same passwords. The privileged EXEC password is **class**, and **cisco** is the console and vty password.

Router R1 Configuration:

```
conf t
hostname R1
enable secret class
no ip domain lookup
key chain EIGRP-KEYS
 key 1
   key-string cisco123

line con 0
 password cisco
 login
 logging synchronous
line vty 0 4
 password cisco
 login
banner motd @
   Unauthorized Access is Prohibited! @
interface lo1
 description Connection to Branch 11
 ip add 172.16.11.1 255.255.255.0
interface lo2
 description Connection to Branch 12
 ip add 172.16.12.1 255.255.255.0
```

```
interface lo3
 description Connection to Branch 13
 ip add 172.16.13.1 255.255.255.0
interface lo4
 description Connection to Branch 14
 ip add 172.16.14.1 255.255.255.0
interface g0/0
 description R1 LAN Connection
 ip add 192.168.1.1 255.255.255.0
 no shutdown
interface s0/0/0
 description Serial Link to R2
 clock rate 128000

 ip add 192.168.12.1 255.255.255.252
 ip authentication mode eigrp 1 md5
 ip authentication key-chain eigrp 1 EIGRP-KEYS
 ip hello-interval eigrp 1 30
 ip hold-time eigrp 1 90
 ip bandwidth-percent eigrp 1 40

 no shutdown
interface s0/0/1
 description Serial Link to R3
 bandwidth 128
 ip add 192.168.13.1 255.255.255.252
 ip authentication mode eigrp 1 md5
 ip authentication key-chain eigrp 1 EIGRP-KEYS
 ip bandwidth-percent eigrp 1 40

 no shutdown
router eigrp 1
 router-id 1.1.1.1
 network 192.168.1.0 0.0.0.255
 network 192.168.12.0 0.0.0.3
 network 192.168.13.0 0.0.0.3
 network 172.16.0.0 0.0.255.255
```

```
    passive-interface g0/0
    auto-summary

    end
```

Router R2 Configuration:

```
    conf t
    hostname R2
    enable secret class
    no ip domain lookup
    key chain EIGRP-KEYS
     key 1
       key-string Cisco123
    line con 0
     password cisco
     login
     logging synchronous
    line vty 0 4
     password cisco
     login
    banner motd @
       Unauthorized Access is Prohibited! @
    interface g0/0
     description R2 LAN Connection
     ip add 192.168.2.1 255.255.255.0
     no shutdown
    interface s0/0/0
     description Serial Link to R1
     bandwidth 128
     ip add 192.168.12.2 255.255.255.252
     ip authentication mode eigrp 1 md5
     ip authentication key-chain eigrp 1 EIGRP-KEYS
     ip bandwidth-percent eigrp 1 40
     ip hello-interval eigrp 1 30
     ip hold-time eigrp 1 90
     no shutdown
    interface s0/0/1
     description Serial Link to R3
     bandwidth 128
```

```
   ip add 192.168.23.1 255.255.255.252
   ip authentication mode eigrp 1 md5


   ip bandwidth-percent eigrp 1 40
   ip hello-interval eigrp 1 30
   ip hold-time eigrp 1 90
   no shutdown
  interface lo0
   ip add 209.165.200.225 255.255.255.252
   description Connection to ISP
  router eigrp 1
   router-id 2.2.2.2
   network 192.168.2.0 0.0.0.255
   network 192.168.12.0 0.0.0.3
   network 192.168.23.0 0.0.0.3
   passive-interface g0/0


  ip route 0.0.0.0 0.0.0.0 lo0
  end
```

Router R3 Configuration:

```
  conf t
  hostname R3
  enable secret class
  no ip domain lookup
  key chain EIGRP-KEYS
   key 1
    key-string Cisco123
  line con 0
   password cisco
   login
   logging synchronous
  line vty 0 4
   password cisco
   login
  banner motd @
    Unauthorized Access is Prohibited! @
  interface lo3
```

```
   description Connection to Branch 33
   ip add 172.16.33.1 255.255.255.0
 interface lo4
   description Connection to Branch 34
   ip add 172.16.34.1 255.255.255.0
 interface lo5
   description Connection to Branch 35
   ip add 172.16.35.1 255.255.255.0
 interface lo6
   description Connection to Branch 36
   ip add 172.16.36.1 255.255.255.0
 interface g0/0
   description R3 LAN Connection
   ip add 192.168.3.1 255.255.255.0
   no shutdown
 interface s0/0/0
   description Serial Link to R1
   ip add 192.168.13.2 255.255.255.252
   ip authentication mode eigrp 1 md5
   ip authentication key-chain eigrp 1 EIGRP-KEYS

   ip hello-interval eigrp 1 30
   ip hold-time eigrp 1 90


   clock rate 128000
   bandwidth 128
   no shutdown
 interface s0/0/1
   description Serial Link to R2
   bandwidth 128
   ip add 192.168.23.2 255.255.255.252
   ip authentication mode eigrp 1 md5
   ip authentication key-chain eigrp 1 eigrp-keys

 ! ip bandwidth-percent eigrp 1 40
   ip hello-interval eigrp 1 30
   ip hold-time eigrp 1 90


   no shutdown
```

```
router eigrp 1
 router-id 3.3.3.3
 network 192.168.3.0 0.0.0.255
 network 192.168.13.0 0.0.0.3
 network 192.168.23.0 0.0.0.3
 network 172.16.0.0 0.0.255.255
 passive-interface g0/0
 auto-summary

end
```

Step 4: Verify end-to-end connectivity.

Note: It may be necessary to disable the PC firewall to ping between PCs.

Step 5: Save the configuration on all routers.

Part 2: Troubleshoot EIGRP

In Part 2, verify that all routers have established neighbor adjacencies, and that all network routes are available.

Additional EIGRP Requirements:

- All serial interface clock rates should be set at 128 Kb/s and a matching bandwidth setting should be available to allow EIGRP cost metrics to be calculated correctly.

- Manual route summarization of the branch networks, simulated by using Loopback interfaces on R1 and R3, should be utilized. The automatic summarization feature of EIGRP should not be used.

- EIGRP should redistribute the static default route to the Internet. This is simulated by using Loopback interface 0 on R2.

- EIGRP should be configured to use no more than **40** percent of the available bandwidth on the serial interfaces.

- EIGRP Hello/Hold timer intervals should be set to **30/90** on all serial interfaces.

- All serial interfaces should be configured with MD5 authentication, using key chain **EIGRP-KEYS**, with a key-string of **Cisco123**.

List the commands used during your EIGRP troubleshooting process:

_____

_____

_____

_____

List the changes made to resolve the EIGRP issues. If no problems were found on the device, then respond with "no problems were found".

R1 Router:

_____

_____

_____

_____

R2 Router:

_____

_____

_____

_____

R3 Router:

_____

_____

_____

_____

Reflection

1. How can the **auto-summary** command create routing issues in EIGRP?

   _____

   _____

   _____

   _____

2. What advantages are provided by manually summarizing the branch routes (loopback interfaces on R1 and R3) in this network?

   _____

   _____

3. Why would you want to change the EIGRP Hello and Hold time intervals on an interface?

   _____

   _____

Router Interface Summary Table

Router Interface Summary				
Router Model	**Ethernet Interface #1**	**Ethernet Interface #2**	**Serial Interface #1**	**Serial Interface #2**
1800	Fast Ethernet 0/0 (F0/0)	Fast Ethernet 0/1 (F0/1)	Serial 0/0/0 (S0/0/0)	Serial 0/0/1 (S0/0/1)
1900	Gigabit Ethernet 0/0 (G0/0)	Gigabit Ethernet 0/1 (G0/1)	Serial 0/0/0 (S0/0/0)	Serial 0/0/1 (S0/0/1)
2801	Fast Ethernet 0/0 (F0/0)	Fast Ethernet 0/1 (F0/1)	Serial 0/1/0 (S0/1/0)	Serial 0/1/1 (S0/1/1)
2811	Fast Ethernet 0/0 (F0/0)	Fast Ethernet 0/1 (F0/1)	Serial 0/0/0 (S0/0/0)	Serial 0/0/1 (S0/0/1)
2900	Gigabit Ethernet 0/0 (G0/0)	Gigabit Ethernet 0/1 (G0/1)	Serial 0/0/0 (S0/0/0)	Serial 0/0/1 (S0/0/1)

Note: To find out how the router is configured, look at the interfaces to identify the type of router and how many interfaces the router has. There is no way to effectively list all the combinations of configurations for each router class. This table includes identifiers for the possible combinations of Ethernet and Serial interfaces in the device. The table does not include any other type of interface, even though a specific router may contain one. An example of this might be an ISDN BRI interface. The string in parenthesis is the legal abbreviation that can be used in Cisco IOS commands to represent the interface.

8.3.1.1 Class Activity – Tweaking EIGRP

Objectives

Implement advanced EIGRP features to enhance operation in a small- to medium-sized business network.

Scenario

The purpose of this activity is to review EIGRP routing protocol fine-tuning concepts.

You will work with a partner to design one EIGRP topology. This topology will be the basis for two parts of the activity. The first will use default settings for all configurations and the second will incorporate, at least, three of the following fine-tuning EIGRP options:

- Manual summary route

- Default routes

- Default routes propagation

- Hello interval timer settings

Refer to the labs, Packet Tracer activities, and interactive activities to help you as you progress through this modeling activity.

Directions are listed on the PDF file for this activity. Share your completed work with another group. You may wish to save a copy of this activity to a portfolio.

Resources

- Packet Tracer software or real network lab equipment
- Word processing program

Directions

Step 1: Design a WAN and LAN topology.

a. Use Packet Tracer to design a network with two routers (1941 model, suggested). If necessary, add NICs to the routers to provide connectivity to the routers to provide for, at least, two LANs for each router. Add, at least, one PC to each LAN.

b. Address the networks using either an IPv4 or IPv6 addressing scheme. VLSM may or may not be used per group discretion. If you use a full VLSM-addressed network, you will need to turn off auto-summarization from the beginning of your configuration design.

c. Configure the topology using basic EIGRP default settings.

d. Make sure all PCs can ping each other to prove connectivity. If not, work to make this so.

e. Save your work.

Step 2: Copy the topology.

a. Using your cursor, highlight the entire EIGRP-configured topology.

b. Press **Ctrl+C** to copy the highlighted topology.

c. Use **Ctrl+V** to paste a full copy of the topology to the Packet Tracer desktop. You will now have displayed two exact EIGRP-configured topologies. You will use the topology copy to tweak the network.

d. While highlighted, move the copied topology to a different location on the Packet Tracer desktop to create room between the two for configuration purposes.

Step 3: Configure fine-tuning features on the copied topology.

a. Choose three of the bulleted items from the Scenario section of this activity. Configure your changes on the copied topology. **Note**: By changing the Hello interval times, network instability may occur. You should be able to configure it; however, notice adjacencies status changing if you do choose this configuration option.

b. Save your work to avoid losing your configuration.

Step 4: Use verification commands to compare and contrast your default and fine-tuned configurations.

a. Use, at least, three output commands to compare and contrast the two topologies, and copy them to a word processing software program. For example, some useful commands include:

- `show ip route`
- `show running-configuration`
- `show ip protocols, show ip eigrp neighbors`

b. Share your work with another group. Explain how you changed the second topology from the first configured example. Justify what happened when you configured the three EIGRP fine-tuning options.

Chapter 9 — IOS Images and Licensing

9.0.1.2 Class Activity – IOS Detection

Objective

Manage IOS system image files to increase network reliability in a small- to medium-sized business network.

Scenario

Your school or university has just received a donation of Cisco routers and switches. You transport them from your shipping and receiving department to your Cisco networking lab and start sorting them into switch and router groups.

After all the equipment has been sorted, you cannot wait to turn them on to see if they really work. Once you do power them up, you find out that all of the equipment operating systems have been erased! Because computers use different operating systems, you think that routers and switches also use different internetworking operating systems (or IOS) as well.

One good thing you notice is that most of the routers are either models 1941 or 2911. The switch models are either 2960 or 3560. You have worked with this type of equipment in the past and know you can research which IOS is appropriate to purchase for each model. You also know that documenting hardware features, serial numbers, and MAC addresses is very important to do whenever you add networking equipment to any network topology.

Refer to the accompanying PDF for directions on how to proceed with this modeling activity. Save your work and share the data you found with another group or the entire class.

Resources

- Packet Tracer software
- Internet connectivity

Directions

Step 1:   Create a switch and router matrix for documenting hardware and software information.

a. Design a matrix to record information about your two router models, 1941 and 2911. Both models are included in your Packet Tracer software. Record the following information in your matrix:

1) The system serial numbers of the equipment

2) The Cisco IOS type and version shown for each model

3) The name of the preferred system image file

4) How much NVRAM is present on the routers

5) How many and which types of interfaces are built in to the routers

b. Design a matrix to record information about your two switch models, 2960 and 3560, from Packet Tracer. Record the following information in your matrix:

1) The system serial number for this type of equipment

2) The Cisco IOS type and version shown for these models

3) The name of the preferred SW image

4) How much NVRAM is present on the models

5) How many and which types of interfaces are built in to the switches

Step 2:   Open Packet Tracer.

a.   Place one router and switch for each router and switch model you will research on the desktop.

b.   Open the router or switch models on Packet Tracer and use the **show version** command to display operating system and other information about your equipment.

c.   Read and record the information found in Step 2b to your matrix designs.

Step 3:   Visit http://www.cisco.com for further model research content.

a.   Sign in to your account at cisco.com. If you do not have an account, create one.

b.   Research your router and switch models for additional feature sets available for the models.

c.   Note the physical hardware designs of the devices. Check if additional network cards can be installed; if so, record what types of cards can be installed for your router and switch models.

d.   Mention some of these facts below in your two matrix designs.

Step 4:   Document the information you found to share with the class or another group of students.

9.3.1.1 Class Activity – Powerful Protocols

Objective

A review of EIGRP and OSPF routing protocol configuration and verification commands.

Scenario

At the end of this course, you are asked to complete two Capstone Projects where you will create, configure, and verify two network topologies using the two main routing protocols taught in this course, EIGRP and OSPF.

To make things easier, you decide to create a chart of configuration and verification commands to use for these two design projects. To help devise the protocol charts, ask another student in the class to help you.

Refer to the PDF for this chapter for directions on how to create a design for this modeling project. When complete, share your work with another group or with the class. You may also want to save the files created for this project in a network portfolio for future reference.

Resources

- Previous curriculum chapter content for EIGRP and OSPF
- Word processing software

Directions

Step 1: Create a matrix for each routing protocol (EIGRP and OSPF).

a. Within each routing protocol matrix, design two sections.

1) one section for configuration commands

2) one section for verification or **show** commands

b. Use a word processing program to save your matrix designs, one for EIGRP and one for OSPF.

Step 2: Review the chapters in this curriculum.

a. Refer to the different sections and activities presented in the curriculum.

1) Content

2) Labs

3) Packet Tracer Activities

b. Record configuration commands for each protocol on their respective matrix. **Note**: Some commands are universal, and some are used only for IPv4 or IPv6.

c. Record verification commands used for each protocol on their respective matrix. **Note**: Some of these commands are universal, and some are used only with IPv4or IPv6.

d. Leave extra, blank rows for the group or classroom portion of this activity.

Step 3: Meet as a class or with another group.

a. Compare configuration commands.

b. Compare verification commands.

c. Add any commands to each matrix mentioned in the full- or group-setting that you did not record in your own group.

d. Save your work for use with the two Capstone projects which summarize this entire course.

9.3.1.2 – EIGRP Capstone Project

Objectives

In this Capstone Project activity, you will demonstrate your ability to:

- Design, configure, verify, and secure EIGRP, IPv4 or IPv6 on a network
- Design a VLSM addressing scheme for the devices connected to the LANs
- Present your design using network documentation from your Capstone Project network

Scenario

You are a network engineer for your small- to medium-sized business. You and your team have been asked to design an IPv4 or IPv6 network that uses the EIGRP routing protocol.

The network consists of four branches that is connected to a headquarters router. The headquarters then connects to an ISP router.

Your job is to create an EIGRP-based, VLSM addressed network scheme using IPv4 or IPv6 to accommodate the number of hosts requested for this Capstone Project.

Required Resources

- Packet Tracer software

- Word processing or presentation software

Step 1:   Design the network topology.

a.   Network equipment:

1) Six routers

(a) Four branch routers

(b) One headquarters router

(c) One ISP router

2) Switches to support the LANS

b.   LANs:

1) Two LANs per branch router

(a) Two LANs with 500 hosts

(b) One LAN serving 120 hosts

(c) One LAN with 200 hosts

(d) Two LANS with 80 hosts

(e) One LAN with 60 hosts

(f) One LAN with 30 hosts

2) One, three-host LAN assigned to the ISP router for server connectivity (DNS, Web, and TFTP).

Step 2:   Devise the network addressing scheme.

a.   Use any RFC 1918 Class B address that will accommodate the specifications listed in Step 1.

b.   ISPs LAN connection will use a different IPv4 network number to indicate Internet or telecommunications connectivity to the servers.

c.   Use VLSM efficiently to conserve addresses and allow for scalability.

d.   Apply the network address scheme to hosts and LAN and WAN interfaces.

Step 3:   Implement the EIGRP routing protocol on your network

a.   Requirements:

1)   Advertise directly connected networks using the wildcard mask.

2)   Disable automatic summarization.

3)   Disable routing updates from being sent across the LAN interfaces.

4)   Implement one, named extended ACL on the network.

b.   Recommendations (choose two):

1)   Selectively implement EIGRP summary routes.

2)   Modify the EIGRP hello-timers.

3)   Modify the bandwidth of the interfaces.

Step 4:   Configure basic security

a.   Restrict access to the console connection.

b.   Configure encrypted passwords.

c.   Restrict access to the VTY connections.

d.   Configure a banner warning.

Step 5:   Backup the configurations of each router to the TFTP server.

Step 6:   Verify the network.

a.   Validate connectivity by pinging all devices.

b.   Use five **show** commands to verify EIGRP configuration.

Step 7:   Present your Capstone Project to the class and be able to answer questions from your peers and Instructor.

9.3.1.3 – OSPF Capstone Project

Objectives

- Configure basic OSPFv2 to enable internetwork communications in a small- to medium-sized IPv4 business network.
- Implement advanced OSPF features to enhance operation in a small- to medium-sized business network.
- Implement multiarea OSPF for IPv4 to enable internetwork communications in a small- to medium-sized business network.
- Configure basic OSPFv3 to enable internetwork communications in a small- to medium-sized IPv6 business network.

Scenario

Your company has made the decision to implement the OSPF routing protocol on its network. You have decided that you need to review the concepts related to OSPF in order to make a smooth transition to this protocol.

Create a network using Packet Tracer. Configure the network with these OSPF routing protocol options:

- Multiarea OSPFv2
- Single-area OSPFv3
- Bandwidth
- Cost
- Authentication
- Default routes
- DR and BDR elections for segments

Required Resources

- Packet Tracer
- Student/group-created rubric for assessment of the assignment

Step 1:   Design and build a network from scratch.

    a.   Your design must include three routers connected to a multi-access network in area 0 for use with IPv4.

       1) Enable authentication.

       2) Establish the DR and BDR using the `router id` command.

Step 2:   Add one additional router with two connections to area 0, representing another OSPF area.

Step 3:   Configure the bandwidth or cost to favor one route.

Step 4:   Add a network containing end devices and a passive OSPF interface.

Step 5:   Add a route to a default network such as the Internet.

Step 6:   Add an IPv6 addressing scheme on the routers and configure OSPFv3.

    a.   Enable IPv6 unicast routing.

    b.   Establish the DR and BDR using the `router id` command.

    c.   Do not configure timers, bandwidth, cost, default routes, or authentication.